# Europeanizing Contention

# Protest, Culture and Society



Protest movements have been recognized as significant contributors to processes of political participation and transformations of culture and value systems, as well as to the development of both a national and transnational civil society.

This series brings together the various innovative approaches to phenomena of social change, protest and dissent which have emerged in recent years, from an interdisciplinary perspective. It contextualizes social protest and cultures of dissent in larger political processes and socio-cultural transformations by examining the influence of historical trajectories and the response of various segments of society, political and legal institutions on a national and international level. In doing so, the series offers a more comprehensive and multi-dimensional view of historical and cultural change in the twentieth and twenty-first century.

**Volume 1**
*Voices of the Valley, Voices of the Straits: How Protest Creates Communities*
Donatella della Porta and Gianni Piazza

**Volume 2**
*Transformations and Crises: The Left and the Nation in Denmark and Sweden, 1956–1980*
Thomas Ekman Jørgensen

**Volume 3**
*Changing the World, Changing Oneself: Political Protest and Collective Identities in West Germany and the U.S. in the 1960s and 1970s*
Edited by Belinda Davis, Wilfried Mausbach, Martin Klimke, and Carla MacDougall

**Volume 4**
*The Transnational Condition: Protest Dynamics in an Entangled Europe*
Edited by Simon Teune

**Volume 5**
*Protest Beyond Borders: Contentious Politics in Europe since 1945*
Edited by Hara Kouki and Eduardo Romanos

**Volume 6**
*Between the Avant-Garde and the Everyday: Subversive Politics in Europe from 1957 to the Present*
Edited by Timothy Brown and Lorena Anton

**Volume 7**
*Between Prague Spring and French May: Opposition and Revolt in Europe, 1960–1980*
Edited by Martin Klimke, Jacco Pekelder, and Joachim Scharloth

**Volume 8**
*The Third World in the Global 1960s*
Edited by Samantha Christiansen and Zachary A. Scarlett

**Volume 9**
*The German Student Movement and the Literary Imagination: Transnational Memories of Protest and Dissent*
Susanne Rinner

**Volume 10**
*Children of the Dictatorship: Student Resistance, Cultural Politics, and the 'Long 1960s' in Greece*
Kostis Kornetis

**Volume 11**
*Media and Revolt: Strategies and Performances from the 1960s to the Present*
Edited by Kathrin Fahlenbrach, Erling Sivertsen, and Rolf Werenskjold

**Volume 12**
*Europeanizing Contention: The Protest Against 'Fortress Europe' in France and Germany*
Pierre Monforte

# Europeanizing Contention

## The Protest against 'Fortress Europe' in France and Germany

By

Pierre Monforte

berghahn
NEW YORK • OXFORD
www.berghahnbooks.com

First published in 2014 by
Berghahn Books
www.berghahnbooks.com



Library of Congress Cataloging-in-Publication Data
Monforte, Pierre.
Europeanizing contention: the protest against "fortress Europe" in France and Germany / by Pierre Monforte. -- First Edition.
pages cm. -- (Protest, culture & society; Volume 12)
Includes bibliographical references.
ISBN 978-0-85745-996-1 (hardback: alk. paper) -- ISBN 978-0-85745-997-8 (institutional ebook) 1. Social movements--Political aspects--France. 2. Social movements--Political aspects--Germany. 3. Emigration and immigration--Government policy--Case studies. 4. Social media--Political aspects. I. Title.
HM881.M66 2014 303.48'40944--dc23
2013042954

British Library Cataloguing in Publication Data
A catalogue record for this book is available from the British Library
Printed on acid-free paper

ISBN 978-0-85745-996-1 (hardback)
ISBN 978-0-85745-997-8 (institutional ebook)

# Contents

# Tables and Figures

## Tables



## Figures

# Acknowledgements

This book is the result of a long personal and academic journey that brought me to many different places. It could not have been written without the support of the people and institutions that welcomed and supported me throughout the journey.

I would particularly like to thank my PhD supervisor, Donatella della Porta, for offering steady support, trust and inspiration over my four years of doctoral research at the European University Institute in Florence. I am also very grateful to my co-supervisor, Virginie Guiraudon, for following my work with great attention and patience and encouraging me in many ways. In addition to the great quality of their supervision, Donatella and Virginie offered extremely appreciated consideration and kindness. I am profoundly indebted to them.

I would also like to address my most sincere gratitude to Pascale Dufour for her friendly support and encouragement during my post-doctoral stay in Montreal. I thank François Crépeau, Jane Jenson and Eric Montpetit who made me feel welcome at the Université de Montréal. I would like to thank Didier Chabanet, Andrew Geddes, Jérôme Valluy and the anonymous reviewers for giving me precious comments on draft chapters and earlier versions of this book. I am also grateful to Martin Klimke, Kathrin Fahlenbrach, Joachim Scharloth and to the production team at Berghahn Books for their help during the final writing process.

This research would not have been possible without the support of the French Egide programme and the European Commission during my stays in Florence, Paris and Berlin. I also received financial support from the CERIUM and the CPDS during my stay in Montreal.

I feel great admiration for the activists dedicating their time and energy to the social movements that I studied. The context in which they act is becoming increasingly threatening and I have immense respect for their political and intellectual courage. I want to take this opportunity to thank in particular all activists of the *Gisti* and *Migreurop*. I humbly wish that this book may help to show the importance and relevance of their mobilization.

Many of the people I met at the EUI and at the Université de Montréal have become close friends. I greet them all and I hope that we will share many more experiences despite the distance. I finally wish to thank my family in Paris, Munich and Barcelona for their support and patience. Since I started this research in 2004, I have had many good moments and some more difficult ones. Nuria and our son Gabriel helped me in the difficult times. They also brought me all the happiest moments I had in these years.

# Introduction

## The Europeanization of Social Movements and Immigration and Asylum Policies

### Europeanization 'from below' and 'from the borders'

Since the beginning of the 1990s, European Union member-states have defined and implemented a set of common norms related to immigration and asylum policies.[1] Giving priority to security and control measures (especially since September 2001), EU power-holders involved in this process have created the framework of a 'fortress Europe' (Geddes 2000). The most symbolic example of this is probably the creation of the FRONTEX agency in October 2004. This agency responds to the demand of the EU member-states to have a common corps of frontier guards: it organizes and supervises their cooperation with regard to the control of their external borders. Thus, it coordinates military forces deployed in specific zones, such as the maritime route between Senegal and the Canary Islands, in order to intercept migrants' boats and bring them back to their point of departure. The adoption of the European directive on 'returns' is another illustration of this process.[2] In June 2008, the majority of the European deputies approved the directive proposal negotiated by the European institutions since September 2005. As stipulated in this proposal, member-states can now detain undocumented migrants (including unaccompanied minors) for a period of up to eighteen months, put in place a five-year entry ban to European territory for returned migrants, or expel undocumented migrants to a country other than their country of origin (the 'transit countries').

At the same time, the dramatic attempts of migrants to enter the EU territory have been widely commented upon by the political class and by mainstream media all over Europe: images such as the camp of Sangatte or Lampedusa, the lines of barbed-wires around Ceuta and Melilla, and the *Cayucos* arriving in the Canary Islands have become illustrations of what is presented as a danger which justifies increasing security and control measures in the eyes of the public opinion. Thus, in preparation of the French presidency of the European Union starting in July 2008, delegates of the French government travelled to most European capitals to present their primary objective for this presidency: a 'European pact on immigration' based on measures such as the fight against illegal migrations and the reinforcement of borders controls. During this European tour, this pact was systematically justified through references to uncontrolled flows of migrants at the Southern borders of Europe, and, even if it is far from being true, this vision is widely relayed by the mainstream media. In brief, immigration and asylum are becoming European issues, both in the political agenda and in the mainstream media. And in the way in which they are defined, both agendas create and reinforce the image of the 'fortress Europe'.

Social movements have been reacting against this process. They have been working at the European level to protest against the way in which EU immigration and asylum policies are defined and implemented. In particular, activists have criticized the proliferation of detention centres for migrants in the European territory, the militarization of EU external borders, the externalization of asylum procedures and the increase of expulsion procedures. For example, on 31 January 2004, a few months after the second European Social Forum in Paris, hundreds of associations and networks of activists from different European countries organized a 'European day of action against detention centres for foreigners and for the regularization of undocumented migrants'. This initiative was repeated in April 2005 and October 2006 (one year after several migrants were killed by the frontier-guards at the Spanish-Moroccan border in Melilla, during their attempt to reach the Spanish territory). Demonstrations and symbolic actions were organized simultaneously in around forty European cities and claims related to the European dimension of immigration and asylum policies were formulated. In 2008, associations from all over Europe carried out a long-term campaign against the directive on 'returns', which they called the 'outrageous directive'. They opened a website (www.outrageousdirective.org), carried out a lobbying campaign addressed at European deputies, organized several demonstrations (in May 2008 in Brussels and in June 2008 in Paris), and launched an 'Appeal to the Members of the European Parliament' which was signed by around 1,300 associations, 40,000 individuals and 500 political figures. Moreover, in order to protest against the European Union's Council of Ministers, which met in Paris in October 2008 to discuss the 'European pact on immigration and asylum', many of these associations organized a 'counter-summit and an alternative forum on migrations and development' ('For a Europe of openness and solidarity') 'in order to make the voices of French, European and African civil society heard'.[3]

Social movements are crucial actors in the process of construction of modern nation-states (Bright and Harding 1984). Movements began to organize at the national level when modern European nation-states were formed, and they participated in the construction of boundaries between the 'legitimate state politics' and those 'outside the sphere of the state'. In doing so, social movements participate in the definition of the state itself. This process lies at the core of Charles Tilly's (1978, 1984, 2004) analysis of social movements in Europe. Tilly shows that the construction of modern nation-states in Europe coincides with an evolution in the locus and forms of protest: the old form of protest, based on spontaneous charivaris and riots which emerged exclusively at the local level, was progressively replaced by more routinized collective actions organized by national social movements. Tilly offers a general reflection on the construction of modern nation-states: he observes the historical evolution of protest in order to analyse the transformations in the forms of governments. In doing so, he provides an analysis of the construction of nation-states 'from below'. Following this general perspective, this book aims to analyse the processes through which social movements move from the local or national level to the European level. In doing so, it aims to propose an analysis of Europeanization 'from below': my general objective is to reflect on the construction of the European Union and on the European forms of governance emerging from it.

This study addresses then the question of the European Union's borders. As one focuses on the asylum issue, one is indeed situated at the border between different governments in an international system. This is made explicit in the definition of the 1951 Geneva Convention on the status of refugees:

> A refugee is 'A person who owing to a well-founded fear of being persecuted for reasons of race, religion, nationality, membership of a particular social group or political opinion, is outside the country of his nationality and is unable or, owing to such fear, is unwilling to avail himself of the protection of that country; or who, not having a nationality and being outside the country of his former habitual residence as a result of such events, is unable or, owing to such fear, is unwilling to return to it'.[4]

A refugee is a person who is 'outside the country of its nationality' and who cannot return to it. Therefore, the government that recognizes the refugee status of a person has to define what constitutes the 'inside' and the 'outside' of its own country: if refugees are persons who are outside their own country, it means that they have crossed a border and that they have arrived 'inside' another country. Immigration (being forced or not) includes by definition a 'transfer of jurisdiction' (Zolberg 1981). A government must therefore define its own borders in order to guarantee protection to individuals seeking it: its decision to give and to guarantee asylum status fundamentally depends on this act of definition. In this regard, the definition and implementation of asylum policies are intrinsically linked to states' sovereignty. The definition of the concept of asylum, which has been retained by a resolution of the Institute for International Law in September 1950,[5] is as follows:

> The term 'asylum' designates the protection that a State gives in its territory or in another location, which comes under some of its component, to an individual, which has come for this protection.[6]

The term 'asylum' describes a relationship between the state and an individual, and has to be considered as a state prerogative. It is the state that decides to give its protection to an individual who seeks it. Moreover, asylum policy is also intrinsically linked to the sovereignty of the state at the level of the policy's own implementation. Indeed, the protection that is given is based on the idea of territory: if it can be secured it is because (to quote Max Weber) the state offering it holds 'the monopoly over legitimate violence in a given territory'. Asylum policy, in terms of its definition as well as its implementation, is thus a highly symbolic attribute of state's sovereignty. This has led Hannah Arendt (1951: 278) to write (be it more generally on migration policies) that '[s]overeignty is nowhere more absolute than in matters of emigration, naturalization, nationality and expulsion'. This question is not exclusively a geographical issue: asylum policies (and more generally immigration policies) do not only relate to the definition of governments' external borders but also to the definition of internal borders within societies. Governments establish a categorization of individuals who live in a territory through the attribution of different residence and citizenship statuses. In the definition and implementation of immigration and asylum policies, the state defines state-membership – the national – and state-nonmembership – the foreigner. Thus, the notion of nationality has emerged, as developed by Brubaker (1992), when states have seen the necessity of dividing responsibility for certain categories of people (such as the poor migrant): by categorizing the poor migrants as foreigners (or non-nationals), a state holds another state responsible for them and can thus deny their right to stay in its territory.

The definition of external and internal borders is related to the process of construction of nation-states. Since the nineteenth century, European nation-states have progressively exercised and increased their power by establishing an intensive effort at categorizing the individuals residing in their territory (categorization as national or foreigner, as refugee or 'economic' migrant, as 'legal' or 'illegal' migrant, etc.). The construction and implementation of immigration and asylum policies has thus played a crucial role in the transfer of power relations from the local to the national level. Focusing on the French case, Noiriel (1998) shows that at the end of the nineteenth century, the 'national' became the major criteria for the distinction of different categories of individuals in a territory. A study focusing on immigration and asylum leads one to reflect on the process of the construction of nation-states. Focusing on the asylum issue at the European level, and on the process of the harmonization of asylum policies, one must analyse how the European Union authorities define the 'inside' and the 'outside' of Europe,[7] and how European external and internal borders are defined and implemented: it is the perspective of a process of Europeanization 'from the borders'.

## The Europeanization of immigration and asylum policies and its effects on social movements

The research agenda on Europeanization (Caporaso et al. 2000; Graziano and Vink 2006; Ladrech 1994; Radaelli 2001) has developed since the mid-1990s in order to address European politics as a multilevel framework. This agenda is based on the conception of European politics as a process rather than as a fixed institutional structure, and it emphasizes the importance of change in politics. Moreover, this agenda encompasses the study of both organizations and individuals, in an attempt to analyse how actors can define, use, adapt to, or translate European norms and practices at the local or national level. The concept of Europeanization refers to:

> Processes of (a) construction (b) diffusion and (c) institutionalization of formal and informal rules, procedures, policy paradigms, styles, 'ways of doing things' and shared beliefs and norms which are first defined and consolidated in the making of EU public policy and politics and then incorporated in the logic of domestic discourse, identities, political structures and public policies. (Radaelli 2001: 108)

This research agenda therefore complements those studies that consider the EU from a strictly institutional or legal point of view, allowing a less 'aerian view' (Smith 1999). It also enables researchers to consider the impact of national contexts in the definition and implementation of European politics.

The central question addressed in this study is that of the consequences of a specific Europeanization process (immigration and asylum policies) on social movements: to which extent do social movements Europeanize when a policy is Europeanizing? And, if so, how do they do this? To address this question, a brief summary on the Europeanization of immigration and asylum policies is required.

## From Schengen to FRONTEX: the construction of a multilevel framework on immigration and asylum policies

The process of Europeanization of immigration and asylum policies is not a simple transfer of power to the European Union, but more precisely a sharing of competences between EU member-states and the EU institutions. In other words, it does not imply a loss of sovereignty for the member-states; it does imply a change in the locus of political activity, but does not change the fact that European nation-states remain determinant power-holders in this domain. This leads us to highlight three major trends of this process: it is multilevel, polycentric, and externalized. First of all, it is multilevelled as it involves both the European and national political arenas. Secondly, it is both vertical and horizontal: it is guided by a neo-functionalist as well as an inter-governmental logic. This leads to a polycentric framework because various actors (such as the member-states, the Council of ministers, the Commission, the European Parliament or various ad hoc groups and agencies) are involved. These actors do not necessarily share the same interests. It is also a 'variable geometry' process as some member-states Europeanize faster than others. Finally, it is externalized because it directly enrols third countries in the control of migrations.

The signature of the Schengen agreements in 1985 constituted one of the first steps of the intergovernmental cooperation in the domains of immigration and asylum. These agreements paved the way for an opening of the European Union's internal borders, and in many states civil servants responsible for immigration policies saw an opportunity for a strengthening of the EU's external borders (Guild 2000; Guiraudon 2003). Schengen rapidly became a laboratory for the definition of new measures for migration controls on the part of member-states' ministries of Interior (Bigo and Guild 2005). The Europeanization of immigration and asylum policies was thus guided by a 'securitarian' framework (Lavenex 2001). This framework was then implemented in the early 1990s with the adoption of measures and instruments such as the Schengen Information System[8] and the Dublin convention.[9] These were adopted through a strictly intergovernmental logic, and until the Amsterdam Treaty came into force in 1999, Schengen was not part of the European Union legal framework. With the Amsterdam Treaty, part of the immigration and asylum policies became communitarized. Moreover, during the Tampere Summit in October 1999, member-states declared their intention to harmonize immigration and asylum policies, and they devised a programme in different steps for this purpose: the first step was related to the definition of a set of minimal norms; and the second step to the definition of common policies. However, the legal framework for the harmonization of these policies remained mainly intergovernmental: member-states had to adopt directives unanimously at the Council of ministers; the European Commission shared the competency to propose directives with the member-states; the European Parliament was only consulted. After the adoption of the Den Haag programme in 2004, the framework for the Europeanization of immigration and asylum policies became more supranational (except for those policies related to legal immigration, visas and police cooperation). Directives and regulations were adopted through the codecision procedure: the European Commission has the monopoly on legislative initiative; the European Parliament and the member-states (at the qualified majority) share the competence for their adoption.

This process has led to the construction of a Europeanized immigration and asylum policy, which is mainly based on a restrictive view on these matters. As mentioned above, the priority given to control policies has indeed created the framework of a 'fortress Europe' (Geddes 2000). However, not all the actors involved in this follow the same logic. In comparison with the member-states and the Justice and Home Affairs Council, the European Parliament and the Commission have in the past argued for more liberal immigration and asylum policies (Guiraudon 2010). The priority given to immigration controls is due to the decisive role played by the ministries of Interior of some member-states. Indeed, the ministries responsible for immigration controls in France, Germany and Italy have viewed the international cooperation as an opportunity to avoid obstacles (courts, political parties, some ministries, social movements etc.) that prevent them from devising restrictive policies. Following this strategy of 'venue-shopping' through vertical policy-making (Guiraudon 2000), these member-states have created multiple ad-hoc working groups (such as the High Level Working Group or the PRÜM Treaty) which permitted them to guide the Europeanization process. These member-states, followed by the European Commission, have moreover opted for an externalization of immigration control policies. First of all, through the conclusion of readmission agreements, third countries are asked to facilitate the procedure for the deportation of migrants. Then, third countries (countries of transit or countries of origin) are also asked to control their own borders and to impede emigration (Lavenex 2006).

This multilevel, polycentric and externalized process illustrates the fact that the Europeanization of public policies is not linear: it is the result of the interactions between various actors and can take different modes. As is stressed in the literature on the modes of Europeanization of civil society organizations, the same can be said about social movements.

## The modes of Europeanization of social movements: from domestication to the construction of transnational movements

Until the end of the 1990s, studies on collective action in the European Union were generally guided by a static perspective (della Porta 2003). Much research has been carried out on the mobilization of European umbrella structures (European social movement organizations) or international non-governmental organizations and lobby groups acting in Brussels. Yet little has been written about the relations between these groups and those active at the national level. More generally, little has been written about the effects of European integration on the social movements which are traditionally active at the national level. The general assumption has been that national challengers were supposed to mobilize exclusively at the national level whereas European challengers were supposed to act exclusively at the European level. The issue of the dynamics of 'Europeanization from the inside'[10] is thus still a relatively open question (della Porta and Caiani 2009).

In fact, empirical studies have proven that the collective actions devised by national social movement organizations constitute most of the mobilizations around European Union policies (Imig and Tarrow 2001). Since the end of the 1990s, several studies have explored this question through the distinction of different modes of Europeanization (Balme, Chabanet and Wright 2002; della Porta 2003; della Porta and Caiani 2009; Imig and Tarrow 2001). I propose to explore this question further through a typology based on four dimensions:

- the networks through which collective actions emerge: they can be national, European and centralized in Brussels, or transnational;
- the frames on which they are based: European policies can be considered as more liberal, more restrictive, or as following the spirit of national policies;
- the repertoire of collective action on which they are based: this can be corporatist, pluralist or based on protest (Balme and Chabanet 2002);
- the strategies of protest: to pressurize national or European institutions or both at the same time.

These four dimensions allow us to distinguish four different modes of Europeanization (table 1):

**Domestication**: social movements ascribe some of the responsibility for a problematic situation to the European Union, but they continue nonetheless to mobilize at the national level. Their actions target national institutions, but they have a European dimension because they are constructed in reaction to decisions taken at the European level. They aim thus to pressurize European institutions indirectly, through their national governments (see also Balme and Chabanet 2002; della Porta and Caiani 2009). These mobilizations are mainly based on protest and emerge through national networks.

**Externalization**: social movements traditionally active at the national level target European institutions in order to put pressure on their own government indirectly. This strategy is similar to the 'boomerang effect' presented by Keck and Sikkink (1998). They can also use opportunities available at the European level (such as European funds) in order to ameliorate their situation at the national or local level (see also Balme and Chabanet 2002; della Porta 2003). In this mode of Europeanization, national social movement organizations are usually involved in supranational coalitions that represent them at the EU level, and collective actions are based on a corporatist repertoire or on a pluralist repertoire that consists of lobbying strategies and juridical actions. European institutions are thus perceived as being close allies that can be used against national governments, and European policies are considered as more liberal than national policies.

The construction of **multilevel social movements**: national social movements become actively involved in networks coordinated by a centralized supranational structure (most of the time based in Brussels). Unlike the previous mode however, European institutions are not considered as allies that can be used against national governments, and European policies are not considered as being more liberal than national policies. These networks aim to pressurize both European and national institutions through the construction of multilevel campaigns: the European central structures target European institutions principally through lobbying techniques whereas national social movement organizations target their own government through their traditional repertoire of collective action.

The construction of **transnational social movements**: movements target European and national institutions through transnational protest. These transnational social movements are composed of national social movement organizations coordinated through formal structures (transnational groups) or loose networks (see also Tarrow 2001). Unlike the previous mode, this process leads social movements traditionally active at the national level

**Table 1** The modes of Europeanization of social movements

| | Network | Frames | Repertoire | Strategies |
|---|---|---|---|---|
| Domestication | National | European policies are perceived as being more restrictive than, or in the continuity of, national policies | Protest | Pressurize European institutions through the national level |
| Externalization | European, centralized in Brussels | European policies are perceived as being more liberal than national policies | Pluralist or corporatist | Pressurize national institutions through the European level; use opportunities opened at the European level |
| Construction of multilevel movements | European, centralized in Brussels | European policies are perceived as being more restrictive than, or in the continuity of, national policies | Mainly pluralist at the European level; pluralist or protest at the national level | Pressurize national and European institutions simultaneously |
| Construction of transnational movements | Transnational | European policies are perceived as being more restrictive than, or in the continuity of, national policies | Protest | Pressurize national and European institutions simultaneously |

to directly target European institutions and to define networks and collective actions addressing various polities (European or national) simultaneously (rather than through a multilevel framework). Also, in contrast to the previous mode, protest is central in this process.

The perspectives opened up by the application of this typology are important. In particular, it leads to more general reflections on the European integration process (Imig and Tarrow 2001; della Porta and Caiani 2009). For instance, the observation of the process of domestication of collective action could confirm the definition of the European Union through a 'liberal inter-governmentalist' theory (Milward 1992; Moravcsik 1998)

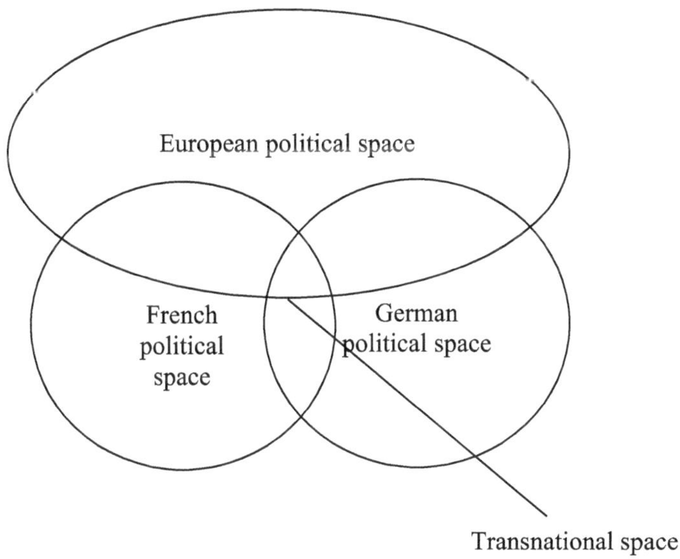


**Figure 1.** A multilevel configuration on collective action in Europe

in which the nation-states continue to be the most significant actors. On the other hand, the observation of the externalization of movements, or of the construction of multi-level movements, would corroborate the theories analysing the European Union as a system of multilevel governance (Hooghe and Marks 2001; Kohler-Koch and Eising 1999): the actors of a social movement construct cross-level mobilizations, as the European policy-making is in itself multilevelled. Finally, the possible emergence of transnational movements could be a sign of the emergence of a supranational state, as neo-functionalists (Haas 1964) would argue.

This typology leads us to underline that European collective actions can take place in different political spaces, and that they can address different actors. Considering the relation between two national political spaces (France and Germany) and the European political space, this view on European collective actions can be represented by figure 1.

As indicated in this figure, European collective actions can take place in the European, national or transnational political spaces. In these different political spaces, these actions can address European institutions, national governments or both simultaneously. Moreover, as suggested in the typology above, the situation in one particular political space is generally the result of a specific Europeanization process:

- In the European political space, collective actions are constructed by groups, with constituents in at least two European states, engaged in a direct interaction with power-holders directly involved in the negotiations on the harmonization of asylum policies (mostly within the frame of the European Union institutions). This type of collective action is the result of processes of externalization and of construction of multilevel movements.
- In the transnational space, collective actions are constructed by groups, with constituents in at least two European states, and are achieved in at least two European states simultaneously. They have as their subject an issue that is defined at the European level, but they do not necessarily address the European institutions directly. This type of collective action is the result of processes of construction of transnational movements.
- In the national political space, European collective actions are constructed by groups engaged in an interaction with power-holders of one European state, which is involved in the negotiations on the harmonization of asylum policies. This type of collective action is the result of processes of domestication.

As I will discuss below, these perspectives need to be explored further, and the differences and similarities between the European and national polities for the mobilization of social movements need to be considered.

## Social movements and the European Union: an institutionalization of protest?

Do social movement organizations Europeanize? If they do, do they Europeanize to the same extent and through the same modes of Europeanization, in particular if they have different features? Do they tend to change their identity during the process? These are the first questions that will be addressed in this book.

As noted by della Porta and Caini (2009), the conclusions drawn in the studies related to the Europeanization of social movements depend fundamentally on their empirical focus. Research analysing the protest-events reported in the national press have observed that nation-states remain the main targets of social movements. They have concluded that the European Union does not play a significant role in social movements. However, research focusing on public interest groups gravitating around European institutions has concluded that a new polity has emerged. It has also shown that the inclusion of civil society organizations is highly selective and that those relying on protest do not access this specific field. Although they lead to distinct conclusions, both streams of study (the first being mainly related to social movements studies and the second to European policy-making) share the idea that protest which targets European institutions remains exceptional: groups relying on protest do not target the European Union, or do not have access to it.

Several authors have empirically shown the low level of Europeanization of social movements. Using quantitative observations, Imig and Tarrow (2001), and Rucht (2002) have underlined that social movements rarely targeted EU institutions in the 1980s and the 1990s. In this regard, transnational movements of protest like the 'European marches against unemployment, precariousness and exclusion' at the end of the 1990s were seen as exceptional and very limited in time (Lefébure and Lagneau 2002; Chabanet 2008). Thus, in their analysis of protest events from 1984 to 1998, Imig and Tarrow (2001) have shown that only five per cent of them had a European dimension. Rucht (2002) has formulated several possible explanations for this low level of Europeanization of protest. First, as nation-states remain the dominant actors in the European Union, social movements are more effective when they target them. Also, the EU is extremely complex in terms of its policy-making; activists do not know the relevant targets and are not aware of the effective channels of influence (see also Ruzza 2004; Lahusen 2004). In addition, activists have practical difficulties in organizing themselves at the European level: they do not speak the same languages, they do not have sufficient material resources to organize transnationally, and they have different national conflict styles. Finally, there is no 'transnational European public' in which their claims could resonate.

The non-governmental actors that react to European public policies are above all professionalized organizations acting through direct contact with the European institutions in Brussels, having important resources, and privileging non-protesting types of collective actions. This is empirically sustained by several studies which have proved that NGOs and lobby groups are over-represented, in comparison to groups with more 'grass-roots' origins, among the organizations active in Brussels (Aspinwall and Greenwood 1997; Balme and Chabanet 2008; Greenwood 1997; Clayes et al. 1998; Marks and McAdam 1996). They thus deduce that mobilizations follow a process of 'NGOization' as soon as they are concerned with a European policy issue (Grossman and Saurugger 2006; Marks and McAdam 1996; Nugent 1999). From this perspective, actors with a profile that is different from the lobby groups and NGOs established in Brussels rarely mobilize on EU policy issues. Associations having a more 'grass-roots' profile only construct European mobilizations on the occasion of particular events like the European Social Forums, the counter-summits or demonstrations in Brussels. This idea is sustained by studies on the transnationalization of social movements that are inspired by the theory of political opportunity structure (POS) (Kriesi et al. 1995) or by the resource mobilization theory (RMT) (McAdam, McCarthy and Zald 1996).

The fundamental idea that lies at the core of the studies based on the concept of POS is that the context of progressive enforcement of global or European decision centres would create new types of constraints and opportunities for social movements. Consequently, they explore the hypothesis that, depending on the features of these new political opportunity structures, only some particular types of social movement organizations are able to transnationalize or Europeanize. Some authors have observed that because international institutions and the EU are more open to lobbying than to other types of collective action, only the actors that can adapt to this form of collective action are able to profit from the opportunities offered in this arena (Greenwood 1997; Smith, Chatfield and Pagnucco 1997; Marks and McAdam 1996; Bandy and Smith 2005). It has also been asserted that because EU policies are defined in highly technical terms, SMOs relying on technical and pragmatic discourses have more chance of influencing EU institutions than those relying on principled and ideological discourses (Balme and Chabanet 2008; Geddes and Guiraudon 2004; Ruzza 2004). Other authors, basing their approach on RMT, have argued that only actors disposing of significant material and specific symbolic resources are able to construct mobilizations at the European level (Giugni and Passy 2002; Imig and Tarrow 2001; Rootes 2002; Rohrschneider and Dalton 2002). Indeed, these mobilizations are based on the coordination of SMOs across national boundaries, and they generally require a great amount of material resources (Rohrschneider and Dalton 2002). Moreover, a high level of expertise among activists is needed in order to construct collective actions on EU policies which are defined through complex policy-making mechanisms (Grossman and Saurugger 2006; Rootes 2002). It has also been stated that national associations with high levels of formalization and professionalization are richer in resources than local associations with more informal organizational structures. They are thus better able to construct transnational or European mobilizations (Keck and Sikkink 1998; Giugni and Passy 2002; Rohrschneider and Dalton 2002; Tarrow 2005).

From the perspective of these studies, the specificities of the opportunities opened at the international or European level, and the constraints linked to the construction of collective actions at these levels, favour NGOs and lobby groups, and hinder the Europeanization of more 'grass-roots' groups. Grass-roots groups tend thus to remain at the national or local level or, if they 'shift their claims from the national to the European level', they tend to change their characteristics in order to 'model their repertoires of action around the forms of collective action that work the best at that level' (Imig and Tarrow 2001: 9). Activism around European public policies is therefore often described as exclusionary or elitist. Focusing on the organizations active around EU immigration policies, Favell (2000), Geddes (1998) and Guiraudon (2001) have shown that they have significant resources, are very professionalized and construct collective actions based on lobbying techniques (Geddes and Guiraudon 2004). Moreover, they benefit from the support (also financial) of the European Commission, which is open to their claims. Consequently, they have developed specific practices (a 'habitus'), which are linked to their location in Brussels (Favell 2000), and which lead to the exclusion of 'grass-roots' associations traditionally active at the local or national level (Guiraudon 2001).

Connected to the idea of an 'NGOization' of the mobilizations around EU policy issues, some studies have shown that – in a cross-national comparative perspective – SMOs coming from a national context in which movements are well organized have experienced different processes of Europeanization than SMOs coming from contexts in which movements are fragmented (Imig and Tarrow 2001; della Porta and Caiani 2007). Indeed, SMOs belonging to well-organized movements have better access to resources that they can use to Europeanize because resources are easily pooled in these movements. However, SMOs belonging to fragmented social movements tend to act on their own, and so dispose of fewer resources.

The idea of cross-national variations in the processes of Europeanization of social movement organizations is then sustained by studies insisting on the strategies of SMOs. Here, two alternative ideas can be presented, which relate the political opportunity structure in which a SMO is embedded (at the national level) to its process of Europeanization. On the one hand, SMOs coming from a closed political opportunity structure tend to have different processes of Europeanization than those coming from a more open POS (della Porta 2003). The first tend to explore more easily the European (or transnational) level in an attempt to trigger the 'boomerang effect' (Keck and Sikkink 1998). On the contrary, SMOs coming from more open POS tend to stay at the national level because they have the opportunities of presenting forward their claims in their traditional context of mobilization. On the other hand, authors (Kriesi et al. 1995; Giugni 2004; Koopmans 1995) have shown that SMOs involved in closed POS tend to rely more often on protesting types of repertoires of collective actions and to be less well endowed in resources. One might thus observe that SMOs coming from closed POS have more difficulty in Europeanizing than those coming from open POS where social movements tend to rely on more formalized repertoires of collective actions and have more resources. This leads to the observation of an over-representation of organizations coming from Northern European countries and an under-representation of organizations coming from Mediterranean countries in Brussels (Balme and Chabanet 2008). These two ideas are alternative: they lead to different conclusions. However, they lead us to expect that cross-national differences in terms of POS can explain cross-national differences in terms of processes of Europeanization of SMOs.

As has been highlighted here, most of the studies related to the Europeanization of social movements were carried out in late 1990s and early 2000s. Moreover, most of these studies relied on data from the 1980s and 1990s. More recently, some studies have proposed different conclusions. They have taken into account the evolution of social movements in the European Union since the beginning of the 2000s and have observed their increasing European dimension, as well as the increase of protest at the EU level (Agrikoliansky and Sommier 2005; della Porta et al. 2006; della Porta and Caiani 2009; Tarrow 2005). In particular, these authors have shown that the European Union is not necessarily defined in an instrumental way by social movement activists. Thus, relying on a constructivist view of the Europeanization processes, della Porta and Caiani (2009) argue that the construction of European social movements is part of a larger phenomenon, which is the emergence of a (non-consensual) European public sphere. Simply stated, it is the idea that debates on Europe are growing within civil society, and that citizens increasingly recognize the influence of European institutions on key political issues (Diez Medrano 2008). In fact, European institutions do not only have an influence on policy-making, but they also produce norms that influence actors' identities, and bring the European Union as a common general referential (or frame) in public debates (Diez Medrano 2003; Jorgensen and Wiener 2001). As this European public sphere has become increasingly present, it has also become less consensual (Risse 2003). The Europeanization of social movements and the construction of protest at the European level can thus be seen as a consequence of the emergence of a critical European public sphere. The analysis proposed in this book will follow this direction, analysing the construction of European social movements as well as the emergence of protest at the European level. I will stress the fact that this phenomenon is recent (since the end of the 1990s) and related to the Europeanization of the public sphere as it targets European institutions through public opinion rather than directly. More generally, the analysis proposed here is consonant with studies which study the European Union through the perspective of political sociology (Favell and Guiraudon 2009; Georgakakis 2008). This perspective leads us to underline the centrality of relational dynamics in Europeanization processes. In particular, studies inspired by Pierre Bourdieu's concept of 'field' (Adler-Nissen 2011; Bigo 1996; Cohen and Vauchez 2007; Favell 2000; Guiraudon 2002) have shown how, through the construction of Europeanized networks in which new values, forms of action, capital and 'habitus' are defined, institutional and non-institutional agents follow strategies of generation of new forms of social power at the EU level. These perspectives are important for the analysis of European social movements. They lead to an analysis of the strategies through which coalitions are constructed across borders and dynamics of distinction are created. More generally, this leads to an understanding of European social movements as actors which embody Europe as an 'everyday practice' (Favell and Guiraudon 2009: 570).

## Comparing the Europeanization of the French and German pro-asylum movements

Do social movements that come from distinct national contexts Europeanize differently? This is the other main question addressed in this book. In this perspective, the French and German comparison proves to be fruitful. The literature shows that these two cases are contrasted in terms of immigration and asylum policies and the general features of social movements.

First, this comparison is justified by the fact that both countries have a 'history' of asylum.[11] In France and Germany, the asylum issue has led to much public debate and state intervention.[12] This has been the case since the end of the eighteenth century in France (Noiriel 1998), and since the end of the nineteenth century in Germany (Herbert 2001). Moreover, although the numbers have decreased considerably in the last decade, these two countries have received most of the asylum-seekers and refugees that have come to Europe since the 1950s.[13] Consequently, the asylum issue traditionally tends to be more salient in the public sphere in France and Germany than in any other European country (Lavenex 2001). As a matter of fact, the social movements based in these two countries are part of this history. As will be developed in chapter two, there is a history of mobilization around the asylum issue that is independent from the actual context (which is influenced by the process of Europeanization). This criterion is fundamental for the longitudinal perspective of this study as it allows for the retracing of the history of these movements, and for a comparison of their features before and after the start of the Europeanization process. One must moreover add that since the 1980s, France and Germany have been among the leading countries in the European process of harmonization of immigration and asylum policies.[14] As one of the objectives of this research is to offer a more general reflection on the process of European integration, it has seemed logical to focus on cases that constitute crucial actors in this process.

Finally, and most importantly, the decision to focus on the French and German pro-asylum movements is justified by the differences in the national settings in which they mobilize. Two main streams of research should be mentioned: the comparative studies on citizenship and on asylum and immigration policies in European states; and the cross-national comparative studies on social movements in Europe.

Considering the comparative literature on citizenship and on asylum and immigration policies, the French and German pro-asylum movements are characterized by different degrees of embeddedness in society. In both countries, the asylum issue has traditionally held a different significance in the public sphere, which has had consequences for their ability to mobilize.

In Germany, the shape of asylum policies has been strongly linked, in public debates, to moral and ethical considerations related to the experience of the Third Reich (Lavenex 1999). These considerations led to a humanitarian definition of asylum: refugees were considered as victims and had to be protected through a generous policy. As I will discuss in chapter two, this perception prevailed until the beginning of the 1990s. However, an understanding of the way in which the asylum issue is traditionally framed in the German public sphere would not be complete if we failed to take account of the characteristics of citizenship. In fact, even if the definition of citizenship is not directly linked to the notion of asylum, the general features of the citizenship regime shape the way in which a society perceives the entry and the stay of migrants in general (Koopmans et al. 2005). It thus affects the general significance of the asylum issue in a country's public sphere. In this sense, the humanitarian perception of the asylum issue which has emerged since the Second World War in Germany has to be understood to be counterbalanced by an exclusive definition of citizenship expressed through the principle of 'jus-sanguini' that prevailed until the end of the 1990s (Brubaker 1992; Koopmans et al. 2005) and by the self-representation of Germany as a 'no-immigration' country (Bade 2000; Herbert 2001; Kastoryano 1996; Lavenex 1999). Until the end of the 1990s, immigrants were considered as 'guest-workers' and the 'jus-sangui' law impeded their political inclusion (Brubaker 1992). This has led to an 'institutionalized separateness' of migrants in society (Brubaker 2001), which has persisted despite recent changes to public policy (Borkert and Bosswick 2007: Koopmans et al. 2005; Heckmann 2003).[15] The view of the asylum issue in Germany is thus in a constant tension between the principles set out in the immediate post-war period and the exclusive definition of citizenship. In this regard, asylum has been traditionally perceived as an exceptional right in German society (in the sense that it is an exception to the general representation of Germany as a 'no-immigration' country). In France, on the other hand, the asylum issue traditionally tends to be perceived as a more global issue. Here again, the reference to history is necessary, as the matter of asylum is rooted in the constitution of France as a Republic: the right to asylum was adopted in the Constitution of the first French Republic (1793). The notion of asylum in France has been historically framed as a question of international relations: behind the promotion of the right to asylum, there was the self-perception of the 'pays des droits de l'Homme' of the 'terre d'asile' (Lavenex 1999; Noiriel 1998). There was the idea that the French example constituted a sort of universal model, an 'international engagement'. The difference between the French and German cases is reinforced by the fact that both countries have differentiated notions of citizenship. Nationality law and citizenship in France are based on the notion of '*jus soli*' and are therefore traditionally more inclusive (Brubaker 1992). Finally, France has a much longer history of immigration than Germany and the asylum issue has thus tended to be generally linked in the public debates with the question of immigration and, by extension, with the question of the external relations of France with the countries of origin (Weil 1995).[16]

In brief, the asylum issue is historically more embedded in society in France (it is related to various issues) than in Germany where it is considered as an exceptional right (and thus a more isolated issue).[17] In their cross-national comparative study on the anti-nuclear movement in Western Europe, Koopmans and Duyvendak (1994) proved that the general presentation of an issue in the public sphere (the 'political construction of an issue') influenced the way in which social movements found support for their cause. As I will develop in the second chapter, due to these differences in terms of the perception of the asylum issue in the public sphere, the French pro-asylum movement is traditionally less isolated in society than the German one: the cause of the asylum-seekers and refugees resonates more in the public sphere and the movement has therefore fewer difficulties in constructing stable networks of support.

The French-German comparison is then justified by comparative studies on social movements in Europe, which have shown that both countries are characterized by different forms of contention (Kriesi et al. 1995). German social movements have been described as being less turned towards disruptive forms of collective actions and less ideological than French movements, where the social question in particular is more salient. As I will develop in chapter one, my empirical analysis proves that this holds partially true for the pro-asylum movement. Both French and German movements are composed of different types of social movement organizations: some are close to NGOs and privilege strategies of compromise with public authorities whereas others are rather grass-roots groups who privilege protest. In France, grass-roots groups have significant immaterial resources and a wide scope of mobilization, and they therefore occupy an important position in the pro-asylum movement. However, in Germany, grass-roots groups have few resources and they tend to act more at the local level. They therefore occupy a more minor position in the pro-asylum movement in comparison with a small group of NGOs. Moreover, various comparative studies have shown that due to the different characteristics of the French and German institutional regimes (the French regime being centralized and the German being federal), German social movements tend to be more fragmented in geographical terms than French movements (Kriesi et al. 1995). This difference is clear when we look at the pro-asylum movements in the two countries. In Germany, even if asylum policies are defined at the federal level, Länder have the financial responsibility for their implementation. However, in France asylum policies are defined and implemented at the national level. This has consequences on the pro-asylum movements. As I will develop in chapter one, this is one of the factors that make the French pro-asylum movement more stable than the German one, which is characterized by geographical division.

Considering these differences, one might expect that French and German pro-asylum movements Europeanize to different degrees and via different paths. Thus, in line with analyses presenting European mobilization as an exclusionary process, one might expect that the French movement, being more embedded in society, would Europeanize more than the German movement. Conversely, following analyses showing the absence of protest at the EU level, one might expect that the German movement, where NGOs occupy a predominant position, Europeanize more than the French movement, in which protest is more central. Also, considering institutional factors, one might expect that the German movement, already addressing different institutional levels (regional and national), would have more facilities, thus enabling it to move to a higher level of mobilization than the French one, which addresses more exclusively the national level. Then, following Diez Medrano (2003), who has stressed the historical and cultural dimensions affecting the attitudes of the public opinion to European integration, one might expect that the different perceptions of the asylum issue in the French and German public sphere might have an influence on the Europeanization of the pro-asylum movements. One might thus observe that historical references to the Third Reich in Germany might lead the pro-asylum movement to be more critical of EU policies than the movement in France, where a more international view on asylum prevails. In sum, this comparison will lead to explore which are the resources, strategies, and institutional, historical and cultural dimensions that make it possible for a social movement to move from the national to the European level.

The analysis presented in this book will show the differences in the degrees and forms of Europeanization of the main social movement organizations which are part of French and German pro-asylum movements. I will show that particular attention should be paid to the resources, repertoires of collective action and ideas on which these SMOs traditionally rely and thus stress the impact of their national environment and history. But this book will also highlight the important similarities in the processes of Europeanization of French and German social movements. In so doing, I will show that the European polity is not only an institutional target but also a new common space of mobilization in which new solidarities, new resources and new ideas emerge, and where social movements can consequently overcome national differences.

## Methods and sources

Transnational social movements are formed by 'socially mobilized groups, with constituents in at least two states, engaged in sustained contentious interactions with power-holders in at least one state other than their own, or against an international institution or a multinational economic actor' (Tarrow 2002: 34).

From the perspective of this definition, this book focuses on the entire set of 'socially mobilized groups' which 'engage in sustained contentious interactions' with power-holders involved in the European process of harmonization of immigration and asylum policies. However, it is important to specify that the focus will not be limited to the analysis of 'contentious' types of interactions. Indeed, the core of this analysis deals with the process through which the Europeanization of a social movement occurs. One of the aims of this work is to examine whether this process will lead a SMO to change the form of its collective actions. Therefore the analysis cannot be carried out without acknowledging non-contentious forms of collective actions (for instance, lobbying techniques). For example, when it Europeanizes, a social movement organization which traditionally privileges protest at the national level can choose to diversify its range of collective action and become part of a lobby campaign or ally with NGOs. For this reason, I use Tarrow's definition in a flexible way as far as the forms of 'contention' are concerned. This book will thus analyse empirically grass-roots social movement organizations as well as more professionalized groups such as non-governmental organizations. Both have as a common aim to act publicly for the defence of refugees and asylum-seekers and to address institutions on this basis. As I will develop further, both types of organizations are often in competition, even conflict, but they can define alliances in specific campaigns, and they generally recognize each other as being active in the same field. Both SMOs and NGOs are thus the components of a broader pro-asylum movement.

The sample of organizations selected for the empirical analysis is representative of French and German pro-asylum movements: I have chosen to retain the groups that have played an important role in these movements since the beginning of the 1990s.[18] In order to constitute this sample, a first selection was made during a period of participant observation in France from September 2003 to July 2004.[19] This selection was then adjusted throughout the empirical analysis of the important collective actions that have been constructed around the asylum issue in France since the beginning of the 1990s. A similar approach was followed for the German case. I defined a first set of organizations through the analysis of the main collective actions that have been constructed around the asylum issue since the beginning of the 1990s. The composition of this panel was subsequently adjusted in the course of the interviews that took place in Berlin from February to August 2006.[20]

The French organizations that have been selected are:

- *Act Up Paris*
- *Amnesty International Section Française* (*AISF*)
- *Cimade*
- *Coordination Nationale des Sans-Papiers* (*CNSP*)
- *Fédération des Associations de Solidarité avec les Travailleurs Immigrés* (*FASTI*)
- *Forum Réfugiés*
- *France Terre d'Asile* (*FTDA*)
- *Groupe d'Information et de Soutien des Immigrés* (*Gisti*)
- *Ligue des droits de l'Homme* (*LdH*)
- *Mouvement contre le Racisme et pour l'Amitié entre les Peuples* (*MRAP*)
- *Secours Catholique*

The German organizations that have been selected are:

- *Aktionsbündnis Gegen Abschiebung Rhein-Main*
- *Amnesty International Deutschland*
- *Arbeiterwohlfahrt* (*AWO*)

- *Bayerischer Flüchtlingsrat*
- *Caritas Deutschland*
- *Diakonisches Werk der EKD* (*Diakonie*)
- *Flüchtlingsrat Berlin*
- *Flüchtlingsrat Hamburg*
- *Kanak Attak*
- *Karawane für die Rechte der Flüchtlinge und MigrantInnen* (*Karawane*) (including in particular *The Voice Refugee Forum*)
- *Kein Mensch ist Illegal* (*KMII*) (*and No Lager since 2004*)
- *Pro Asyl*

In the course of their process of Europeanization, these associations have constructed or integrated organizations or networks which mobilize at the EU level. These structures have thus also been studied, and are listed as follows.

European coalitions of associations and European networks:

- The *Churches' Commission for Migrants in Europe* (*CCME*)
- The *European Council on Refugees and Exiles* (*ECRE*)
- The *European Coalition for Foreigners' Right to Family Life*
- The *European Network Against Racism* (*ENAR*)
- The *Frassanito* network
- The *Migreurop* network
- The *No Border* network
- The *Platform for International Cooperation on Undocumented Migrants* (*PICUM*)
- The *United* network

European delegations of international NGOs and lobby groups:

- *Amnesty International – European Office* (*AI-EU*)
- *Caritas Europa*
- *Human Rights Watch* (*HRW*)
- The *Jesuit Refugee Service* (*JRS*)
- The *Migration Policy Group* (*MPG*)

The Europeanization of these groups has been analysed through the triangulation of various methods and data. The definition of these methods is based on the idea that the process of Europeanization of a social movement organization is made up of three decisive (and intrinsically linked) stages, or steps:

- the Europeanization of their networks: the progressive construction of linkages across the borders of member-states;
- the Europeanization of their perception (which is captured through the concept of cognitive frames):[21] the progressive construction of a common perception of the European Union as a necessary target for collective action;
- the Europeanization of the collective action: the progressive definition of a common collective action addressing the power-holders involved in the European integration process.

The Europeanization of networks is the first and most evident sign of the Europeanization of a social movement: the construction of inter-organizational and inter-personal linkages across borders is the basic element that allows the Europeanization of protest (della Porta et al. 2006; Rootes 2004). In the course of the construction of Europeanized networks, common (Europeanized) perceptions are defined: social movement organizations and activists from different countries construct shared views on the European Union which go beyond national or local particularisms (Balme and Chabanet 2002). Finally, the Europeanization of collective actions is made possible by the existence of Europeanized networks and is justified by the definition of common perceptions: these two elements allow social movement organizations and activists from different countries to construct joint collective actions at the EU level (Balme and Chabanet 2002). These different stages are not separate: I will show that the Europeanization of collective action has an influence on the Europeanization of networks. Through the construction of Europeanized collective actions, organizations will extend and/or consolidate their linkages across borders. The Europeanization of collective actions has also an influence on perceptions: through the construction of Europeanized collective actions, organizations are led to deepen their common perceptions. Likewise, the Europeanization of perceptions has an influence on the Europeanization of networks: through the definition of common perceptions, organizations are able to better define the shape of their European networks. For example, depending on the perceptions that emerge, some groups will play a more central role in the network, others will be less present, and still others will choose to quit these networks if they are in disagreement with the other groups.

My methods of data collection and analysis aimed at analysing these three dimensions systematically from 1999 to 2008.[22]

First, the Europeanization of networks was analysed through the observation of the web of ties of cooperation forged by the groups mobilizing on the asylum issue across borders. In this sense, the focus of this analysis is on 'horizontal networks', i.e. on the ties between networks, rather than with policy-makers and institutional actors as in 'vertical networks' (Cinalli 2004). One clear indicator of the possible Europeanization of the SMOs is their involvement in one or several European social movement organizations (European coalitions of associations, European delegation of an international NGO or European networks of activists). The presence and the nature of these linkages were identified through the information obtained in the associations' websites and mailing lists. This information was then complemented with a set of twenty-nine in-depth semi-structured interviews (see below): I asked respondents to identify their main partners at the European level and to comment on the shape of their European networks.

The Europeanization of discourses has been analysed through the concept of 'frame'. A frame is an 'interpretation of the reality' which justifies a collective action by presenting 'who we are', by presenting a social phenomenon as a problematic situation, by imputing responsibility for this situation, and by presenting the means to solve the problem (Snow et al. 1986; see also Gamson 1992; Snow and Benford 2000; Cefaï and Trom 2001). Snow and Benford (1988) have thus distinguished three basic framing tasks:

- diagnostic framing: it presents a situation as problematic; it tells what is good or wrong and implies the attribution of a responsibility;
- prognostic framing: it presents a solution to the problem presented in the diagnosis;
- motivational framing: it gives people a reason and an incentive to mobilize. This task strongly connects with identity-building: it seeks to 'transform actors' identities in a way which favors action' (della Porta and Diani 2006: 79).

The Europeanization of the frames was examined on the basis of a selection of organizational documents, which were produced between 1999 and 2008, and also analysed through the interviews. Around 400 relevant documents were analysed in total. This data was found in the websites of the associations (there was often a section related to 'European developments') and in their archives. The analysis aimed at identifying the Europeanization of the 'diagnostic', 'prognostic' and 'motivational' frames of these groups. Several indicators were identified and observed through an open-coding method. Concerning the 'motivational frame', one relevant indicator of the Europeanization of an association is a frequent reference to the groups with which it has constructed linkages across the states' boundaries. Regarding the 'diagnostic frame', the indicator may be a reference to a global 'problematic situation' in the European Union, or a reference to related situations and/or events in other European countries. Finally, the expression of a need to construct a joint collective action with actors from other European States, or the expression of a need to modify the European legislation and/or the modes of negotiation in the European sphere, have also been considered as important indicators of the Europeanization of the 'prognostic frame'. This analysis was complemented by the interviews. In particular, I asked questions relating to perceptions of European immigration and asylum policies or to views about their possibilities of mobilizing at the EU level.

Finally, the Europeanization of collective actions was observed through a protest-event analysis. As the aim is to observe the process of Europeanization of associations that are constituted at the national level, this analysis took into account the Europeanized collective actions that were constructed by these associations themselves as well as the collective actions of the European networks (informal or structured) to which they belong. Concerning the second type of collective action, it is important to acknowledge the different degrees of involvement of the member-associations in the process of construction of a collective action. Indeed, in many cases, a European collective action is constructed and implemented by the secretariat of a centralized network, without a strong involvement of the member-associations. For this reason, it would be a methodological error to analyse the Europeanization of a SMO only through the activities of the European network to which it belongs. I have thus combined this protest-event analysis with my network analysis. The network analysis led me to distinguish three degrees of involvement of the SMO in the construction of a European collective action (within the framework of a European network):

- a strong degree of involvement: a participation in the phase of construction and elaboration of collective action (for example, the writing of a joint communiqué);
- an intermediary degree of involvement: a participation in the phase of implementation, the final stage of construction of collective action (such as the signature of a joint communiqué);
- a low degree of involvement: the delegation of power to a European secretariat or office (when an association is part of a European network, however without participating in the construction or implementation of its collective actions).

This typology has enabled me to have an accurate view of the processes of Europeanization of collective actions. As the aim was to analyse comparatively the role of each of the SMOs studied at the EU level, a comprehensive list of all the Europeanized collective actions in which they were involved from 1999 to 2008 has been made (seventy-two protest-events were counted in total). The events that were analysed were those reported in the associations' websites and mailing lists, in their publications (calls and communiqués) and in their internal literature (in particular the annual reports).[23] This data was complemented by the interviews: respondents were asked to describe the main protest-event organized at the European level.

Among the methods used in this research, two in particular are fundamental: document analysis (for frame-analysis and protest-event analysis) and in-depth semi-structured interviews (see the list of interviews at the end of the book). In the course of my empirical research, I have thus relied on two main sources: written documents and oral conversations. The use of these two sources has the advantage of situating the actors of social movements directly at the core of the empirical analysis. I aim to observe social movement organizations 'from the inside': how – as collective actors – they organize themselves, how they think, and how they act at the European level. Therefore, I choose sources in which associations present themselves directly (through the 'official' voice of the documents that they publish or through the voice of activists).[24]

However, it is important to specify that the researcher inevitably faces difficulties in dealing with these sources. Throughout my empirical research I have faced two main difficulties. The first was the need to situate each of the documents and interviews in its particular context. The ideas presented in the documents and interviews are often related to a set of events that are affecting the life of the association or the activist being interviewed (Johnston 2002). These events may be the recent evolution of asylum policies, a change of government, the financial situation of the association, its collective work with another association; the recruitment of new activists, etc. These sets of events may have a decisive influence on the collective identity of the association (at least in the long term). The difficulty is thus to single out these particular events and to analyse whether their influence on the life of the associations is fundamental or not. In other words, the difficulty is to understand the data on which I rely in its particular context. For that, a good historical knowledge of the events that may affect the life of the associations (in particular the evolution of the legislation related to immigration asylum policies) was needed. I will present the significance of these events in the course of chapters one and two. Then, concerning the documents in particular, I privileged the analysis of texts that are characterized by a high level of abstraction and that are thus less influenced by the particular context in which they were produced. Moreover, I relied on a set of data that was significant enough to avoid problems of context dependence. Concerning the interviews, I stressed in the beginning of each of them what my research objectives were. I made it clear to each interviewee that my analysis related to the evolution of its organization in the long term and not only in the period in which the interview took place.[25]

The second difficulty concerned more particularly the interviews. As I have outlined above, my analysis focuses on the meso-level: I want to analyse SMOs. During the interviews, it was thus particularly important for me to distinguish the personal view of the interviewee (which can be critical vis-à-vis its own association) from the presentation of the association to an external observer (the researcher). I therefore had to remind the interviewees of the general objectives of my research when necessary. Moreover, as often as I could, I referred during the interviews to factual information relating to the history of the association (for example, I referred to a mobilization that occurred in the past, and asked if this type of collective action was usual or exceptional for the association). Although gaining the trust of the activists proved to be extremely useful for my research, this task tended to be more difficult when the level of confidence was high between the interviewee and the interviewer. In this case, the interviewee sometimes tended to be critical vis-à-vis his/her own organization and would let his/her own voice prevail over the 'official' voice of the association. In this case, again, I reminded the interviewee of the general objectives of my research.

## The structure of the book

In this general introduction, I have presented and discussed the literature relating to the harmonization of asylum policies and the Europeanization of social movements. I have shown how these two fields of study can be related in order to define a theoretical framework on Europeanization 'from below' and 'from the borders'. I have then explained why and how I chose to compare French and German pro-asylum movements.

Chapters one and two focus on the analysis of French and German pro-asylum movements in their traditional context of mobilization.

First, chapter one proposes a global and longitudinal comparison of French and German pro-asylum movements since the beginning of the 1990s. Insisting on the cross-national comparative perspective (thus situated at the macro-level), I address the fundamental questions of knowing if (and why) French and German movements are made of different inter-organizational dynamics and if (and why) they have different types of allies.

Then, chapter two moves to the meso-level in order to propose a systematic comparison of the fundamental features of the groups that constitute the French and German pro-asylum movement. More precisely, I attempt to highlight the differences that separate different groups of associations in these two countries.

Chapters three and four present the empirical results on the processes of Europeanization of these movements. These chapters show that associations mobilizing around the same issue do not follow a unique process of Europeanization: they have different levels and modes of Europeanization. Chapter three presents the results concerning their levels of Europeanization and chapter four presents those concerning their modes of Europeanization. Throughout these chapters, I relate these empirical results with those presented in chapters one and two. I address in detail the four fundamental research questions presented in this introduction. Do social movement organizations Europeanize? Do social movement organizations having different features tend to have different levels and modes of Europeanization? Do they tend to change the features of their collective identity when they move from the national to the European level? Do social movement organizations coming from different national contexts of mobilization tend to have different levels and modes of Europeanization?

In chapter five, I emphasize the strategies of the actors in order to explain the processes of Europeanization of French and German pro-asylum groups. First, I focus on the groups of non-governmental organizations mobilizing around the asylum issue exclusively at the European level (in Brussels) since the beginning of the 1990s. I relate social movement studies to the Bourdieusian concept of 'field' in order to explain the dynamics of the field of mobilization on European asylum policies. Then, I move back to the components of French and German social movements. I show how they have developed various strategies of Europeanization and how these are related to the particular dynamics of interaction within the field of mobilizations on EU's asylum policies. I offer an explanatory scheme for the Europeanization of social movement organizations which is centred on their strategies.

In the conclusion, I summarize and put into perspective the main findings of the combined empirical and theoretical analyses. I discuss the contribution of a study on Europeanization 'from below' and 'from the borders' in order to gain a greater understanding of the evolution of power relations in the European Union.

## Notes

1 This study is more specifically focused on asylum policies as it is in this domain that EU institutions have gained more power. However, asylum policies are highly dependent on immigration policies more generally, and so they should not be conceived as separate. Indeed, many of the organizations that I study have mobilized

not only for the inclusion of asylum-seekers and refugees, but more generally for the inclusion of migrants (and also of undocumented migrants).

2 Directive 2008/115/EC of the European Parliament and of the Council of 16 December 2008 on common standards and procedures in Member States for returning illegally staying third-country nationals.

3 'First call for mobilization for a counter-summit and an alternative forum on "Migrations and Development". For a Europe of openness and solidarity', May 2008.

4 Article 1 of the 1951 United Nations Convention Relating to the Status of Refugees as amended by the 1967 Protocol.

5 As there is no conventional definition of this concept, this resolution is generally considered as a reference.

6 Quoted by Bouteillet-Paquet (2001: 33).

7 Since 2003 European member-states have formally agreed on the fact that they cannot give the status of refugee to an EU citizen.

8 The SIS is an informatic centralized system in which immigrants who do not have legal authorization to enter the EU territory are registered.

9 The Dublin convention (1990) specifies that asylum-seekers have to submit an application for the refugee status in the first EU country in which they arrived.

10 This image has been borrowed from the two chapters related to 'Transnationalism From the Inside' in della Porta and Diani (2004: 20–70).

11 See the work of German and French historians on this issue: Bade (2000); Herbert (2001); Noiriel (1998).

12 On the contrary for example to Southern-European countries, where the asylum issue has become salient only recently.

13 See the statistics published on UNHCR's website: http://www.unhcr.org/statistics.html.

14 Great-Britain is also a crucial actor in this process, but it represents a particular case as it is one of the two member-states (with Ireland) that did not sign the Schengen agreements.

15 A new nationality law was adopted in 1999; it makes it easier for immigrants living in Germany on a long-term basis, and their children, to acquire German citizenship.

16 As shown by Sandra Lavenex (1999), these differences in the general perception of the asylum issue in the public debates in France and in Germany persisted until the mid-1990s. They then started to become convergent with the emergence of a 'securitarian frame' in the political debates related to asylum in both countries.

17 It is important to specify that the question of the degree of embeddedness in society does not mean that the asylum issue is more or less salient in the French and German public spheres. It suggests rather that the public debates on asylum are more likely to be linked with debates related to other issues in France than in Germany (see below for more on this point).

18 I will show why, during the developments related to the history of these social movements, the beginning of the 1990s is a crucial period for the pro-asylum movement in both countries.

19 During this period, I worked as a volunteer for a French association (*Gisti*) and was involved in its daily activities. I also participated in many formal and informal

meetings of representatives of the French pro-asylum movement. This association is a major component of the European network *Migreurop*, and so I have actively participated in many meetings with activists from different European or African countries. Although I consider this experience to have been part of my research process, I would not qualify it as a method of 'theory-driven participant observation' (Lichterman 2002). Indeed, if I undertook 'participation' during this period (I was actively involved in the activities of this organization and its networks), I did not conduct 'theory-driven observation' as it is usually understood by the methods of participant observation. I did not enter the field with a theoretical framework that I intended to 'test': at this stage, I had only a general idea of the analysis that I wanted to carry out. I think that this experience helped me to gain a background in-depth knowledge of my field of research.

20 It is important to specify that *Amnesty International Section Française*, *Amnesty International Deutschland*, the *Ligue des droits de l'Homme*, the *Deutscher Caritasverband*, the *Secours Catholique* and *Diakonie* represent particular cases. They are the national branches of international organizations (respectively *Amnesty International*, *Fédération Internationale des Ligues des droits de l'Homme*, *Caritas* and *Diaconia*). Therefore, unlike the other SMOs analysed, they already have Europeanized networks. However, it was important to include them in this panel as they all represent crucial actors in French and German pro-asylum movements. Moreover, depending on the context in which they are embedded, the national branches of these international organizations do not necessarily play the same role in each country. Thus, the *Ligue des Droits de l'Homme* is a crucial actor in mobilizations on the asylum issue in France, whereas its German counterpart – the *Deutsche Liga für Menschenrechte* – does not play an important role in this domain (it has thus not been integrated in the panel of German associations).

21 See the definition below.

22 1999 was a crucial year for the construction of European immigration and asylum policies. The Amsterdam Treaty came into force in May 1999, and part of the immigration and asylum policies became communitarized. And in October, member-states formulated the Tampere Program for common EU immigration and asylum policies.

23 Unlike most of the studies based on protest-event analysis, I have relied on reports made by the SMOs directly rather than on press reports. I chose this specific strategy because it allowed me to have a more comprehensive list of all the Europeanized actions in which these organizations were involved. Indeed, as is shown by Earl et al. (2004), news agencies and newspapers report only a minor part of protest events and tend to focus on those which are highly visible. Also, as newspapers tend to privilege information related to national politics (Lefébure and Lagneau 2002), selection biases are even more important with regard to European collective actions.

24 The activists selected for the interviews are those who, in each selected SMOs, are the most involved in European networks. As I will develop below, they represent a minority of the people active in these SMOs. They were identified during the period of participant observation and through a snowball strategy. The semi-structured questionnaires included closed and open questions on strategies of networking, communication and collective actions at the national and European level. Particular

attention was paid to the strategic continuities or ruptures between the national and European level. More generally, interviewees were asked to present their views about the process of harmonization of immigration and asylum policies, and about the evolution of their organization in this context. Finally, the interviews addressed activists' general ideas on the inclusion of migrants and refugees as well as their personal experience of activism.

25 I also had to remind my interviewees of my research objectives on several occasions, when they focused too much on the presentation of the association in its immediate context.

Chapter 1

# The Evolution of French and German Pro-asylum Movements since the Beginning of the 1990s

The first step in this study is to analyse French and German pro-asylum movements in a comparative perspective. Chapters one and two present this analysis. Following the theoretical framework developed in the introduction, two levels of analysis will be presented simultaneously. The analysis presented in this chapter is situated at the macro-level. I will provide a historical analysis of French and German pro-asylum movements, and I will focus on two dimensions that have an influence on their Europeanization: their inter-organizational cohesion and their level of embeddedness in society. The focus is then moved to the meso-level: chapter two presents a more detailed comparison of the different organizations which make up these movements. Again, several dimensions that have an influence on their Europeanization will be discussed: their frames, repertoires of collective action, resources, organizational structures and geographical scope of mobilization.

Indeed, the shift from one level of analysis to the other leads to very different – and complementary – perspectives when comparing social movements which are active in different political environments. A focus on the macro-level leads us to stress the main characteristics of the movements. It highlights the general differences between social movements from different countries, and it permits us to identify the elements of the national context that have an influence on these movements. Conversely, a focus on the meso-level leads to an emphasis on the diversity of social movements. This leads us to stress the internal dynamics that can be observed within these social movements.

As I will show in this chapter and the following one, some elements of the national contexts can help us to understand some general features of the mobilizations around a particular issue. However, much more than the national political space in which they are embedded, it is the strategies and the dynamics of interactions of social movement organizations that progressively shape their identity. In other words, it is in the course of their interactions in a particular context that SMOs are led to define their profile and the differences that distinguish one from another. The use of the concept of 'multi-organizational field' (Curtis and Zurcher 1973) enables us to relate the analysis of contextual and interactional factors. Following Curtis and Zurcher (1973), a multi-organizational field consists in general terms of a network of organizations which interact on a regular basis in order to mobilize around a specific cause. The localization of contestation into a particular sphere of activities (or field) within the social world permits us to analyse and to link together internal dimensions (the definition of multi-organizational coalitions and inter-organizational divisions) and external dimensions (the relations between the actors of this field with actors of other fields such as the political field, the journalistic field, the trade unions field or the social movements mobilizing around other issues). Moreover, it permits the handling and linking together of the macro-level (the shape of a social movement) and meso-level (the features of the social movement organizations which comprise it). Following these perspectives, I propose to define the 'multi-organizational field' as a sphere of protesting activities, with a certain degree of autonomy from other spheres of activities, in which the social movement organizations that mobilize regularly around a particular issue interact in order to construct multi-organizational coalitions and in which inter-organizational divisions can occur.

The mobilizations constructed by this inter-organizational field are rooted in history. In France for example, the *Cimade* (created in the 1930s) and the *Ligue des droits de l'Homme* (created in 1898) actively addressed the French government in order to promote an extensive definition of the term 'refugee' at the international conference in Evian in 1938 and during the negotiations of the Geneva Convention in 1951. It has seemed however sensible to limit the analysis to the history of the mobilizations since the beginning of the 1990s. Indeed, it is since this period that the European governments – seeing a growing number of asylum seekers arriving in their country – have started to adopt restrictive measures on asylum (Crépeau 1995). This period therefore constitutes an important shift and it is since that period that the actual dynamics of the pro-asylum movements began to be progressively shaped in France and in Germany. The following developments therefore analyse the evolution of French and German pro-asylum movements from the beginning of the 1990s to the mid-2000s in a comparative perspective.[1]

Throughout this period, French and German pro-asylum movements have had different forms. Two dimensions in particular can be underlined: the internal cohesion of the movement (the density and durability of the multi-organizational coalitions), and its embeddedness in society (the diversity and stability of its alliances). Indeed, the French movement is made up of dense and durable coalitions and is supported by diverse allies, whereas the German movement is more fragmented and isolated. These differences are related to contextual dimensions as well as to the strategies of the actors, both factors being interrelated. I will stress two contextual factors which differentiate the French and German cases: the salience of the asylum issue in the political field (or in other words, the degree of politicization of the asylum issue); and the occurrence of a cycle of protest.[2]

## The French case: a movement made up of dense inter-associative coalitions and diversified allies

Since the beginning of the 1990s, asylum policies have been subject to numerous changes in France: from 1991 to 2006, no fewer than seven significant reforms were implemented. The frequency of these reforms and the degradation of the conditions of immigrants, refugees and asylum-seekers subsequent to them have led to the emergence and consolidation of a significant field of mobilization around these issues. Within this field, a group of associations have progressively constructed and consolidated multi-organizational coalitions which have played a leading role.

The first mobilizations specifically relating to the asylum issue took place in 1991–1992. From April 1991 to September 1992, following the restrictive reform of the French Office for the Protection of Refugees and Stateless Persons (*Office Français pour la Protection des Réfugiés et Apatrides*, *OFPRA*),[3] around 1,500 asylum-seekers who were refused the status of refugee ('*déboutés du droit d'asile*') carried out hunger-strikes all over the country (Siméant 1998).[4] They were supported by associations traditionally mobilized for the defence of immigrants and/or against racism,[5] and by associations who specialized in the material support of asylum seekers (in particular, *Forum Réfugiés* in the Rhône-Alpes region). These two groups of associations soon began to communicate with each other, and they contested the reform of *OFPRA* by launching systematic court appeals against the decisions taken by it. They also addressed the government through the launching of several calls and joint communiqués, and through the organization of regular demonstrations. In July 1991, the government responded to this movement by regularizing some of the asylum-seekers. Of the 50,000 to 100,000 individuals who were concerned by the reform, around 17,000 were regularized. The fact that only a relatively small number of them were granted a regular status explains why the hunger-strikes continued until September 1992. However, following this regularization process, those protestors who had started a hunger-strike were not supported to the same degree by the associations. The coalition of associations quickly became split on the question of whether the migrants who continued their action should be supported, and *FASTI* subsequently became the only association to be active in the Information and Solidarity Network.

Since this experience, mobilizations against immigration policies (in which the associations of the Information and Solidarity Network had been involved since the closure of the borders in the early 1970s) have become systematically linked with those against asylum policies. These associations argue that immigration and asylum policy reforms should be addressed together as they both result in migrants having to live with a precarious or even undocumented residence status.[6] This argument is all the more salient (unlike in Germany, as we will see) as the discourse developed by the successive governments that carried out reforms in these matters systematically maintained confusion between immigration and asylum policies (Crépeau 1995). Following this episode, the movements mobilizing around the asylum issue comprised associations mobilizing specifically around the asylum issue as well as associations that addressed immigration policies more generally (Abdallah 2000).

The mobilizations organized after the introduction of new immigration legislation in 1993[7] were similar to those which had taken place two years earlier. By focusing on the fight against 'illegal immigration' and on the facilitation of deportation procedures, this reform led to a mobilization that concerned all types of migrants (family of migrants whose reunification was made more difficult, undocumented migrants risking deportation, or 'déboutés du droit d'asile' living without residence permits) (Noiriel 1998). The group of associations that formed the Information and Solidarity Network in the 1980s began to collaborate again and to construct joint collective actions (Abdallah 2000). Joint press conferences and communiqués were organized, in particular by *Gisti*, *Cimade*, *MRAP*, the *Ligue des droits de l'Homme* and *FASTI*. Moreover, this coalition launched more durable initiatives that implied collective work in the long term. It coordinated support for mixed couples in 1993 and participated in the construction of the Collective for the Reception of the Algerian Asylum-Seekers and Exiles in France (*Collectif pour l'accueil en France des demandeurs d'asile et exilés d'Algérie*) in 1994. However, the associations who specialized in the reception of asylum-seekers (in particular *France Terre d'Asile* and *Forum Réfugiés*) did not participate in these campaigns.

In August 1996, the hunger-strike carried out by a group of *sans-papiers* (undocumented migrants) in the Saint-Bernard church in Paris was the most dramatic point of a mobilization that had no precedent in such issues

(Costa-Lascoux 1997; Laubenthal 2007; Siméant 1998). The mobilization began in March 1996, as 300 undocumented migrants occupied the Saint-Ambroise church, demanding to be regularized. Evacuated by the police, they then decided to occupy a building in Paris where they were joined by a large coalition of allies. These allies included associations that had led previous mobilizations (such as *Gisti*, *Cimade*, *MRAP*, *FASTI* and the *Ligue des droits de l'Homme*),[8] as well as a significant coalition of organizations and actors from other fields (see below). It was following unsuccessful negotiations with the Minister of the Interior that a group of *sans-papiers* started a hunger-strike at the Saint-Bernard church in July. In August, the church was evacuated by a significant contingent of police, and several protestors were deported to their country of origin in the following weeks. The huge impact of this event in the media contributed to a larger mobilization of public opinion (Balibar et al. 1999). Protest demonstrations were organized in the days that followed, and the groups of *sans-papiers* and their allies continued to construct joint collective actions (occupations, marches, hunger-strikes, and several press campaigns). At the end of 1996, this movement took on another dimension as the government launched new legislation relating to the work and residence of undocumented migrants. A strong mobilization emerged, focusing in particular on the question of the lodging-certificates.[9] In February 1997, several petitions were launched, and a call written by sixty-six young French film-directors advocating civil disobedience rapidly gained much media attention. In the following days, a demonstration of around 100,000 people was organized in Paris. In the context of the legislative campaign in 1997, the impact of these mobilizations became even more important. Those involved in the movement saw an important opportunity to put pressure on the political parties that were campaigning. Thus, from May to June 1997, several groups of *sans-papiers* organized a march from Angoulême to Paris in order to address public opinion and those involved in the electoral campaign. Moreover, two years after the presidential elections in 1995 (in which the *Front National* obtained a significant result), this movement was strengthened by a concern about the growing success of the extreme-right party and extreme-right ideas.[10] Thus, the new legislation proposed by the government was often compared by the actors of the movement with the laws of the Vichy regime, and the Minister of the Interior was often accused of trying to attract the electorate of the *Front National*. The new law, which concerned the work and residence of undocumented migrants, was eventually adopted by the parliament in 1997 but the article relating to the lodging-certificates was omitted. Following the legislative elections in spring 1997, a coalition government consisting of the Socialist, Communist and Green parties was formed, and a programme of regularization of undocumented migrants was rapidly launched. Moreover, negotiations were started for a new general legislation on immigration and asylum. The *sans-papiers* and the organizations supporting their mobilization maintained pressure in order to obtain an abrogation of the laws passed by the previous government and a global regularization of undocumented migrants (in contrast to the case-by-case regularization proposed by the government). Thus, in July 1997, a group of associations (including *Gisti*, *Act Up-Paris* and *FASTI*) published a communiqué asking for 'freedom of circulation'.[11] In December 1997, the government proposed a new reform on immigration and asylum.[12] Soon after, the organizations acting with the *sans-papiers* launched new collective actions. Several joint communiqués, calls, and press campaigns were launched by *Gisti*, *FASTI*, *Act Up-Paris*, the *Ligue des droits de l'Homme*, *Cimade* and *CNSP* (*Coordination Nationale des Sans-Papiers*, recently created by the different groups of *sans-papiers*). Notwithstanding these actions, the reform was adopted in May 1998.

In September 1999, the opening of the centre of Sangatte[13] was the point of departure for new mobilizations. In October 2001, a 'campaign of support for the refugees from Sangatte to Calais' was organized by the *Ligue des droits de l'Homme*, *Cimade*, *Gisti*, several collectives of *sans-papiers*, together with many other allies (see below). On November 2002, a group of member-associations (*Amnesty International Section Française*, *Gisti*, the *Ligue des droits de l'Homme*, *MRAP*) of the newly created French Coalition for Asylum Right (*Coordination Française pour le Droit d'Asile*, *CFDA*)[14] launched a communiqué demanding the full application of the principles included in the Geneva Convention.[15] Moreover, associations like the *Ligue des droits de l'Homme*, *Gisti*, *Cimade*, *Amnesty International Section Française* and *Forum Réfugiés* carried out several campaigns of observation and published studies intended to show the public exactly 'who' the migrants in Sangatte were (Carrère 2002). The aim was to criticize the analysis offered by the government and by the mainstream media who tended to present the individuals in Sangatte as 'clandestine' without explaining their situation. When the centre was closed in the winter of 2002–2003, these associations (and in particular *Amnesty International Section Française*) denounced this 'non-solution'.[16] In March 2003, they jointly launched a call for a demonstration in Paris. Sangatte was one of the main events that intensified the collective work of the pro-asylum movement in France. Joint efforts were perceived as necessary as their aim was to mobilize on a phenomenon that was difficult to grasp (the centre of Sangatte being difficult to access). A more intense cooperation was therefore needed in order to exchange information and to render this reality visible to the public. This is why much of the collective action carried out by the associations during this period has taken the form of joint studies and seminars. As I will develop below, this collaboration and the exchanges of ideas on Sangatte became the point of departure for the launching of the European network *Migreurop*.

In 2003, the introduction of a new reform of immigration and asylum policies[17] led to new mobilizations by these associations. After a lobbying campaign that did not lead to considerable results, the associations of *CFDA* started a long-term public campaign. Several joint communiqués, calls and publications were published. In May 2003, *CNSP*, *Gisti*, the *Ligue des droits de l'Homme* and *MRAP* launched a call[18] that was signed by around 300 associations, and a public meeting was organized in Paris in October. However, although the general frame of these mobilizations was similar to the actions carried out in 1996–1997 (the call for civil disobedience against the measures related to acts of solidarity with migrants), public opinion did not mobilize to the same degree. Participation in the demonstration organized in July 2003 (on the opening of the parliamentary debates on the project of law) was relatively low. The new legislation was eventually adopted in the winter of 2003.

In 2004, the increasing number of arrests of undocumented migrants' children and families near schools led to spontaneous collective actions on the part of teachers, parents and citizens at the local level. These initiatives led to the creation, in June 2004, of the Education Without Borders Network (*Réseau Education Sans Frontières, RESF*). Sixty-nine associations[19] and twenty-two trade union movements became part of this network, which rapidly gained in importance: local groups were created throughout the whole territory, and the media provided it with a large audience (Mathieu 2010). The call for the creation of the network[20] was widespread and the movement grew in popularity in the eyes of the public. During the same period, a group of undocumented migrants started a hunger-strike in Lille to protest against a risk of deportation. A demonstration was organized by the *RESF* network in several cities in February 2005, and several occupations were organized by a local collective of *sans-papiers* in Paris (*9e collectif des sans-papiers*). In March 2005, twelve undocumented migrants started a hunger-strike in Paris and occupations were organized in several cities during the same period. In June 2005 and February 2006, *RESF* organized demonstrations to demand the regularization of undocumented students, and it launched a petition in May 2006.[21] In 2006, these mobilizations took on another dimension as the French Minister of the Interior announced a new project of reform on immigration and asylum.[22] This period of intense mobilization was the moment in which the associations that were the most involved (*Gisti*, *Cimade*, *Ligue des Droits de l'Homme*, *MRAP*, *Act Up Paris*,

*FASTI*, etc.) formalized further their collective work. Thus, in February 2006, they launched a petition[23] and created a new network: United Against Disposable Immigration (*Uni(e)s contre une immigration jetable, UCIJ*). The petition was signed by around 105,000 people and the movement rapidly expanded. A joint press campaign and several demonstrations were organized. However, the law modifying the immigration and asylum policies was adopted in July 2006. Also in June 2006, in response to the mobilizations of the *RESF* network, the French government announced the regularization of some of the undocumented migrants living in France. This process was, however, considered largely insufficient by the *RESF* network (out of 30,000 families that sought regularization, only 6,000 obtained it), which continued to mobilize. At the same time, the expulsion of African families who had been occupying a building in Cachan for three years encouraged a link between the mobilizations on the immigration and asylum issue with growing claims for a new housing policy in France. These families were actively supported by the associations of the *RESF* and *Uni(e)s contre une immigration jetable* networks. A new press campaign was launched and at the same time, several migrants started a hunger-strike. An agreement with the government was eventually reached in October.[24]

As is shown in this historical overview, the majority of French associations mobilizing on the asylum issue have progressively intensified their collective work since the beginning of the 1990s. Throughout this period, from one campaign to the other, they have constructed increasingly durable and dense coalitions and have formulated increasingly extensive claims. In the beginning, these coalitions and claims were essentially short-term (dealing, for example, with the construction of a campaign for the regularization of undocumented migrants). But due to their intensive collaboration, these associations were progressively able to formulate common frames that went beyond this immediate claim, demanding, for example, a re-appraisal of immigration and asylum policies and of North-South relations.[25] However, two important associations that specialized in the reception of asylum seekers (*Forum Réfugiés* and *France Terre d'Asile*) remained outside these coalitions. This analysis resonates with the more general idea that frames, ideas and discourses (what makes the cohesion of a movement) are not given 'a priori' (della Porta and Piazza 2008; Fillieule 2006). They emerge progressively during the course of the mobilizations, through the interactions between diverse actors. Thus, as is argued by Fillieule (2006: 208), 'sometimes, mobilization precedes the construction of a frame [. . .], which, quite often, is formed during the action, defining itself through the interactions between mobilized groups and the targets of mobilization and power' (author's translation). As I will now discuss, this process is also related to a strategy of alliance with actors from diverse fields. This strategy is facilitated by the context of emergence of a new cycle of protest.

Since the beginning of the 1990s, the French pro-asylum movement has benefited from the support of diverse types of allies. This includes the involvement of figures of the political, artistic, juridical and academic fields as well as those from trade unions and churches. This has been even more evident since the movement of the 'sans-papiers' in 1996–1997. This period coincides with the emergence of a cycle of protest in which the fight against exclusion was central (Crettiez and Sommier 2006). In this context, the actors involved in the pro-asylum movement have managed to place their movement as one of the crucial components of this cycle of protest. This strategy has enabled them to gain and to consolidate durable and diverse allies.

The variety of the allies of this movement was already visible in the beginning of the 1990s. Thus, in December 1990, in support of the mobilizations against the reform of OFPRA, a group of artists and political and public figures launched a 'call for asylum right',[26] which rapidly made a significant impact in the media. In 1991, a figure from the Catholic Church (l'abbé Pierre, who had initiated a movement of solidarity for better housing conditions in the 1950s) demonstrated his solidarity with the asylum-seekers by going on hunger-strike for several days. This had a strong impact on the movement as it was immediately after this that the media coverage increased substantially (Siméant 1998). This movement was also supported by trade unions. Thus, in 1990, the *CFDT*, the *CGT* and the *CFTC* tried to negotiate with the government for the regularization of the asylum-seekers, and they also organized several public meetings. However, when the asylum-seekers started to privilege the hunger-strike as their principal mode of collective action, trade unions quickly distanced themselves from the movement (Siméant 1998). One must finally mention the support of the French communist party (*PCF*) who, through its newspaper (*L'Humanité*), contributed to the visibility of the movement in the media. The *PCF* saw the movement of the 'déboutés du droit d'asile' as an opportunity to criticize the government, in anticipation of the next legislative elections (1993).

The *sans-papiers* movement in 1996–1997 is probably the most notable example of the significance and diversity of the allies mobilizing on this issue (Laubenthal 2007). As in 1990–1991, several religious figures played an important role in these mobilizations: churches (Saint Ambroise and Saint Bernard) were chosen by protestors as strategic places for their mobilization because they knew that they would find important support from religious figures. Moreover, during this period, the movement gained the support of figures in the artistic field. This involvement was confirmed with the call launched by sixty-six young film-directors and by the presence of a delegation of *sans-papiers* at the Cannes festival in 1997. After this period, the support of the artistic field on the immigration and asylum issue remained constant. Numerous concerts and public events showing solidarity with this movement were organized. More recently, in 2006, many figures from artistic and sporting fields have publicly manifested their solidarity with those evicted from the squat in Cachan. Trade unions were also crucial allies for this movement. Indeed, two years after the general strikes of December 1995, organized in protest against the reforms of public services, the *CGT*, the *CFDT* and more radical trade unions like *SUD* and the *CNT*, were in a period of intense confrontation with the government. The active support of the *sans-papiers* movement was seen as a way to extend this opposition. Moreover, several of the militants of the associations who mobilized on the asylum issue also share an affiliation to a trade union. Thus, in a note published ten years after the mobilizations, the *CGT* underlined its role in this movement. It framed its involvement in this movement as being related to a more general fight against precariousness and so bridges the claims formulated by the *sans-papiers* with its own claims:

> The notion of 'sans-papiers' appeared in 1996, when Africans decided to start a long fight in order to have the right to live in France, to work, to contribute to social security and have the various benefits resulting from it, to have decent housing, to be medically treated . . . in short, to be considered as human beings.
>
> The CGT immediately made this fight its own fight: these foreigners who are in an irregular situation are above all salaried employees and, as such, they are fully integrated in our trade union organization.
>
> Now that the CGT is working to build a conception of the salaried employee statute that gives him security in all aspects of his life, how can we ignore the precariousness, the permanent fear, in which these foreigners are living?[27]

Some political figures played a significant role during the mobilizations of the *sans-papiers*. Thus, the leaders of parties such as *Les Verts*, *Ligue Communiste Révolutionnaire* (*LCR*) and *Parti Communiste Français* (*PCF*), and some members of the *Parti Socialiste* visited the *sans-papiers* who were on hunger-strike and contributed to the emergence of public debates on this issue. The historical links between some associations mobilized on this issue and some political parties (the most obvious example is probably the *MRAP* and the *PCF*) partly explain why these political parties rapidly manifested their solidarity with the movement. Moreover, this crisis was seen as an important opportunity for these parties to show their opposition to the right-wing government, and this became even more evident after the start of the legislative electoral campaign in 1997.

However, with the return of the Left to power in the spring 1997, the support of political parties and some trade unions became more problematic (Cissé 1999). This is this clearly underlined in an analysis published by one of the leaders of the *sans-papiers* movement in 1998:

> What can be observed today – and this can be qualified as a division – results from the behaviour of some organizations and some members of our support. We noticed that since November 1997, when some French organizations tried to take many more initiatives and to control the fight of the *sans-papiers*, that is to channel it so that it doesn't overflow. [. . .] And this is something that we have faced since the Left came back to power. I think that the French communist party in particular has tried to control our fight, through some support that was closed to us. [. . .] French organizations have supported the claims that were convenient for them, that is, the claims that were not too extremist, those that didn't demand 'papers for all', those that didn't criticize the laws adopted by Chevènement, etc. These are the claims that they wanted to support because, at some point (I am thinking about the CGT and the PCF), they have become part of the power-holders. Recently we have thus noticed some changes of position on the part of organizations such as the CGT.[28]

Following the return of the Right to power in 2002, the support of trade unions and of Left-wing parties (or figures from these parties) became more visible again. Trade unions are fully involved in the activities of the *Uni(*e)s *Contre une Immigration Jetable* and *Réseau Education Sans Frontières* networks (twenty-two trade unions are part of *RESF*). Thus, symbolically, the first important meeting of the *UCIJ* network took place at the headquarters of the *CGT* in Paris. Concerning the political field, many figures from Left-wing parties have made public declarations of support to these networks during this period. In 2006, during a pre-electoral period, some of them also visited those living in the squat in Cachan and publicly manifested their solidarity.

The support of intellectuals and academics was also important. Several people from this field served as intermediaries in the negotiations between the *sans-papiers* and the government in 1996. Other intellectuals have also actively supported the movement through numerous public interventions and through participation in the joint collective actions initiated by the movement. Since this period, the involvement of intellectuals and academics has remained an important characteristic of the pro-asylum movement. Thus, reflections and militant arenas like the Centre of Studies and Initiatives on International Solidarities (*Centre d'Etudes et D'initiatives de Solidarités Internationales, CEDETIM*) allow for the construction of linkages between the two fields. The juridical field has also brought important support to the pro-asylum movement. Thus, as shown by Israël (2003), the involvement of lawyers in *Gisti* in particular (and also in the *Ligue des droits de l'Homme, Amnesty International Section Française, Cimade* and *MRAP*) has allowed these associations to gain a high level of juridical expertise.

Finally, the media have been significant allies to the movement of the *sans-papiers*. The photos of the expulsion from the Saint-Bernard church published in *Libération* became symbolic of the movement, and their impact on public opinion was very important. Since this period, the French media has provided extensive coverage of mobilizations on the asylum issue. Since 1996–1997, journalists in *Le Monde* or *Libération* have specialized in covering immigration policies and they have established regular contact with the activists involved in the *sans-papiers* movement. The wide media coverage of this movement can be partly explained by the important role that new technologies have played. As was mentioned in an interview with an activist,[29] the creation in the spring of 1996 of a website (http://pajol.eu.org/) reporting all the activities of the movement provided an important tool which gave the movement a much-needed visibility: it was widely used by journalists who wanted to report on the *sans-papiers*.

The existence of a network of diversified allies is thus an important feature of the French pro-asylum movement. This has created a feeling of support which is clearly expressed in a joint communiqué which was launched by most of the associations mobilizing around the asylum issue in October 2007, through the emphasis on the daily 'resistance' of diverse actors of civil society:

> [T]his government is flirting with racism and xenophobia and, at the end, these are our fundamental rights that are being reduced.
>
> But France is above all represented by the actions of its inhabitants! The multiple initiatives of solidarity with and around the condition of the foreigners, immigrants and *sans-papiers* will be at the core of our demonstration on the 20th of October. Yes, there is the protection of the *sans-papiers*, there is the daily mobilization of pupils' parents against the expulsion of children, there are the reactions of the neighbourhood when a raid is organized by the police,

> there are the initiatives of the researchers and academics, there is the basis of trade unionism that is present in the working places and that supports the initiatives of so many professions, there is, there is . . . and all this gives to solidarity and resistance the face of action. This action – multiple and diversified – will take the form of street demonstrations and also – throughout France – of gatherings, debates, concerts, meetings. . .[30]

The significance of the *sans-papiers* movement led observers and analysts to describe it as one of the major moments of a new cycle of protest that started with the strikes in December 1995, and that encompasses new categories of social movements (Péchu 1996). These new movements represent all populations who are being excluded and who lack political representation (the undocumented, unemployed, homeless . . .) (Maurer and Pierru 2001). In contrast to previous mobilizations around immigration and asylum issues, the movement of the *sans-papiers* in 1996–1997 has therefore been defined as being connected to other issues. Indeed, the associations that comprised it described themselves systematically as being not only representatives of the undocumented migrants living in France, but more generally, of all populations that are excluded by traditional political parties. Thus, in April 1997, in the context of the ongoing legislative campaign, *Act Up-Paris* launched a call that was signed (among others) by several associations active in the field of immigration and asylum (in particular *Gisti*, *CNSP*, and *FASTI*). This call showed the links between the immigration issue and the more general issue of exclusion:

> The official Left will not win the elections without us. Because we are the real Left. We are the Left that is fighting and that has always been fighting on the field for its own living conditions and for those of everyone.
>
> For the immigrants, the unemployed, homosexuals, women, the homeless; for those with HIV, the drug addicted, prisoners; for all those who suffer every day from exploitation, repression, discrimination.
>
> We are the Left which went to demonstrate in December 1995 to defend social protection and public services, the Left which supports the *sans-papiers* and demonstrates against the Debré law, the Left which defends the entertainment workers, which blocks the extreme right in the streets of Strasbourg; the Left which goes in the street against the badly-hidden unemployment of almost 5 million persons in France, and which goes on strike when Vilvorde's factory is closed.[31]

In the events taking place in 1996–1997, one can observe an evolution of the movement on immigration and asylum. The group of associations that were the most active share the idea that these mobilizations should not be disconnected from other mobilizations. Moreover, these associations started to promote the idea that their demands should not be only of an immediate nature (such as the regularization of the group of migrants who started a collective action), but should be more general and more politicized (in the sense that they imply a profound change of the whole orientation of immigration and asylum policies): the regularization of all undocumented migrants, and the wider opening of borders. Thus, in 1997, *Gisti* launched a general reflection on the opening of borders and on freedom of circulation, and these objectives became the most central claims of the association. This also lies behind the creation of the *Coordination Nationale des Sans-Papiers* (*CNSP*): the different local groups of *sans-papiers* saw the need to create a national coalition that would represent their long-term demands and not only the immediate claims that were put forward through their dominant forms of collective actions (collective hunger-strikes and occupations). Through this strategy, important allies could be found in other fields of mobilizations. Thus, links could be made with actors from movements on housing issues (such as *Droit Au Logement*) and on unemployment (*Action contre le Chômage* . . .). This dynamic was still visible in the mid-2000s. In April and May 2006, the movement on immigration and asylum issues joined the protest against the 'Contrat Première Embauche' (CPE):[32] the *Uni(e)s contre une immigration jetable* network called for participation in demonstrations against the CPE in the name of a global fight against precariousness.

Thus, the emergence of a cycle of protest does not only relate to a change in the frequency and intensity of protest during a certain period. It also corresponds to a change in the features of the movements that are part of this cycle of protest. In other words, it is not only a quantitative change, but also a qualitative one. The cycle of protest in which the pro-asylum movement plays a central role corresponds to a period of intense interaction with diverse allies: actors from social movements mobilized around different issues and actors from different fields.[33] Through this interaction, the actors of the pro-asylum movement have extended, diversified and consolidated their network of allies. They have also evolved in the formulation of their demands: these have become more politicized and geared towards longer-term aims. However, it is important to note that two important French associations, who specialize in the reception of asylum-seekers (*France Terre d'Asile* and *Forum Réfugiés*), do not follow this trend.

More generally, this historical overview leads us to conclude that the interaction of the actors comprising a specific multi-organizational field determines its degree of cohesion and embeddedness in society. The dynamics of this interaction depend on the strategies of SMOs in the particular context in which they take place. In particular, the frequency of the legislative reforms relating to immigration and asylum policies has led French associations to construct and consolidate multi-associative coalitions. Moreover, the occurrence of a cycle of protest in the mid-1990s has allowed these associations to construct and consolidate a diversified network of allies.

## The German case: a fragmented and isolated movement

In comparison with the French case, the mobilizations around the asylum issue in Germany have followed a very different evolution since the beginning of the 1990s. The reform of the Fundamental Law in 1993 and the racist attacks occurring in the same period provoked significant mobilizations on the part of a strong anti-racist movement that managed to involve numerous and diverse allies. However, after this, the pro-asylum movement faced great difficulties in constructing dense and durable coalitions and its support has been relatively limited. This is due to the fact that – in contrast to the French case – the period after 1993 was characterized by a low degree of politicization of the asylum issue (only one minor reform of asylum policies has been implemented, in 2005) and by the absence of a cycle of protest. These elements have strongly influenced the dynamics of interaction within the German pro-asylum movement and between the actors of this field and those of other social fields.

The mobilizations on asylum emerged at the beginning of the 1990s in a particular context in Germany. Since 1988, the Right-wing party *CDU-CSU*, aware of the growing number of asylum-seekers in Germany, proposed a change to the Fundamental Law's article on asylum (article 16), which it considered too generous. For that, a coalition was needed in the Parliament (two-thirds of the majority in the Bundestag is needed to amend the Fundamental Law). As the Liberal *FDP* and the Social-Democrat *SPD* were reluctant, the *CDU-CSU* decided to give this issue a higher priority in public debates. Thus, in anticipation of the legislative elections in December 1990, the 'asylum campaign' (*Asylkampagne*) became one of the principal issues in public debates (Herbert 2001). Soon, the mass media (in particular, the tabloids *Bild-Zeitung* and *Welt am Sonntag*) launched a campaign that stigmatized asylum-seekers and refugees as 'smugglers' that would endanger the welfare state (Prantl 1993). The 'asylum campaign' did not stop with the elections in 1990 and with German unification; in fact, it became more intense and polemical. Thus, in November 1992, in order to put pressure on the Left-wing deputies in the Bundestag, Helmut Kohl announced that he would declare a state of emergency if no compromise could be found regarding the reform of article 16 (the declaration of a state of emergency allows an amendment to the Fundamental Law with a simple majority in the Bundestag). He explained that the state of emergency would allow the government to take any measure that could stop the 'flows of asylum-seekers' and permit the deportation of a large number of migrants. This declaration further intensified the overall climate of stigmatization and criminalization of asylum-seekers and refugees on the part of the political class and the media (Niehr 2000). At the same time, acts of violence against foreigners, asylum-seekers and refugees increased dramatically, in particular in East Germany. In the summer of 1991, the *Süddeutsche Zeitung* reported that the number of attacks against migrants reached seventy-eight on a single day (Herbert 2001: 304). Between March and August 1992, four foreigners were killed by groups of far-Right activists in East Germany. In the summer of 1992, a group of thousands of young people near Rostock, encouraged by the local population, attacked several times in the same week a residence where asylum-seekers were living. In November 1992, the house of a Turkish family was burned by two skinheads in Mölln, in the North of Germany (Schönbach 1993); three people were killed. In May 1993, five people were killed in a similar attack in Solingen.

Mobilizations began following the negotiations in the Bundestag. Since its creation in 1986, *Pro Asyl* represented the most important and almost unique organization active on the asylum issue at the national level (Bojadzijev 2002). The Refugee Councils (*Flüchtlingsräte*) mobilized exclusively at the regional level, and organizations like *Amnesty International Deutschland*, *Caritas* or *Diakonie* only occasionally acted on this issue. Therefore *Pro Asyl* was alone when it launched, in 1988, a lobbying campaign aiming at defending article 16 of the Fundamental Law (Herbert 2001). The deputies of the *SPD*, *Die Grünen* and the *FDP* were contacted and asked to oppose the restriction proposed by the *CDU-CSU*. Several associations (in particular *Caritas*, *Diakonie*, *Arbeiterwohlfahrt* and *Amnesty International Deutschland*) soon joined the work being carried out by *Pro Asyl*. Thus began an intense period of cooperation: the associations launched a common lobbying campaign and they published several joint communiqués during a brief period of time. Moreover, wide inter-associative coalitions were created at the local level. The Refugee Councils, active in every region, gathered together around them many anti-racist associations and launched numerous information campaigns and demonstrations. After the wave of racist attacks in 1992–1993, large coalitions of actors from diverse fields were formed both at the local and national level. In the winter of

1992, several demonstrations were organized, with high numbers of participants. Thus, on 8 November, 300,000 people demonstrated in Berlin; on 14 November, more than 100,000 demonstrated in Bonn. On 6 December 1992, following the racist attack in Mölln, massive demonstrations were organized in several cities. In Munich, 400,000 people marched with candles and formed a forty-five-kilometres long demonstration. The amendment of article 16 of the Fundamental Law was eventually passed at the Bundestag in May 1993. Conforming to this new legislation, a list of 'safe third-countries' was adopted and the right to asylum was considerably restricted. *Pro Asyl, Caritas, Diakonie* and the *Flüchtlingsräte* criticized this decision in several communiqués. *Pro Asyl* then continued its mobilization by presenting systematic appeals at the German Constitutional Court to contest refusals of the demands for asylum. However, these collective actions did not lead to a change in the nature of the new article 16 of the Fundamental Law, and they were not as well supported by public opinion.

After 1993, and throughout the rest of the 1990s, few mobilizations have addressed the asylum issue with such intensity (Koopmans et al. 2005). The principal organizations active on this issue during this period (*Pro Asyl, Caritas, Diakonie, Amnesty International,* the *Arbeiterwohlfahrt,* and the Refugee Councils at the regional level) launched several campaigns in the course of the 1990s, but they had little impact on the political class and a low profile in public opinion. During this period, this group of organizations mobilized mainly through the method of task-division. Each one specialized in a particular aspect of asylum policies and constructed a collective action on its own. Therefore *Pro Asyl* mainly specialized in the (juridical) defence of the terms of the Geneva Convention. *Caritas* and *Diakonie* mainly specialized in the question of the integration of refugees and on the promotion of minimum rights for undocumented migrants. *Amnesty International Deutschland* specialized in the application of the principle of 'non-refoulement' and acted mainly against the deportation of migrants. The *Arbeiterwohlfahrt* specialized in the conditions of reception of asylum-seekers. And the Refugee Councils specialized mainly in the provision of juridical and practical help to asylum-seekers at the local level. Thus, in 1996–1997, the association *Pro Asyl* launched its own lobbying and juridical campaign against the introduction of the notion of 'manifestly unfounded demand of asylum'.[34] During the same period, *Caritas Deutschland* launched a lobbying campaign to guarantee for asylum-seekers the same minimum wage as prevailed before the 1993 reform. It also lobbied for refugees to have the right to subsidies for their children's education. All the campaigns that were carried out during this period were centred on lobbying strategies: they mainly addressed the federal government or the deputies of the Bundestag, and made little impact on the media and public opinion. Grass-roots mobilizations which privilege more contentious types of collective action take place almost exclusively at the local level (Bojadzijev 2002). This is for example the case with the association *The Voice – Refugee Forum* which was created in 1994 by a group of refugees, and which was – during this period – exclusively active in Thüringen. This is also the case with some of the local associations which are grouped around the Refugee Councils at the regional level.

In 1999, in order to increase their interactions, *Pro Asyl, Caritas Deutschland, Diakonie, Amnesty International Deutschland,* and the *Arbeiterwohlfahrt* (together with other associations and the German representation of the *UNHCR*) created the Information Coalition on Asylum (*Informationsverbund Asyl*). This network is similar to the French *CFDA*: it aims at facilitating greater exchange between associations through the organization of regular meetings. As a result of this initiative, these organizations managed to meet on a more regular basis, and could thus achieve a better sharing of information. During the war in Kosovo in 1999, the associations involved in this network launched several initiatives to address public opinion and the government in favour of the refugees coming from the former Yugoslavia. Then, in 2000–2001, Gerhard Schröder's government launched the negotiations for a reform of immigration and asylum policies (*Zuwanderungsgesetz*). In this context, most of the associations active in the Information Coalition on Asylum (and in particular *Pro Asyl, Caritas, Diakonie* and *Amnesty International*) launched a lobbying campaign for the recognition of non-state persecution in the status of refugee.

During the same period, *Pro Asyl* launched a campaign for the granting of a stable residence permit for persons who had requested refugee status and who had resided in Germany for a long time (the 'de-facto refugees').[35] This campaign was supported by a large coalition of associations and attracted the attention of the media and of a section of public opinion. In 2001, the first draft of the project of law did not take these demands into account, and the two campaigns were intensified (Fritz and Groner 2004). In 2005, the final agreement on the immigration law eventually introduced the principle of recognition of non-state persecution.[36] However, no progress has been made with regard to the 'right to stay' for the 'de-facto refugees'. Several calls were launched and some demonstrations were organized. In particular, a demonstration was held in Nuremberg in November 2006, when the Ministers of the Interior of all German regions gathered together to seek agreement on this issue. As the agreement reached by the ministers was considered by the associations to be rather disappointing, they decided to continue with their campaign. In spite of the coordination of these campaigns, the relationships between the SMOs which comprised the Information Coalition on

Asylum were still characterized by a division of labour. On a daily basis, these associations continued to specialize on a particular issue and to act on this basis. Thus, the organization of these campaigns by the same group of actors does not signify the existence of stable inter-associative coalitions. Thus, in comparison with the French case, very few communiqués and calls were produced jointly after the mobilizations in 1993. Consequently, the content of the demands formulated by these associations has been relatively unchanging over time. In contrast with the French case, their demands have been more of a short-term nature during this period: they have been constructed in the framework of a particular campaign on a specific dimension of asylum policies (for example, the 'right to stay') and they rarely go beyond the scope of that campaign.

In parallel with this group of associations, new organizations and networks emerged towards the end of the 1990s. Conscious of the limits of their geographical scope, local, grass-roots associations launched initiatives to build wider networks. In 1997, the network *Kein Mensch Ist Illegal* was created in Kassel. Following the network's initial call, more than 200 local groups and organizations joined.[37] At the same time, a group of activists from Berlin created the anti-racist association *Kanak Attak* (1998). Moreover, in the late 1990s, several associations that had been created by refugees (in particular the association *The Voice – Refugee Forum*) and by groups showing solidarity with refugees started to establish linkages across German regions. This resulted in the creation of the *Karawane für die Rechte der Flüchlinge und MigrantInnen* network (Caravan for the Rights of Refugees and Migrants). This is a relatively loose network that is active in several German cities and regions (Berlin, Bielefeld, Bremen, Göttingen, Hamburg, Jena, Munich, Nordrhein-Westfalen and Nuremberg in particular). The objective of these organizations was to construct collective actions that would coordinate at the national level actions carried out at the local level. Most of these collective actions belonged to a contentious repertoire. For example, every year, the activists involved in these networks participated in the organization of a 'border-camping' initiative. An initial camp took place at the German-Polish-Czech border in Rothenburg in the summer of 1998. It was then followed by camps near Frankfurt airport, at the German-Polish border in Zittau and Forst, and at the French-German border in Strasbourg. These camps gathered together activists from all parts of Germany (and in the case of Strasbourg in July 2002, from other parts of Europe) who organized public debates and violent symbolic actions.[38] Inspired by the experience of the *sans-papiers* movement (activists from the German movement rapidly made contact with the leaders of the movement in France), the organizations taking part in these camps also intended to challenge the more established associations by making demands that looked towards the long-term (such as the regularization of all undocumented migrants or the reappraisal of North-South relationships).

In the early 2000s, the main issues addressed by these different networks were the 'obligation of residence' (the *Residenzpflicht*, the legislation that obliges asylum-seekers to stay in a determined geographical zone and which prevents them from working during the processing of their demand),[39] the deportations, and the regularization of migrants. In 1999, following the death of a migrant during his deportation, a national campaign focusing on the role of aviation companies was launched ('deportation-class campaign').[40] This campaign consisted mainly of symbolic actions at Frankfurt airport which brought together small groups of activists. In this context, the *Aktionsbündnis Gegen Abschiebung Rhein-Main* network (Actions Coordination Against Deportation Rhein-Main) was created by activists of *Kein Mensch Ist Illegal*. In 2003, a campaign demanding the regularization of undocumented migrants was launched by activists of *Kanak Attak* together with other associations. Public events (seminars, conferences and artistic interventions) were organized, and several communiqués and calls were published. In 2003–2004, the campaign against the rule on the obligation of residence resulted in the creation of the *No Lager* network by activists from *Kein Mensch Ist Illegal*.[41] This network is mainly active in North and East Germany, and it privileges the organization of actions of civil disobedience against the detention of migrants.

However, despite the efforts of these new networks to create denser and more durable coalitions at the national level, their scope of mobilization remains principally local. This is obviously the case for the Refugee Councils, which are active in each German region. Moreover, the *Kein Mensch Ist Illegal* network is no longer active as such (only one organization – *Kein Mensch Ist Illegal Köln* – still represents the network). Due to limited amounts of material and human resources, the association *Kanak Attak* is almost exclusively active in Berlin, and the *No Lager* network in Brandenburg, Mecklenburg-Vorpommern, Hamburg and Bremen. The *Aktiv Gegen Abschiebung* association is exclusively active in the region of Frankfurt. The same can be said of the *Karawane für die Rechte der Flüchlinge und MigrantInnen* network: the member-associations are situated in several German regions; however, the coordination between them remains difficult. The network is mainly activated by *The Voice – Refugee Forum* association (exclusively active in the region of Jena) and by the *Carava.net* association (exclusively active in Munich). It is only through events such as the marches across Germany (such as the 'Karawane-Tour' in 2007) that member-associations have the opportunity to really federate.

As shown in the historical review, the period after 1992–1993 contrasts with the period of intense mobilizations at the end of the 1980s and beginning of the 1990s. Since this time, the German pro-asylum movement has had difficulties in constructing durable coalitions. In particular, two divisions have impeded any lasting collective work: a division in terms of tasks and a geographical one. In comparison with the French case, the low profile of the asylum issue in the political sphere (only one minor legislative reform has been concerned with this issue since the constitutional reform in 1993) has led German associations to interact more sporadically. Moreover, as will be developed below, the fact that Germany is a federal state has played a role.

The contrast between the French and German cases is confirmed by the analysis of the strategies of interaction of the groups comprising this movement with actors of other fields. Indeed, in comparison with the French case, the German movement is characterized by a relative isolation in society. In the early 1990s, the mobilizations enabled the construction of a wide alliance against racism: the actors involved in the pro-asylum movement managed to gather around themselves a large and diversified range of allies. This alliance was however ephemeral: following these mobilizations, they did not manage to consolidate these networks of allies. This is mainly due to the fact that the pro-asylum movement is not involved in the context of a cycle of protest.

It was the association *Pro Asyl* that carried out, in the first instance, the campaign for the defence of asylum right at the end of the 1980s and beginning of the 1990s. This organization soon defined a strategy aiming at the construction of a large coalition of non-governmental actors. Thus, in January 1989, it launched a call to 'all power-holders and public figures':

> Call launched through the media to all power-holders and public figures from politics, science, economy and culture, from the churches, trade unions, humanitarian organizations, media, associations and sporting organizations, from the spiritual and educational fields. Pro Asyl calls you to: GIVE YOUR VOICE TO PEOPLE WHO DON'T HAVE ONE! ADDRESS THE GOVERNMENT![42]

This call is very representative of the overall shape of the pro-asylum movement during this period. In contrast to the collective action taking place in France in the early 1990s, the aim was not only to oppose government policy. The denunciation concerned not only the revision of article 16 of the Fundamental Law, but also the political discourse of stigmatization of asylum seekers and refugees which caused a radicalization of a part of society. It was thus considered necessary to form the largest possible coalition which would assemble people who were able to speak up for moderation, to 'educate' against racism. This strategy became even more central with the beginning of the anti-immigrant campaign in the media in 1990 (Herbert 2001). In fact, in contrast to the French associations, the associations mobilizing in Germany shared the feeling that their opinion represented only a small minority in German society. Thus, on 7 December 1992, after the deputies had agreed on a first compromise on the reform of asylum right, *Pro Asyl* declared that:

> The article 16a of the Fundamental Law that is planned by the deputies is a victory of the street and a defeat of the state of law.[43]

The significance of the formulation 'victory of the street' is great. It means that a campaign relating to asylum rights should take place at two different levels: the protest against restrictive measures taken by the government; and the more general mobilization against what was perceived as the intolerant tendencies in German society. This led the associations of the pro-asylum movement to form a large coalition of actors from diverse horizons. Thus, in December 1991, the Coalition of German Trade Unions (*Deutsche GewerkschaftsBund, DGB*) launched a call against racism and for the protection of asylum-seekers and refugees. In September 1992, several academic, religious, trade union and political figures (the latter from the *SPD* or *Die Grünen*) launched a call (together with *Pro Asyl* and all Refugee Councils) against the revision of article 16.[44] However, these mobilizations had little impact in the German institutions. One of the reasons is that they did not benefit from good coverage by the media, who – for the most part – relayed a discourse of criminalization of migrants (Herbert 2001). Another reason is that the different fields supporting the anti-racist movement were themselves strongly divided. Thus, throughout the period, the discussions between those in the *SPD* party were tense. And when the majority of the *SPD* deputies accepted the 'compromise on asylum' (Asylkompromiss) in December 1992, harsh criticism came from within the party.

After this period of intense mobilization, the pro-asylum movement has found it difficult to find allies from other fields. Trade unions have been relatively absent from the mobilizations on this issue since 1993. The Coalition of German Trade Unions took a position against the reform of immigration and asylum policies in the early 2000s. It is also involved in the campaign for the right to stay. However, this has not led to such a regular dynamic of collaboration as in the French case. Also, in comparison to the French case, there have been relatively few allies from the political field. Thus, during the years of the Red-Green coalition (1998–2006), associations found little support from Left-wing parties. During the negotiations surrounding the reform in the early 2000s, a few members of these parties have sporadically referred to the associations that were carrying out lobbying (*Pro-Asyl*, *Caritas*, *Diakonie* . . .). These expressions of support have, however, been relatively isolated in the political arena.

Churches have remained important allies of the pro-asylum movement in Germany. In 1994, they created an ecumenical organization (*Asyl in der Kirche*) that aimed to offer an ultimate recourse to asylum-seekers coming to Germany (Morgenstern 2003).[45] The investment of the Churches in the pro-asylum movement remains, however, mostly limited to the support of two particular associations: *Caritas* and *Diakonie*. Churches participated in the activities of *Kein Mensch Ist Illegal* at the time of its creation (in particular in the framework of the *Wanderkirchenasyl* network in Nordrhein-Westfalen). However, their involvement in this network soon decreased.

Concerning the artistic field, local scenes have actively supported the pro-asylum movement (like the *GRIPS* theatre in Berlin during the campaign for the right to stay). Several artists of the musical and cinematographic scene have also supported the *Pro-Asyl* association: several documentaries and discs have been produced in support of the association. However, this support has had less impact than in the French case. Moreover, in comparison with the French case, there has been little involvement of the academic field, especially since 1993. As an exception, however, one can mention the existence of the Research Centre on Exile and Migration (*Forschungsgesellschaft Flucht und Migration*) that presents itself in an activist perspective: important links have been made with activists from associations such as *No Lager* or *Kanak Attak*.

In contrast with the French case, the links between the pro-asylum movement and the journalistic field are also much more limited. German associations communicate far less with the press; this is evident in the results of the document analysis that was carried out in a comparative perspective,[46] which shows that German associations have launched press communiqués much less often than French associations over the same period. Consequently, no newspaper of the German mainstream press has covered the mobilizations of the pro-asylum movement with as much regularity as in France.

The fact that the mobilizations on the asylum issue have not coincided with periods of intense mobilizations in other fields also rendered difficult the links between the pro-asylum movement and other movements. As a matter of fact, examples of bridging between the pro-asylum movement and other social movements (as could be observed in France since the mid-1990s) are rare in Germany (with the mobilizations against the G8 summit in Heiligendamm in 2007 possibly representing an exception).[47]

Finally, the German rule on the obligation of residence (Residenzpflicht) also has an influence on its degree of embeddedness in society. The French example shows indeed that the choice of the location where a collective action (in particular a hunger-strike) could be started was a highly strategic one that took into consideration the possible impact on the media and the possible support that could follow the action. In Germany, due to the mobility restrictions imposed by this law, the pro-asylum movement experienced difficulties in finding equivalent allies and media coverage. Thus, in its self-presentation, *The Voice Refugee Forum* association (the main association of the *Karawane für die Rechte der MigrantInnen und Flüchtlinge* network) underlines the consequences of this rule and perceives the abolition of this law as a first condition for the organization of a stronger movement:

> Since 1982, which is more than twenty years ago, the residential obligation law has been restricting the freedom, personal and political rights of thousands of asylum seekers prejudicially. 'Residenzpflicht' criminalizes and discriminates. It makes refugees the object of humiliating racist controls and puts them under psychological and material pressure. [. . .]
>
> Germany is the only country in Europe where refugees are criminalized by the law of the movement restriction (Residenzpflicht). This law shows that refugees in Germany are meant to be socially isolated, not only being kept in faraway camps in the middle of forests, in addition, the restriction of movement by the 'Residenzpflicht' law excludes refugees from mainstream societies by not allowing them to mix with the general populace, fellow refugees and migrants who may be living in other cities.
>
> The Restriction law movement keeps refugees from seeing their doctors, their lawyers, their friends and relatives and for some of them worst of all from continuing the political activities that made them flee their country in the first instance. The government law is gagging us in a way.[48]

## Conclusions

The analysis presented in this chapter shows that the French and German multi-organizational fields on asylum have been mobilizing in contrasting contexts and have followed different evolutions. Three main aspects have been underlined:

First, the French and German movements are characterized by different forms of cooperation. In France, the associations comprising this movement have progressively formed dense and durable coalitions. Through the recent creation of the *Uni(e)s contre une immigration jetable* (*UCIJ*) and *Réseau Education Sans Frontières* (*RESF*) networks in 2004, this cooperation finds its most evident illustration. Conversely, in Germany very few collective actions have been constructed jointly by the associations comprising this movement after 1993. Whereas one can observe the regular cooperation of French associations, it is only in exceptional cases (like for the launching of long-term campaigns) that German associations tend to collaborate. In fact, despite the recent initiatives taken by newly created networks, German associations tend to specialize in terms of tasks and in geographical terms.

Second, French and German movements have different types of alliances. In the French case, the associations comprising the movement have managed to gain a diversified and durable support from allies present in other fields. This is the case of trade unions, some figures in the artistic, academic and political fields, of sections of the press, and other social movements. These alliances have widely contributed to the resonance of the mobilizations on immigration and asylum in public opinion, in particular after the mobilizations of the *sans-papiers* in 1996. In the German case, the significant mobilizations which took place in the early 1990s could be organized through the support of an important alliance of heterogeneous actors (churches, political parties and academic figures in particular). However, after this period, the movement has had great difficulty in finding allies in other fields. Thus, trade unions have had little links with the pro-asylum movement. Churches have played an important role, but their support is limited to a small number of associations. Moreover, in comparison with the French case, the German movement is relatively isolated from other movements and other 'causes'.

The analysis developed in this chapter has focused on the degrees of cohesion and embeddedness in society of French and German pro-asylum movements. Throughout the analysis I have, however, underlined another difference between these two cases: mobilizations have been more intense and more frequent in France than in Germany. Since the beginning of the 1990s, French associations have launched a high number of collective actions. And these mobilizations have been at the core of important debates in the public sphere. This is true of the first hunger-strikes carried out by asylum-seekers in 1990–1991, of the mobilizations of the *sans-papiers* in 1996–1997, and of the more recent mobilizations of the *Réseau Education Sans Frontières* network, for example. In Germany, there have been very important mobilizations in the beginning of the 1990s. However, since this period, a limited number of collective actions has been launched, with a relatively low profile in the public sphere.[49]

Therefore, the French movement seems to be more entrenched in society than the German movement. To give a first explanation, I have insisted on two crucial contextual factors: the level of salience of the asylum issue in the political sphere (or in other words its level of politicization), and the occurrence of a cycle of protest.

First, French and German immigration and asylum policies have evolved in different ways since the beginning of the 1990s. Although, in their substance, they have evolved in the same direction (towards more restriction), the changes in legislation have been much more frequent and abrupt (in terms of timing) in France. In Germany, two major changes have occurred (the reform of the Fundamental Law in 1993, and the introduction of new legislation in 2005), and the negotiations required to make these changes possible have taken years. In France, no fewer than seven important reforms have been carried out during the same period, and the phases of negotiation have been much more limited in time. This has led French associations to mobilize with more frequency than in Germany. Moreover, due to the briefness of the periods of negotiations in France, the associations have often had the feeling of being presented with a fait accompli. This has led them to build dense coalitions and to construct more intense mobilizations. In Germany, in contrast, the length of the political negotiations for the reforms have led the associations to privilege less intense mobilizations based on the launching of a limited number of joint campaigns. Moreover, the fact that these reforms have been less frequent than in France explains why German associations have privileged a mode of task-division.

Second, the two countries have faced different levels of contention. In France, a cycle of protest emerged in the mid-1990s; this led the French associations involved in the pro-asylum movement to create important links with other fields of contention and to gain diversified allies. In particular, the movement of the *sans-papiers* in 1996–1997 could be defined as one of the most central movements of this cycle of protest. This has allowed it to construct an important network of allies made up of actors from different fields. Over the years, these links were consolidated through the regular interactions between these different actors. However, in the German case, after the mobilization in 1993, the absence of a cycle of protest did not facilitate the construction of a diversified network of allies. In comparison with the French case, the German field of mobilization relating to the asylum issue remained relatively isolated in society.

Beside these two fundamental elements, I have stressed three other features that have also shaped the pro-asylum movements in both countries.

First, the German and French states have different levels of centralization. In Germany, even if the federal state has the general responsibility for the definition of the asylum policy, the regions play an important role in the reception of asylum-seekers and refugees (in particular in financial terms). It is therefore much less centralized than the French state, where all the responsibility for the definition and implementation of the asylum policy is held at the national level. This factor has influenced the way in which actors of the pro-asylum movement have organized themselves. In Germany, decentralization has led the associations to act through a method of geographical sharing: the construction of coalitions mainly takes place at the local or regional level. On the contrary, centralization in France has led the pro-asylum movement to privilege the construction of coalitions at the national level. There are of course also local initiatives in France, but comparatively, they have less importance than in Germany.

The second element is related to the different nature of the anti-immigrant organizations in both countries. In France, the anti-immigrant movement takes the form of a political party (*Front National*) with a significant electorate. In Germany, this movement mainly takes the form of diffuse violent racist attacks that are at the margins of the democratic system and that take place at the local level (there is one main anti-immigrant party in Germany, the *NPD*, but it is less significant than the *Front National* in France). This dimension has strongly influenced the shape of the movement. Thus, in the French case, the associations often put forward the idea that, by instigating restrictive immigration and asylum policies, the government is attempting to attract the electorate of the *Front National.* This argument is central in the mobilizations against the reforms introduced in 1993, 1996 and in the early 2000s. In France therefore, through a sort of mirror-effect, the presence of a significant anti-immigrant party has led the pro-asylum movement to enter a phase of confrontation against the government. This has thus reinforced its tendency to construct dense and durable coalitions at the national level. Differently, in the German case, the fact that anti-immigrant movements are mainly active at the local level has reinforced the tendency of the pro-asylum movement to construct coalitions locally (with anti-fascist groups in particular).

Finally, in both countries, asylum-seekers, refugees and undocumented migrants have a different place in society. In France, they live at the heart of the cities. Although they risk police controls, they live in the same spaces as French citizens, and this therefore makes them more visible in the public sphere. The situation is different in Germany. In particular, asylum-seekers and undocumented migrants are concerned by the rule of the obligation of residence: they often have to live for years in remote places and are under the permanent control of the police. If they leave the zone in which they live, they risk a fine. Also, in many regions, they must buy food and clothes in particular shops, with vouchers. Asylum-seekers, refugees and undocumented migrants have thus much less visibility in Germany than they do in France: they face more isolation. This fact is significant as it partly explains why the German pro-asylum movement could not construct a network of allies like its counterpart in France. The mobility restrictions in Germany made it more difficult for asylum-seekers and refugees to organize and construct their collective actions in strategic locations where potential allies could be reached.

The influence of these contextual factors is not mechanical: they do not determine in a direct way (through a structural dynamic) the features of French and German movements. French and German pro-asylum movements have different features because, depending on the national context in which they are involved, the actors of these movements have strategically put forward different dynamics of interaction (dynamics of interaction between them, and with other actors). Thus, the occurrence of a cycle of protest in France is not per se a factor which explains why the French movement has established more links with other social fields than the German movement. This factor has had an influence because the actors of the French movement felt that it was strategically necessary to adapt their interaction to this particular context. In brief, the shape of a particular movement is progressively defined through a complex process in which the strategies of interaction of the actors constituting it play a fundamental role. This is what an analysis in terms of multi-organizational field allows us to understand. In the following chapter, I will move the focus of analysis from the macro-level (the general internal and external features of a multi-organizational field) to the meso-level (the features of the organizations comprising this field).

## Notes

1 The historical overview presented in this chapter is based on the analysis of the documents published by the SMOs comprising the pro-asylum movements since the beginning of the 1990s (their communiqués, calls and their internal literature). I analysed around 200 documents published jointly by several SMOs and/or presenting a list of external supports. These documents are representative of the important communiqués and calls that they have published since the beginning of the 1990s. I also analysed their internal literature comparatively (in particular the annual reports). This analysis was complemented by the set of interviews (I asked a series of questions relating to the history of the pro-asylum movements and of the organizations comprising them) and by the use of the secondary literature.

2 Defined by Sidney Tarrow as 'a phase of heightened conflict and contention across the social system that includes: a rapid diffusion of collective action from more mobilized to less mobilized sectors; a quickened pace of innovation in the forms of contention; new or transformed collective action frames; a combination of organized and unorganized participation; and sequences of intensified interactions between challengers and authorities which can end in reform, repression, or sometimes revolution' (Tarrow 1994: 153).
3 The French central administration in charge of the examination of asylum claims.
4 The most important of these took place at the church of Saint-Joseph des Nations in Paris in May 1991.
5 These associations (*FASTI*, *GISTI*, *Cimade*, *MRAP*, and some activists of the *Ligue des droits de l'Homme*) were grouped in a collective network ('Information and Solidarity Network': *Réseau d'information et de solidarité*) that was mobilized against the deportation of undocumented migrants from the 1980s.
6 As will be developed further, this argument is however contested by some of the French associations.
7 This reform restricted the possibility of entrance into French territory though increased controls (in particular controls on the weddings between French and foreigners in order to stamp out 'fake weddings') and it facilitated the expulsion of immigrants living irregularly in France.
8 These associations initiated the 'Gx', a group aiming to provide support for *sans-papiers*.
9 The 'certificats d'hébergements' obliged those who welcomed visitors from third-countries to notify the French authorities of their dates of arrival and departure.
10 In February 1997, the *Front National* won the municipal elections in Vitrolles, in the South of France.
11 'Lettre ouverte à Lionel Jospin', 10 July 1997.
12 Although this reform introduced some more favourable measures, the law passed by the previous government was not abrogated.
13 Sangatte is a town in the North of France in which migrants who wanted to reach the United Kingdom transited, waiting for an opportunity to cross the Channel. In 1999, the French government authorized the Red Cross to run a humanitarian refugee camp as many migrants lived in precarious health conditions for months. However, the housing capacity of the camp was soon overwhelmed and riots broke out. Furthermore, the British government pressured the French government to close the camp. In 2002, after the elections and the change of majority, the new government decided to close the camp.
14 The *Coordination Française pour le Droit d'Asile* (*CFDA*) was created in 2000. It gathers together twenty associations that are active on the asylum issue. However, the tensions between the member-associations are visible, even within this structure. Thus (for different reasons), *MRAP* and *FTDA* do not participate in the working groups of the *CFDA*. When a communiqué is launched by *CFDA*, the member-associations can choose to sign it or not. In this particular case, *Forum Réfugiés*, *France Terre d'Asile* and the *Secours Catholique* chose not to sign this communiqué.
15 *Coordination Française pour le Droit d'Asile*, 'Faux-semblants du droit d'asile à Sangatte-Calais', 27 November 2002.

16 *Coordination Française pour le Droit d'Asile*, 'La non-solution de Sarkozy', 25 September 2002.
17 This reform limits the possibility for migrants to enter into French territory and it facilitates the procedures of deportation. It also introduces the notion of a 'safe third-country'. Moreover, migrants will have to complete an 'integration contract' (*contrat d'intégration*) in order to obtain a safer status.
18 'Manifeste des délinquants de la solidarité. Face à une loi encore plus répressive sur les étrangers, Tous délinquants de la solidarité!'
19 This figure includes the *Ligue des droits de l'Homme*, *Gisti*, *MRAP*, *Act Up-Paris*, *Cimade*, *FASTI*, and several collectives of 'sans-papiers'.
20 *Réseau Education Sans Frontières*, 'Appel à la régularisation des sans-papiers scolarisés', 26 June 2004.
21 *Réseau Education Sans Frontières*, 'Nous les prenons sous notre protection'.
22 This reform makes it more difficult for a migrant to gain access to a stable residence permit, the possibilities of regulation are limited and the conditions for family reunification become stricter. To use the terminology of the Minister of Interior, it intends to fight against 'non-chosen migration' in order to favour 'chosen migration'.
23 'Réforme du droit des migrant(e)s: Une attaque sans précédent. Uni(e)s contre une immigration jetable', 7 February 2006.
24 However, some of the associations denounced the terms of this agreement and continued to address the government on this issue.
25 The 'Lettre ouverte à Lionel Jospin' (July 1997) could have been a turning point in this regard. See below for more developments on this evolution.
26 'Appel pour le droit d'asile', December 1990.
27 See the website www.cgt.fr (author's translation).
28 *Entretien avec Madjiguène Cissé*, 12 November 1998, on the website http://pajol.eu.org/(author's translation).
29 Interview number 22.
30 *CSP – Collectifs de sans-papiers d'Ile de France*, *RESF – Réseau Education sans frontière*, *UCIJ – Uni(e)s contre l'immigration jetable*, 'Journée Nationale de Mobilisation, samedi 20 octobre, Solidarité avec les étrangers dans une résistance réfléchie au nom des droits fondamentaux et de la dignité de la personne humaine', October 2007 (author's translation).
31 'Nous sommes la gauche' (author's translation).
32 The CPE project was a new type of working contract for young people, which was contested by a significant movement of protest on the part of the youth and trade unions. It was eventually abandoned by the government.
33 One example of this is the fact that *Act Up Paris* (an association concerned with the conditions of HIV-affected persons) started to mobilize on immigration and asylum issues during the course of this cycle of protest.
34 The principle of 'manifestly unfounded demand of asylum' allows for a shorter examination of the asylum demands at the airports. In this procedure, the rights of asylum-seekers are particularly limited.
35 'Bleiberechtkampagne – Hier Geblieben!'.

36 This law principally concerned immigration policy; only minor changes relating to asylum policy were introduced (the main one being the recognition of non-state persecution).
37 *Kein Mensch Ist Illegal,* Manifest (1997).
38 In Strasbourg, several activists were arrested after a confrontation with the police in the course of a demonstration against the *Schengen Information System (SIS)*.
39 Due to this legislation, asylum-seekers are forced to live (sometimes for seven or eight years) in accommodations that are completely isolated (most of them are constructed outside cities and are difficult to reach).
40 See the website http://www.deportation-class.com/.
41 As a matter of fact, the *No Lager* network can be considered as the continuation of *Kein Mensch Ist Illegal,* which has largely ceased to be active.
42 *Pro Asyl,* 31 January 1989 (author's translation).
43 *Pro Asyl,* 7 December 1992 (author's translation).
44 'Keine Änderung des Grundrechts auf Asyl!', 30 September 1992.
45 Around hundred asylum-seekers each year can enjoy the status of *Kirchenasyl.*
46 See below.
47 See below.
48 *The Voice Refugee Forum,* 'Information about The Voice Refugee Forum', November 2003.
49 This was demonstrated in a quantitative way by Koopmans et al. (2005).

Chapter 2

# The Components of the French and German Pro-asylum Movements in Comparative Perspective

As was discussed in the introduction, the analysis of the Europeanization of social movements must take into account the features of the organizations comprising them. Indeed, depending on their characteristics at the national level, SMOs might Europeanize to different degrees and through different modes. Also, from a comparative perspective, cross-national differences in terms of repertoires of collective action or organizational cultures may result in different processes of Europeanization. Finally, this focus leads us to analyse the possible transformation of SMOs during the course of their Europeanization. This chapter proposes a systematic approach to the features of those organizations comprising French and German pro-asylum movements. For this, I rely on the concept of collective identity. As defined by Melucci (1989: 34), a collective identity is 'an interactive and shared definition produced by several interacting individuals who are concerned with the orientations of their action as well as the field of opportunities and constraints in which their action takes place'. More precisely, as shown by Polletta and Jasper (2001: 295), collective identities are 'embedded' in the different features that make up a social movement organization: 'strategies, tactics, claims, organizational forms, and deliberative styles'. Also, conversely, collective identities 'influence how such options can be used' (Polletta and Jasper 2001: 295). My aim in this chapter is to 'capture' the collective identities of the components of French and German pro-asylum movements through a discussion of five features: their understanding of reality (their framing); their experience of protest (repertoire of collective action); their resources; their organizational structure; and their territorial establishment (the geographical scope of their mobilization).

The construction of collective identities does not operate in a vacuum. It has to be understood as a process through which the mutual recognition between different actors is facilitated: a collective actor needs to present itself through a specific identity in order to interact with other actors (Melucci

1995). This is an ongoing and fluid process: in the course of these interactions, SMOs will be led to adapt their collective identity. Thus, within a multi-organizational field, social movement organizations will make their collective identity converge in order to construct joint mobilizations: they will, in particular, define progressively common perceptions and common repertoires of collective actions that will permit them to act together in a durable way. In the same way, depending on the actors with which it is cooperating, an association can be led to change the resources on which it bases the construction of its collective action or, for example, to move from the local to the national level.

As was shown in the previous chapter, French and German pro-asylum movements are based on very different dynamics of interaction. One would therefore expect to observe significant cross-national differences between the collective identities of the organizations comprising them. And one would expect to observe that the organizations from these two countries could be clearly distinguished in terms of discourses, repertoires, structure, etc. This idea is in line with the literature, which proposes a cross-national comparison of social movements through the concept of political opportunity structure. Thus, following Kriesi et al. (1995), one could observe that German SMOs tend to rely on more institutionalized repertoires of collective action than in France. Through the detection of different contextual factors,[1] the authors distinguish different 'prevailing strategies' in four European states (France, Germany, Switzerland and the Netherlands). In France, social movement organizations tend to rely mainly on contentious types of collective action. In particular, due to the closure of the 'strong and exclusive French state' (Kriesi et al. 1995: 49), they will more readily protest than implement institutionalized forms of collective action. In Germany, conversely, the 'exclusiveness and repressive strategies of the German authorities' (Kriesi et al. 1995: 51) and the relatively weak state lead to a polarized configuration: SMOs tend to rely mainly on moderate forms of collective action, but a minority of them rely on very disruptive types of protest.

More closely related to the object of this book, Koopmans et al. (2005) have shown in their study on protest concerning citizenship in five European countries (Britain, France, Germany, Switzerland and the Netherlands) that the demands formulated by immigrants and ethnic minorities differ in France and Germany. In the German case, the 'ethnic assimilationist' citizenship regime leads them to construct demands that refer to 'transplanted homelands' affairs: because former guest-workers living in Germany are generally defined as 'foreigners', immigrants tend also to present themselves as such. In the French case, in contrast, the 'restricted cultural pluralism' and the refusal to recognize particularist identities has led immigrants and ethnic minorities to emphasize their allegiance to universal values and to present themselves as French above all.

However, the hypothesis of a clear difference between those French and German SMOs comprising the pro-asylum movements has only been partially confirmed. In this chapter, I will show that in France, as in Germany, mobilizations around the asylum issue are formed by a plurality of (sometimes conflicting) social movement organizations, characterized by widely differentiated features. This does not allow us to distinguish clearly the components of French and German pro-asylum movements. Moreover, the differences separating the associations take very similar forms in these two countries. French and German organizations can be only distinguished in terms of two dimensions: the intensity of the differences between them; and the relative importance of each organization in the movement.

In the first part of this chapter, I will briefly show how the pro-asylum movement belongs to the 'solidarity movement family' (Giugni and Passy 2001). This will permit me to give an initial overview of the different traditions that make up this movement, before presenting in more detail the collective identities of its components.

## The components of the pro-asylum movement and the 'solidarity movement family': a historical overview

In their study on the solidarity movements, Giugni and Passy (2001: 6–7) base the definition of these movements on the notion of 'political altruism' (Passy 1998):

> Political altruism is a form of behaviour based on acts performed by a group or/and on behalf of a group, and not aimed to meet individual interests; it is directed at a political goal of social change or the redefinition of power relations; and individuals involved in this type of social change do not stand to benefit directly from the success deriving from the accomplishment of those goals. Following this definition, the actions performed by the solidarity movement can be characterized as political altruism. Participants in the solidarity movement act collectively with a clear political aim, and their actions are pursued to the benefits of other people.

This definition corresponds to a large extent to the characteristics of the associations mobilizing on the asylum issue. The large majority of them are indeed constituted by individuals who do not benefit from the (possible) 'success deriving from the accomplishment of their goals' (unlike class movements or corporative movements, for example). In this regard, the *Coordination Nationale des Sans-Papiers* in France and the *Karawane für die Rechte der Flüchtlinge und MigrantInnen* in Germany represent the exception: they are composed of individuals who are directly concerned with the demands they formulate. The unity of the pro-asylum movements in France and Germany is defined by the cause on which they mobilize: this cause requires political altruism on the part of the individuals that mobilize around it. This makes this movement part of the 'solidarity movement family' (Giugni and Passy 2001: 6–7).

This does not mean, however, that these movements form a homogeneous entity. Indeed, the solidarity movement historically builds upon different traditions: the 'Christian cosmology', the 'humanist component of the Enlightenment', and the 'socialist tradition' (Giugni and Passy 2001: 8–9):

> The Christian world provides the movement with the idea of helping your neighbour, giving her/him love, assistance, protection, and care. From the humanist component of the Enlightenment, the solidarity movement draws a coherent discourse on the respect for human rights and individual freedom. Finally, the early socialist movement put forth the ideal of a more just and egalitarian society.

The first major associations belonging to these different traditions were created at the end of the nineteenth century and the beginning of the twentieth century. This is the case, for example, with *Caritas* in Germany (created in 1897), the *Ligue des droits de l'Homme* in France (created in 1898), or the *Arbeiterwohlfahrt* in Germany (created in 1919). The first association builds upon the Christian tradition, the second upon the humanist tradition, and the third upon the socialist tradition. The two world wars generated other types of associations, which drew on the resources of the three traditions described above and which aimed to provide assistance and relief to the victims of wars. In contrast to the associations created during the earlier period, these associations did not combine these activities with the formulation of demands addressed to power-holders. Their essential mission was to visit political refugees, give them assistance and monitor their living conditions. An example of this is *Cimade* which was created in France in the 1930s.

Many authors see the 1960s and 1970s as the moment in which 'new social movements' emerged (Melucci 1989, 1995; Touraine 1978, 1984). Social movements active in this period are considered to be 'new' because they give a political sense to questions (ecology, feminism, anti-racism, living conditions in prisons, etc.) that were not seen as political in the past: they go beyond the idea of a protest defined in terms of class. The solidarity movement sector has followed these significant transformations: 'organizations that emerged since then are quite distinct from the old solidarity associations of the late nineteenth century' (Giugni and Passy 2001). In particular, these organizations have a political orientation: their demands are guided by 'a quest for individual emancipation and a deep democratization both of Western and non-Western society'. Moreover, unlike the associations of the older solidarity movement, which based their activities on assistance and relief, they have a repertoire of collective action that combines these former activities with political demands addressed to power-holders. This leads Giugni and Passy (2001) to conclude that the new solidarity movement that emerged in the 1960s and 1970s has gained 'a unity and a political coherence that it lacked before'.

As I will develop below, several associations active in French and German pro-asylum movements since the 1960s–1970s correspond to these evolutions. This is the case with *Amnesty International* (in both countries), *Gisti* in France or *Pro Asyl* in Germany. The idea of the emergence of a 'new solidarity movement' during this period is, however, a question of debate. In particular, two points can be raised. First, the pro-asylum movement does not represent a complete rupture with what occurred before the 1960s–1970s. In fact, the associations that were created earlier are still important actors in these movements. Thus, associations building on the Christian tradition (*Caritas, Diakonie, Secours Catholique*) still play an important role in this field. This is also true of the associations building on the humanist and socialist traditions (even if they have evolved). Moreover, the associations emerging in the 1960s and 1970s are not completely different from those that emerged earlier. As I will develop below, associations such as *Amnesty International* or *Gisti* have many similarities with the *Ligue des droits de l'Homme* in France. The pro-asylum movement of the period before and after the 1960s–1970s is thus characterized more by continuity than rupture. Indeed, I will show that – to a certain extent – this movement is still shaped by the three traditions that led to its emergence. These three traditions have evolved, but the principal ideas that lie behind them continue to represent three different streams – or components – of the movement. Thus I would contest the idea that, since the 1960s–1970s, the pro-asylum movement has found a unity and the coherence that it lacked before. On the contrary, the analysis shows that it is even less coherent than it was before. This is due to the fact that new components joined this movement in the 1970s, 1980s and 1990s. These new components are service-provider associations and militant associations.

Service-provider associations emerged in the 1970s and 1980s in the context of a rise in the number of asylum-seekers in Europe. They are financed by state subsidies to provide juridical assistance to asylum-seekers and for the management of the centres in which they are accommodated (the *Centres d'Accueil pour Demandeurs d'Asile* in France and the *Asylheime* in Germany). They have thus been described as 'para-public associations' (Valluy 2007). Associations like *France Terre d'Asile* and *Forum Réfugiés* in France were created for these missions (in the mid-1970s and in 1982, respectively). Moreover, some associations that belonged to other traditions re-oriented their activities during this period in order to provide these services. This was the case with the *Arbeiterwohlfahrt* (initially belonging to the socialist tradition) and with *Caritas* and *Diakonie* (belonging to the Christian tradition) in Germany. The militant associations emerged in the second half of the 1990s. They clearly positioned themselves at the Left of the political spectrum and their repertoires are oriented towards disruptive forms of collective action. This is the case with associations such as *Act Up* or the *CNSP* in France and *Kein Mensch ist Illegal* or *Kanak Attak* in Germany.

To sum up, French and German pro-asylum movements are made up of five main associative components that have emerged in different periods: religious associations, human rights associations, those mobilizing for a more just and egalitarian society, those focusing on the provision of services, and militant associations. This brief historical overview is thus useful as it highlights the fact that the solidarity movement is not united and coherent. However, it is important to specify that these different categories are not mutually exclusive. Thus, associations like *Pro Asyl* or the *Flünchtingsrat Berlin* in Germany or like *Gisti* or *Cimade* in France can be seen as human rights associations and also as associations mobilizing for a more just and egalitarian society: they have characteristics that belong to both streams. Equally, the German associations *Diakonie* and *Caritas* can be defined as religious associations and also as service-provider associations. Moreover, organizations can move from one category to another over time. For example, *Cimade*, in France, was created in the 1930s as a religious association, with the aim of providing relief to asylum-seekers and refugees. Today, however, it has more in common with human rights associations and with associations mobilizing for a more just and egalitarian society. It still relies to a certain extent on a network of religious activists mobilizing for humanitarian principles (Marcos 2003). However, as I will discuss further, the characteristics of its discourse, its repertoire of collective action and its organizational structure are closer to those of associations like *Gisti* or *Amnesty International* than to those of religious organizations like the *Secours Catholique*. Similarly, the *Arbeiterwohlfahrt* (created after the First World War as a component of the socialist movement in Germany) now has the profile of a service-provider association. For these reasons, this typology needs to be revised. As I will now develop in detail, the systematic analysis of the features of French and German SMOs leads to a different typology.

## Mobilizing 'for the relief of', 'on behalf of', 'together with', or 'as' asylum-seekers and refugees

Three groups of organizations can be distinguished in France and Germany. This distinction is based on two fundamental dimensions of their collective identities: their perception of how public authorities define asylum seekers and refugees, and the justification of their action in the pro-asylum movement (in other words, their definition of 'political altruism'). These two dimensions are reflected in their frames, their repertoires of collective action and their organizational structures and result in important differences in these three aspects. The first group of organizations has a legitimized identity: they specify how public authorities define asylum-seekers and refugees on the basis of humanitarian principles. They act for the relief of groups that they perceive as victims and, as such, accept the official identification of asylum-seekers and refugees. These organizations are religious associations and those who provide services. They have a humanitarian framing, a mainly corporatist repertoire and highly professionalized structures.

The second group of organizations has a principled identity: they criticize and deconstruct the identification of asylum-seekers and refugees made by public authorities. They mobilize on behalf of what they define as populations facing unjust or inhuman policies: immigrants, minorities, the excluded, etc. This group is composed of the human rights associations and those organizations mobilizing for a more just and egalitarian society. They have a more politicized discourse, a mainly pluralist repertoire and structures mixing professionalization and horizontal dynamics.

The third group is made up of organizations that have an oppositional identity: they construct autonomous identifications of asylum-seekers and refugees that radically oppose those made by public authorities. It is made up of (auto-constituted) organizations acting as asylum-seekers and refugees and of other groups acting together with them. They mobilize against processes considered as exclusionary. This group is composed of militant associations. Like the preceding group, they have a politicized discourse, but they have a more protesting repertoire and less professionalized structures. In the following, I will show how the discourses, repertoires of collective action and organizational structures of these three groups make them distinct.

## Different perceptions of the asylum issue

The empirical analysis of the documents produced by French and German SMOs shows that eight different collective action frames can be used to justify their involvement in the pro-asylum movement. These are:

- anti-racism and anti-discrimination (the endangering of asylum right is a consequence – and leads to – an increase of racist and discriminatory discourses and behaviours in society);
- the defence of human rights (states have to guarantee asylum right as a consequence of their existing international engagements);
- the promotion of new human rights (new fundamental rights should be guaranteed to asylum-seekers and refugees);
- international solidarity (the protection of refugees is a help provided by Northern countries to populations from Southern countries);
- the broader opening of the borders (asylum right is endangered by the restrictiveness of the immigration policies);
- the humanitarian frame (the protection of refugees is a moral duty – it focuses on the conditions of reception of asylum-seekers and refugees, and it insists on individual cases);
- the fight against precariousness and social inequalities (the precariousness of the statute of asylum-seekers and immigrants leads to their exploitation);
- the fight against repression/persecution (asylum-seekers and migrants constitute a particular group that is persecuted as such by public authorities).

An association which relies on more than one frame follows a process of 'frame bridging': 'the linkage of two or more ideologically congruent but structurally unconnected frames regarding a particular issue, problem or set of events' (Snow and Benford 1988). In this perspective, the first step of the document analysis has consisted in the systematic classification (through these different frames) of the different arguments presented by an association.[2] Tables 2 and 3 sum up the results of this analysis. They present the number of frames traditionally used by an association in its discourse (showing thus the existence of linkages between different frames) and they underline the frames that are the most fundamental in its discourse (those that correspond to central ideas in the articulation of its discourse and that are the most frequently used in the list of documents that I have analysed). The frames used by an association are represented by one X; the frames that are fundamental in the discourse of an association are represented by two Xs. In the interests of clarity, French and German associations are presented separately:

**Table 2** The collective action frames of French SMOs

| | | Collective action frames | | | | | | | |
|---|---|---|---|---|---|---|---|---|---|
| | | Anti-racism and anti-discrimination | The defence of fundamental rights | The promotion of new fundamental rights | International solidarity | The broader opening of borders | Humanitarian frame | The fight against precariousness and social inequalities | The fight against repression / persecution |
| SMOs | Act Up | X | X | XX | X | XX | | XX | XX |
| | Amnesty International Section Française | X | XX | X (since the beginning of 2000s) | | | | | XX |
| | Cimade | X | XX | XX | X | | | X | XX |
| | CNSP | XX | | X (until 1999–2000) | X (until 1999–2000) | | | XX | XX |
| | FASTI | XX | X | X | XX | XX | | XX | X |
| | Forum Réfugiés | | X | | | | XX | | |
| | France Terre d'Asile | | X | | | | XX | | |
| | Gisti | X | X | XX | X | XX | | XX | XX |
| | Ligue des droits de l'Homme | XX | XX | XX | | X | | XX | XX |
| | MRAP | XX | X | X | X | | | X | XX |
| | Secours Catholique | | X | | | | XX | | |

**Table 3** The collective action frames of German SMOs

| | | Collective action frames | | | | | | | |
|---|---|---|---|---|---|---|---|---|---|
| | | Anti-racism and anti-discrimination | The defence of fundamental rights | The promotion of new fundamental rights | International solidarity | The broader opening of borders | Humanitarian frame | The fight against precariousness and social inequalities | The fight against repression / persecution |
| SMOs | AGA Rhein-Main | XX | X | | | X | | | XX |
| | Amnesty International Deutschland | | XX | X (since beginning of 2000s) | | | | | XX |
| | Arbeiterwohlfahrt | | X | X | | | XX | X | |
| | Bayerischer Flüchtlingsrat | X | XX | X | | | X | XX | |
| | Caritas Deutschland | X | X | X | | | XX | | |
| | Diakonisches Werk der EKD | X | X | X | | | XX | | |
| | Flüchtlingsrat Berlin | XX | X | X | | | X | | XX |
| | Flüchtlingsrat Hamburg | XX | X | XX | | X | | XX | XX |
| | Kanak Attak | XX | | X | | X | | XX | XX |
| | Karawane für die Rechte der Flüchtlinge und MigrantInen | XX | XX | X | XX | | | XX | X |
| | Kein Mensch Ist Illegal | XX | X | X | X | XX | | XX | XX |
| | Pro Asyl | XX | XX | X | | | XX | | |

First, the analysis shows that some cognitive frames are more common than others in French and German pro-asylum movements. This is particularly the case of the frames of the defence of fundamental rights (used by twenty-one associations), the promotion of new fundamental rights (nineteen associations), anti-racism and anti-discrimination (eighteen associations), and the fight against repression and persecution (fifteen associations). On the contrary, the frame of the broader opening of the borders (used by eight associations), the international solidarity frame (eight associations) and the humanitarian frame (nine associations) seem to be more controversial as they are only used by a minority of French and German associations. Some frames are more central than others. When they are used by an association, the frame of the fight against repression and persecution, the humanitarian frame, the fight against precariousness and social inequalities, and anti-racism and anti-discrimination correspond in general to a central argument. Finally, some frames are often bridged together. For example, nine of the eleven associations for whom the frame of anti-racism and anti-discrimination is central also consider the frame of the fight against repression and persecution to be fundamental. Also, all of the associations for whom the frame of international solidarity is central also consider the frame of anti-racism and anti-discrimination to be crucial, and moreover they all consider the frame of the fight against precariousness and social inequalities as fundamental.

In a comparative perspective, there are few differences that clearly distinguish the discourses of French associations from those of German associations. The only difference that can be observed is that some frames are more present in one country than in the other. For instance, the frame of anti-racism and anti-discrimination is more present and more central in the discourse of German associations than in that of French organizations. Also, the frame of the promotion of new fundamental rights is generally more central in the discourse of the French associations than in the discourse of the German associations. It seems that the frame of a broader opening of the borders has been mainly developed in the French context. However, the most important result of this analysis at this stage is the fact that there is no fundamental difference that clearly distinguishes the process of frame bridging of all French SMOs from that of all German associations.

There is, however, a difference between two groups of associations in both countries. On the one hand, one group of SMOs (majoritarian in terms of number) justifies its mobilization by using a large number of frames and therefore follows an extensive process of frame-bridging. These are the human rights associations, the associations mobilizing for a more just and egalitarian society, and militant associations. On the other hand, another group of associations relies on one particular frame (the humanitarian frame) and follows a limited process of frame-bridging. These are religious associations and service-provider associations. This difference is important because it means that these two groups of associations have two distinct discursive logics. The first group justifies its mobilization on the asylum issue through a high level of generalization and abstraction: they view the question of asylum as an issue that concerns society as a whole. The second group justifies its mobilization through a specific discourse (thus at a lower level of generalization and abstraction): they view the asylum issue as a particular question that has to be dealt with through a unique objective (the protection of refugees).

In France, the associations having an extensive process of frame-bridging are *Act Up*, *Gisti*, *FASTI*, *Ligue des droits de l'Homme*, *Cimade*, *MRAP*, *CNSP*,[3] and *Amnesty International Section Française*. In Germany, these are *Kein Mensch Ist Illegal*, *Karawane für die Rechte der Flüchtinge und MigrantInnen*, *Flüchtlingsrat Hamburg*, *Kanak Attak*, *Flüchtlingsrat Berlin*, *Bayerischer Flüchtlingsrat*, *Pro Asyl*, *Amnesty International Deutschland*, and the *Aktionsbündnis Gegen Abschiebung Rhein-Main*.

A good example of this frame-bridging process is the communiqué 'Open letter to Lionel Jospin' that was published by *Gisti*, *FASTI*, and *Act Up* (together with three other associations) in 1997. It is argued that the closure of the borders leads to repression and to the precariousness of migrant populations (as they have to enter and stay in France illegally) as well as to a denial of asylum rights:

> The repression of the admission to stay principally affects foreigners for whom international law (the Geneva Convention on Refugees and the European Convention on Human Rights in particular) and common sense legitimate the entrance. The aim of the Pasqua law was not to penalize members of families. However . . . How could they not be penalized, knowing that repression affects above all those who want to respect legality? A large percentage of the *sans-papiers* prove this reality, be they spouses of foreigners in regular situations or asylum-seekers whose demand has been rejected.[4]

According to these associations, this situation results from a lack of will by Northern countries to fight the problems faced by the people living in Southern countries (and especially in the former colonies). Moreover, this leads to increases in xenophobic movements in France and in Europe:

> Can we abandon the third world to market laws and close the borders to those who are escaping from injustice and poverty? Did M. Chevènement take one single minute to think before saying that

> 'the problems faced by the South have to find solutions in the South, and not in the North'? It is pure stupidity to pretend that because a large part of the problems faced by the South are made worse, or even created and maintained by the North. [. . .] The question of immigration has become a problem because public authorities have considered it for too long as a taboo. We are not naïve, but we think that it is possible to imagine other solutions than repression. This means that your government takes the time to open the conditions for an open debate before adopting laws. This would also allow the demonstration of the absurdity of the theses presented by the *Front National* in this domain.[5]

These associations conclude that this situation can be resolved through the opening of borders (freedom of circulation) and through the promotion of new rights for migrants (in particular, access to labour markets and social protection):

> The defence of freedom of circulation, of the opening of the borders, of equality of rights doesn't correspond at all to a choice going in the direction of ultra-liberalism. But it takes into account the disastrous human consequences due to the progressive triumph of ultra-liberalism in the world. [. . .] In contrast to ultra-liberals, we want foreigners that are pushed to come to us by the consequences of liberalism – and that no law will impede to enter the territory – to have rights (in particular the right to stay and to work) so that they don't remain the excluded of a society that knows exactly how to exploit the irregularity of their statute. [. . .] The respect of the state of law leads to forbidding any kind of discrimination between French and foreigners. So there is no reason to deprive those who live in France from the right to work. [. . .] Also, the principle of equality implies that (like before 1993), the regularity of residence is not a condition for the access to social security.[6]

In Germany, a similar example is the manifesto written by the *Kein Mensch Ist Illegal* network in 1997. It is argued that the closure of borders by the European states leads to a precarious situation for migrants and thus to a constant risk of repression:

> Migrants and refugees are not welcomed in Europe. Because it is almost impossible for them to arrive here in a legal way, the crossing of state borders is only possible through illegal ways, which are often

> linked to deathly dangers. [. . .] So, an increasing number of people are forced to live illegally.
>
> Borders do not only separate territories, borders separate people. Borders occur everywhere: in the administration offices and in the railway station, in the town centres and in the state borders. Borders are everywhere where people have to fear to be asked for documents.
>
> To live under a precarious, unsafe or illegal statute means to live under the permanent fear of denunciation and repression because to be discovered means a condemnation or an immediate expulsion.[7]

The network then argues that the mobilization around immigration is a fight against racism and discrimination, for the defence as well as for the promotion of fundamental rights, and finally a fight against precariousness and social inequalities:

> In the fight against racism and sexism, it is increasingly important to support migrants (in a political and practical way) in their fight against illegalization and for their right to have rights.
>
> Everyone has the right to decide where and how (s)he wants to live. The control of migration and the systematic denial of rights go against the notion of equality in all social and political fields. Human rights have to be respected, whatever the origins and the documents of people.
>
> For these reasons, we demand support for migrants in their way across borders. We demand that migrants be granted work and documents. We demand medical relief, school and training, home and minimal material conditions for migrants.
>
> Because no one is illegal.[8]

These two examples illustrate how, through an extensive process of frame-bridging, the asylum issue is related to several general societal issues: racism, North-South relations, the protection of individual liberties, the growth of precariousness, the defence of fundamental human rights, etc. This particular logic corresponds to a politicized handling of the asylum issue: these discourses present a high level of generalization and of abstraction.

Unlike this first group of SMOs, one group of associations has a limited frame-bridging process and relies mainly on one particular frame: the humanitarian frame. In France, this group is made of the two service-provider associations (*France Terre d'Asile* and *Forum Réfugiés*), and the religious association *Secours Catholique*. Thus, in its introduction, *France Terre d'Asile* defines its activities through a focus on the daily work of assistance and protection of refugees and asylum-seekers:

> France Terre d'Asile was created in 1971 in order to support the daily exercise of asylum rights, in order to monitor carefully the evolution of legal dispositions and administrative practices, in order to participate actively in the reception of refugees and asylum-seekers, and in order to promote a policy of social and professional integration.[9]

In Germany, the organizations having a limited process of frame-bridging are the religious associations *Caritas* and *Diakonie* and the service-provider association *Arbeiterwohlfahrt.* In their documents, the humanitarian frame is bridged with other frames (the defence of fundamental rights and the promotion of new fundamental rights in particular). However, the humanitarian frame is by far the most central. They therefore have to be distinguished – as in the French case – from the organizations that have an extensive frame-bridging process. Thus, when it presents its activities relating to the asylum issue, *Diakonie* frames them as being centred on 'humanitarian' objectives:

> Diakonie works for the respect of humanitarian minimal conditions in the implementation of foreigners' law. It is not possible that, in one of the richest countries in the world, traumatized refugees are expelled. It is not possible that family reunifications are impeded and that the protection of family can thus not be guaranteed. It is not possible that disabled or sick persons are sent back to their countries of origin.[10]

The associations having a limited frame-bridging process present themselves as acting mostly for one purpose: the protection of asylum-seekers and refugees ('Refugees have to be protected' is the slogan of *Forum Réfugiés*). They act for their relief and present their action as being directed towards individuals rather than towards groups of people in society (asylum-seekers and refugees in general, migrants, undocumented migrants, people in a precarious situation, people whose fundamental rights are in danger, etc.) as is the case for the associations having an extensive frame-bridging process. In contrast to a discourse turned towards the denunciation of general societal problems, these associations present themselves as acting through concrete 'everyday actions' for the relief of individuals. The level of generalization and abstraction is thus lower than in the discourse presented by the first group of associations. One can clearly distinguish a discursive logic of 'politicization' of the asylum issue (in the sense that the asylum issue is viewed as a general societal issue) from a process of 'individualization' (in the sense that the asylum issue is viewed through the particular situations of the individuals concerned by it).

A further analysis of the frames used in French and German movements leads to a more specific typology. The examination of the three dimensions of frames (diagnostic, prognostic and motivational) permits us to distinguish three different groups of SMOs: those having a humanitarian framing, a principle-oriented framing, and a subversive framing. The organizations following a process of individualization of discourse have a humanitarian framing, while those having more politicized discourses have principle-oriented and subversive framings.

First, the exploration of the diagnostic and prognostic frames allows us to draw a typology of the frames used by French and German associations. The eight frames which have been described above can be categorized in three 'master frames':[11] the 'call for new political orientations', the 'call for reason' and the 'call for help'. I represent this typology in Table 4.

These three categories are close to the three initial traditions of the solidarity movements, as presented by Giugni and Passy (2001): the call for new political orientations puts forth the idea of a 'more just and egalitarian society', the call for reason promotes 'respect for human rights and individual freedom', and the call for help is based on the idea of 'helping your neighbour, giving her/him love, assistance, protection, and care'.

The first category of frames is represented by the humanitarian frame and by that of international solidarity. These frames are central in the discourse of religious associations and those providing services, and they both contain the central idea of a call for helping individuals who face a situation of emergency. For example, the association *Secours Catholique* writes that its

**Table 4** Typology of the collective action frames on the asylum issue

| | |
|---|---|
| Call for help | International solidarity |
| | Humanitarian frame |
| Call for reason | Anti-racism and anti-discrimination |
| | The defence of fundamental rights |
| | The fight against repression and/or persecution |
| Call for new political orientations | The fight against precariousness and social inequalities |
| | The fight for a broader opening of the borders |
| | The promotion of new fundamental rights |

activities are based on the objective of resolving the 'problems of immediate survival' of 'foreigners being in a difficult situation':

> In France, around 120 000 asylum seekers are waiting for a definitive answer on the part of public authorities. [. . .] The average delay is around one year and a half. In this context, the 106 delegations of the *Secours Catholique* are mobilized in order to answer the demands of foreigners who find themselves in a difficult situation. All over the year, local teams face the problems relating to immediate survival and housing and they have created groups that work on the initiation of the French language.[12]

This idea is linked with the identification of asylum-seekers and refugees as a vulnerable group. Thus, the central argument of *Caritas Deutschland* in its 'general position on asylum and refugee questions' is that it should provide help to 'foreigners' difficult destiny':

> *Caritas* wants to raise comprehension for the difficult destiny of foreigners, to promote their reception, and to propose human relief. *Caritas* looks after the concrete cases of asylum-seekers and refugees with a high number of social and law advisers, psychological help and various other services.[13]

This type of frame is not based on the idea of the defence (or promotion) of general principles and values. It is less oriented towards the general definition of the policy of immigration and asylum than towards its concrete implementation. In other words, it is essentially focused on the immediate situation of individuals rather than on state policy. The idea of a call for help is thus oriented towards political neutrality.[14]

The frames of anti-racism and anti-discrimination, of the defence of fundamental rights, and of the fight against repression and/or persecution are different as they are more principle-oriented. They are the most central in the discourse of organizations mobilizing for a more just and egalitarian society and of human rights associations. Their internal logic is to present a call for reason that is addressed to public authorities. The underlying idea is that public authorities have gone beyond the limits fixed by the principles of democracy and individual freedoms and by their international engagements (the Geneva Convention or the European Convention on Human Rights in particular). Associations using these types of frames demand public authorities to 'be reasonable' and to return to a position of respect of fundamental democratic values and individual liberties. Thus, as it called for a demonstration in March 2001, the *Mouvement contre le Racisme et pour l'Amitié entre les Peuples* (*MRAP*) argued that it would pressure the government to come back to these fundamental principles:

> to get back to the values of solidarity, of respect for the rights of individuals and of reception of refugees which are the foundations of European civilization.[15]

In the same perspective, *Amnesty International Deutschland* justifies its mobilization on the asylum issue as follows:

> The basis of Amnesty International's work on the asylum issue is led by the objective to fight against the forced returns (*refoulement*) of persons who will risk becoming victims of the denial of human rights (torture, 'being made to disappear', non-legal sentences or death penalty). Amnesty International works for the guarantee of a secured statute for these endangered persons.
>
> Amnesty International demands that governments guarantee asylum-seekers a fair and full access to asylum procedures. The organization demands that no asylum-seeker can be expelled without a full examination of his demand.[16]

Finally, the frames of the fight against precariousness and social inequalities, of the broader opening of the borders, and of the promotion of new fundamental rights represent another general category: they are oriented towards the call for new political orientations. They are the most central in the discourse of the more militant organizations. They stress the idea that another asylum and immigration policy should be conceived. For example, one of the demands included in the frame of the fight against precariousness and social inequalities is that all undocumented migrants should be regularized. All the discourses using these types of frames demand a clear break with the asylum and immigration policy that has been implemented since the 1970s in France and Germany (the frame of the broader opening of the borders being maybe the most exemplary). They constitute therefore a strong criticism of the authorities. The analysis shows moreover that they are often combined with the frames that belong to the idea of the call for reason. Thus, in 1999, as they call for a demonstration, the groups of the *Sans-Papiers de Saint Bernard* (initiators of the *CNSP*) write that:

> We observe reality and we see the existence of a large political consensus (built against popular will) against foreigners – in particular

> through the question of documents – and, largely beyond, against the most exploited parts of the population.[17]

This quotation is a good example of the process of bridging between the frame of the fight against precariousness and social inequalities and that of anti-racism and anti-discrimination. In the same sense, the German network *Karawane für die Rechte der Flüchtlinge und MigrantInnen* presents itself as follows:

> The *Karawane für die Rechte der Flüchtlinge und MigrantInnen* is a network which is composed of individuals, groups and organizations of refugees, migrants and Germans. Our founding principles are anti-imperialism and anti-racism. We are engaged in the fight for social and political rights, for equality and for the respect of the fundamental human rights of everyone.[18]

This represents a good example of the process of bridging between the frames of the fight against precariousness and social inequalities, international solidarity, the fight against racism and discrimination, the promotion of new fundamental rights and the defence of fundamental rights.

In comparison with the call for reason, the call for new political orientations is more radical and action-oriented. Its use implies the demand for radical political change whereas the use of the call for reason implies the limitation of policies considered as unjust. Moreover, it is action-oriented as the definition of a prognostic is central. The call for reason is more reactive: it stresses more the definition of a diagnostic. However, these two categories of frames have strong similarities and can be clearly distinguished from the first category (the call for help): they are both political and principle-oriented. The internal logic of the discourse using these frames is to address – in a critical way – the political orientations of the public authorities. The main idea is that the actual state policy towards migrants and refugees endangers fundamental rights, principles and values. These similarities are illustrated by the fact that all associations relying on the first type of frames follow a process of bridging that leads them to rely also on the second type of frames. The reverse is also true.

This highlights a strong ideological difference between the two last groups of organizations and the first group. The associations which rely (almost exclusively) on the humanitarian frame (*Forum Réfugiés*, *France Terre d'Asile* and *Secours Catholique* in France and the *Arbeiterwohlfahrt*, *Caritas* and *Diakonie* in Germany) are ideologically separated from the rest of the associations. Thus, one of the major issues that appeared during the interviews carried out in the two other groups of organizations is that a strictly humanitarian vision of the asylum issue would prevent them from having a 'political' understanding of the situation. In this sense, the associations relying on the idea of a call for help would not see where 'the real problems' are. In fact, in France and in Germany, the group of associations that mainly rely on the frame of the call for help is the only one that assumes the 'humanitarian' label. Thus, in its introduction, *Gisti* underlines the idea that it is defending general political principles rather than taking a 'humanitarian approach':

> *Gisti* is not an association of defence of foreigners (it refuses therefore a 'case-by-case' or humanitarian approach); it aims at fighting for the institution of a full equality of rights between French and foreigners. So people do not always see the role played by the association in the field and in particular in specific and time-limited mobilizations.[19]

In the same vein, and to avoid accusations of 'paternalism', the network *Karawane für die Rechte der Flüchtlinge und MigrantInnen* distances itself from humanitarian types of arguments:

> Important social differences appear when one compares the conditions of an asylum-seeker (who lives isolated and excluded from German society) with those of a German (who does not face this situation of isolation and exclusion). However, Germans are engaged in the *Karawane* at different levels. Their engagement is not based on paternalistic motivations to 'help the poor victims'. The basis of this engagement is the solidarity with the fight of refugees and migrants. This stems from the conviction that society is racist and that the dominant system is unfair. This also derives from an understanding of the responsibility of the German state in the occurrence of the reasons why refugees and migrants have to leave their countries of origin.[20]

This statement has however to be qualified in the German case because several associations combine – to a certain extent – the use of a humanitarian register of discourse with a more politically oriented type of discourse. This is the case of *Caritas*, *Diakonie* and the *Arbeiterwohlfahrt* who rely mainly on the humanitarian frame but who can resort to political types of arguments (the defence of fundamental rights or anti-racism and anti-discrimination in particular). This is also the case with associations like *Pro Asyl*, the *Bayerischer*

*Flüchtlingsrat* and the *Flüchtlingsrat Berlin*, who rely mainly on politically oriented types of frames but who can use more humanitarian arguments. Although one can observe the same line of difference in both countries, the distinction between different groups of associations seems to be stronger in France than in Germany. In this regard, one can reiterate the fact (mentioned in the previous chapter) that, since the beginning of the 1990s, the three groups of French associations (the first one separately from the two others) tend to produce a higher number of joint communiqués and joint calls than German associations. As I will develop below, this tends to increase the differences between these groups of organizations.

These cross-national differences highlight the fact that French and German organizations have different degrees of specialization on the asylum issue (that is the extent to which the asylum issue is considered as being isolated from other issues). In the German case, the discourses formulated by the associations rarely go beyond the asylum issue. Even if most German associations have an agenda of mobilization that does not focus only on the asylum issue, the link between the different issues they handle is rarely made.[21] On the other hand, French associations are more likely to establish links between the asylum issue and other issues on which they mobilize (or on which other associations mobilize). Thus, in a communiqué published by *FASTI*, *Gisti*, *LdH*, and *MRAP* (among other associations and networks) in December 2005,[22] the link is established between the situation faced by young people in poor areas, the projects of laws relating to 'pupils facing academic failure', to 'families in difficulties', to anti-terrorism and that 'directed against foreigners' (evoking thus the legislation on immigration and asylum):

> After fifteen days of spectacular violence, the *cités* and popular areas are not on the front page of the media anymore. Misery, exclusion and discrimination are, however, still present.
>
> Meanwhile, the government has responded with a law of exception, the 'state of emergency', and implements increasingly repressive and unjust measures, which affect foreigners, families in difficulty, pupils facing academic problems. [. . .] One piece of securitarian legislation replaces another. The project of law against terrorism, the announced projects of law on the 'prevention of delinquency' and, once again, on immigration, will stigmatize the same whipping boys as usual.[23]

This example shows that, in their discourses, French associations tend to have a lower degree of specialization on the asylum issue than German associations. However, this is not true of the two French associations whose agenda of mobilization is exclusively related to the asylum issue (*France Terre d'Asile* and *Forum Réfugiés*). These specifications on the differences between the French and German cases have to be kept in mind. As I will develop below, this follows what was said in the last chapter about the evolution of French and German pro-asylum movements since the beginning of the 1990s.

Finally, the frame analysis shows that SMOs belonging to French and German pro-asylum movements define different motivational frames. This relates to two dimensions: the identification of asylum-seekers and refugees (or more exactly the reaction to the identification made by public authorities); and the definition of the relation between its members and asylum-seekers and refugees. In other words, these are the questions about who the organizations act for, and through which legitimacy. It is on the basis of this double identification process that the incentives for mobilization are defined.

A first group of organizations (those that have a humanitarian framing) frame the identity of asylum-seekers and refugees through a categorization that resonates with that traditionally done by public authorities. Asylum-seekers and refugees are defined as a specific social group that is characterized by its vulnerability. This identification is meant to be 'acceptable' to public authorities and public opinion at large: it presents an irrefutable argument that explains their presence in the territory (refuting it would lead one to appear inhumane). The process of identification carried out by these organizations is therefore a process of specification: it specifies who they 'really' are when public authorities deny their identity of asylum-seekers and refugees (for instance when they present them as 'smugglers' or 'illegal'). Thus, when it presents its 'objectives' *France Terre d'Asile* begins with a definition of who is a refugee and underlines the need for 'protection':

> An asylum-seeker is a foreigner in search of protection;
> he fears for his life, he has had to leave his country, and he is no longer protected by the state he is from;
> the refugee status offers him a specific international protection, which has been translated into a particular legislation in France;
> asylum is a long French tradition, and is a moving reality, a human right that can be threatened.[24]

In this perspective, these organizations define their mobilization on the asylum issue as being specific: it is different from those related to the immigration issue or anti-racism, for example. Moreover, they identify their own role in a specific way: they act for the relief of asylum-seekers and refugees.

They situate themselves symbolically between this 'vulnerable' group and public authorities, but they do not claim to represent the identity of asylum-seekers. Rather, they represent their role as being neutral and based on the humanitarian principle of provision of help. Thus, in the same document, alongside its mission of 'action for the respect of asylum right', *France Terre d'Asile* claims a mission of 'solidarity with migrants of right in order to favour their integration':

> Exile causes immense sufferings. Moreover, there is the necessity of starting a new life.
>
> In order to live among us, they need:
>
> - help with their administrative procedures
> - to learn the French language
> - work and shelter
> - a better knowledge of our country and culture.[25]

This (double) process of identification contrasts with that of the second group of organizations: human rights associations and organizations working towards a more just and egalitarian society. The first group of associations reifies an identity (asylum-seekers and refugees) which was defined in the first instance by public authorities. The second group deconstructs this identity through a reference to more general identities. The fight for asylum rights is linked to the fight for the rights of migrants more generally, against racism, for the defence of human rights in general, or against social inequalities. Thus, in its own introduction, the *Flüchtlingsrat Hamburg* demands the regularization of all 'illegalized' migrants, and so links the asylum issue with the immigration issue. Moreover, it evokes their 'human, social, political and economical rights':

> Everyone has human, social, political, and economical rights, independent of his residence status or origins. We stand against the tendency to declare human beings as 'illegals', and we demand the regularization of all illegalized.[26]

In doing so, these organizations do not follow a strategy of identification of asylum-seekers and refugees as an 'acceptable', 'vulnerable' group. Moreover, unlike the first group, these organizations do not act for the relief of asylum-seekers and refugees, but rather on their behalf (and, more generally, on behalf of immigrants, ethnic minorities or victims of human rights abuses). Their role is not presented as being neutral: they claim to represent and to defend an identity that contrasts with that assigned by political authorities. This is explicitly explained by the *Ligue des droits de l'Homme*, when it justifies its use of the term human rights:

> This is why its name is important: it refuses to talk about 'human rights' (droits humains), which is a bad translation from English and doesn't acknowledge the universalism of the word 'mankind' (Homme). The word 'mankind' (Homme) designates all individuals of the human species. It doesn't use the term 'rights of the person' (droits de la personne), which implies a humanitarian and de-politicized vision of rights, and which doesn't take into account the citizen.[27]

Finally, it is in the group composed by militant associations that the process of identification is the most central. Unlike the first group, they do not seek to present asylum-seekers and refugees through an 'acceptable' identity. Moreover, their process of identification is more radical than that of the second group of organizations: they create new forms of identities that fundamentally oppose those traditionally assigned by public authorities. Indeed, their identification of asylum-seekers and refugees is contrary to that of a 'vulnerable' group. For them, asylum-seekers and refugees (and migrants in general) are groups of individuals who are seeking a better life. These associations not only criticize the identification made by public authorities, they also construct collective identities that seek to change the doxa: what can be thought or conceived.

This idea is best illustrated by the concept of 'autonomy of migration', which emerged in the German context. This concept is thought of as a direct challenge to the status that public authorities confer on undocumented migrants and migrants in general. It defines the migrant as the principal agent of his or her destiny. It conceives immigration as a phenomenon that is autonomous from state policies: immigration policies may be more liberal or more restrictive, but people will still cross borders. In the context of restrictive policies, it views the immigration phenomenon as a set of strategies that are defined and implemented by migrants in order to overcome the obstacles created by state border controls:

> When after the end of guest-worker recruitment in the 1970s legal entry to Europe seemed impossible, migrants organized it nonetheless through marriage and family reunion. Migrants fake their papers, states invent new alleged fraud-resistance documents and so on. These struggles imply a certain concept of autonomy, although not in the traditional, emphatic sense. Autonomy of migration

> is not supposed to mean sovereignty of migrants, but rather that migrants are not simply objects of state control – that migrants defy controls and resist racist discrimination.[28]

From this perspective, immigration and the fight against racism are seen as transgressions: when they cross borders, asylum-seekers and refugees (and migrants in general) defy the policies and categories defined by state authorities. In doing so, these organizations present a specific conception of the mobilization against immigration and asylum policies: they 'empower' migrants as they identify them as actors rather than victims, and they value immigration as a subversive act. In other words, in the context of restrictive policies, immigration is in itself an act that is out of the sight of public authorities, and migrants' strategies to cross borders and live in a territory constitute political challenges. This process of identification – the opposite of that made by public authorities – is also implied by the self-definition as *sans-papiers* (undocumented), which emerged in France during the movement in 1996–1997. The use of this term is a reaction against the official designation of migrants who do not have a legal residence status as 'illegals' or 'clandestines'. It is thus a reaction against a stigma. It implies first of all that these groups are able to define new identities: the term has an activist connotation. It also opposes the identification made by public authorities as it implies that it is not the migrant who is responsible for its stigma (as suggested by the terms 'illegals' or 'clandestines') but public authorities (those who do not give them residence permits). Finally, it is also a subversive identification as it indirectly denunciates the fact that individuals are identified on the basis of 'papers'.

These associations identify their own role in different ways than the two first groups of organizations. This role is in line with their objective to empower asylum-seekers and refugees. They consider that asylum-seekers and refugees have the resources necessary to organize themselves and to mobilize on their own. Thus, within this third group of associations, some will identify themselves as organizations which act together with asylum-seekers and refugees (or migrants in general):

> Our campaign against all forms of refugee camps is a struggle against borders. To divide and classify us, to isolate us, to make us accessible, easy to control, and usable. We will not participate in this classification and exclusion of human beings, nor in this separation of societies and the world into zones of poverty and wealth, into those with access to rights and those without rights, into zones of war and of a false peace. We will fight to undermine the foundations

> of the current relationships of domination, of the fences around the refugee camps, and of the visible and invisible borders of those areas, and we want to share our knowledge and our experiences of resistance.[29]

This idea is important as it implies that, unlike the two first groups, these organizations include the participation of asylum-seekers and refugees on a regular basis in their activity. In other words, the individuals who are directly concerned by the mobilizations are directly involved in the process of identification.

Within this third group, some will identify themselves as organizations acting as asylum-seekers and refugees (or migrants in general). These are associations that they have constructed themselves and in which they represent the largest (and often the only) part of the activists. They act on their own behalf and identify themselves as such:

> The politics of the Caravan is drawn, shaped and based on the life experiences and daily realities of our numerous members and colleagues, brothers and sisters both here in Germany and in the home countries.[30]

The associations who are constituted by asylum-seekers and refugees follow a radical process of identification that aims to empower them. However, this process is more ambiguous than for the other associations comprising the third group. Depending on the public they address, they sometimes present themselves as a 'vulnerable' group in need of help (in particular when they address the public at large). However, this identification is not like that of the first group of organizations. As it is coupled with the idea that asylum-seekers and refugees are able to act on their own, this self-identification as vulnerable population rather points to the fact that identities can be re-defined and deployed strategically (Einwohner 2006; Polletta and Jasper 2001). It therefore supports rather than contradicts the idea of an 'empowering' identification.

In conclusion, this frame-analysis has shown the existence of different perceptions of the asylum issue as well as different justifications for mobilization in French and German pro-asylum movements. In both countries, three different groups of organizations compose this multi-organizational field: humanitarian associations; principle-oriented organizations acting for the defence of human rights and for a more just and egalitarian society; and militant organizations. In both countries, the first group of organizations is clearly distinct from the two other groups, which have a politicized framing.

Finally, the comparison shows that the differences between these groups are more pronounced in France than in Germany. These empirical results do not imply that framing processes are carried out in a sort of vacuum. Frames are defined in the course of collective action, within a particular context of mobilization, and through interactions between different social movement organizations and activists (Snow and Benford 1988). Thus, the types of frames defined by an SMO influence its repertoire of collective action, which, in turn, influences its framing process. Nevertheless, these empirical results demonstrate that the framing process is central in the collective identity of an association. I will show in the following section that the differences in terms of framing processes are related (directly or indirectly) to differences in terms of relationship to power-holders, ability to construct inter-organizational coalitions, and organizational structure.

## Different relations with power-holders

Social movement organizations implement different types of repertoire of collective action. Balme and Chabanet (2002) have distinguished three repertoires on the basis of the different degrees of institutionalization of their action: a corporatist, a pluralist and a protesting one. The protesting repertoire corresponds to a low degree of institutionalization. It is opposed to the corporatist one, which is exclusively based on formalized and cooperative interactions with institutions. The pluralist one corresponds to an intermediary level of institutionalization: it is made up of formalized and cooperative interactions, like lobbying, as well as more contentious types of interactions, like juridical actions. These different repertoires are composed of diverse types of collective actions. Considering the empirical analysis of French and German pro-asylum movements, this goes from the regular provision of services (based on state subsidies) to collective hunger-strikes and occupations. Table 5 relates the main types of collective actions constructed in French and German pro-asylum movements to these three repertoires.

The repertoires of collective action of French and German associations were analysed comparatively through a protest-event analysis focusing on two main dimensions: their degree of institutionalization (the extent to which they tend to be close to a corporatist repertoire), and their extensiveness (the variety of collective actions on which they rely). Tables 6 and 7 sum up the results of this analysis (in the interest of readability, the repertoires of French and German associations are presented in different tables). They present the range of collective actions on which they rely on a regular basis and their centrality in the repertoire of each of these associations. Some of

**Table 5** The repertoires of collective action in the French and German pro-asylum movements

| Repertoire of collective action | Type of collective action |
|---|---|
| Protesting | Collective hunger-strike, collective occupation |
| | Violent symbolic action (related to the detention or deportation of migrants) |
| | Demonstration |
| | Launching of a call or a petition |
| | Launching of a communiqué |
| Pluralist | Juridical action |
| | Realization of an independent observation (situation in a detention centre or in a country of origin, for example) |
| | Organization of a conference or a seminar |
| | Lobbying |
| | Juridical help provided to asylum-seekers |
| Corporatist | Answer to calls for proposals for grants or missions launched by the institutions |
| | Provision of services on a regular basis (reception of asylum-seekers with the financial support of the authorities, for example) |

these collective actions (XX) are central for a social movement organization (those on which they rely the most regularly in the list of protest-events that I analysed and for which they have gained a high level of expertise), while others (X) are carried out on a less regular basis.

These empirical results show the existence of two differences between the humanitarian and the more politicized SMOs: in terms of the form and extensiveness of their repertoire. Because of these two differences, these groups of associations have distinct relations with power-holders and different capacities to construct inter-associative coalitions. In France and Germany, humanitarian associations tend to restrict their repertoire to a limited number of collective actions that lead them to a corporatist relation with power-holders. This leads them moreover to privilege the construction of homogeneous coalitions of associations. Conversely, the SMOs acting for the defence of human rights and for a more just and egalitarian society, as well as militant organizations, tend to privilege a wider repertoire, which

**Table 6** Repertoires of collective action of French SMOs

| **Repertoire of collective action** | **Type of collective action** | **Associations** | | | | | | | | | | |
|---|---|---|---|---|---|---|---|---|---|---|---|---|
| | | Act Up Paris | Amnesty International Section Française | Cimade | CNSP | FASTI | Forum Réfugiés | France Terre d'Asile | Gisti | Ligue des droits de l'Homme | MRAP | Secours Catholique |
| Protesting | Collective hunger-strike, collective occupation | | | | XX | | | | | | | |
| | Violent symbolic action | X | | | X | | | | | | | |
| | Demonstration | XX | X | X | XX | XX | | | XX | XX | XX | |
| | Launching of a call or a petition | XX | XX | X | XX | X | | | XX | XX | XX | |
| | Launching of a communiqué | XX | XX | XX | XX | XX | X | X | XX | XX | XX | X |
| Pluralist | Juridical action | | X | X | | | | | XX | X | X | |
| | Realization of an independent observation mission | | XX | X | | | | | X | X | X | XX |

| | | | | | | | | | | | | |
|---|---|---|---|---|---|---|---|---|---|---|---|---|
| | Organization of a conference or a seminar | | X | X | X | X | X | X | XX | XX | XX | |
| | Lobbying | XX | XX | X | | | X | X | | XX | X | X |
| | Juridical help provided to asylum-seekers | | XX | XX | | X | X | X | XX | | | XX |
| Corporatist | Answer to calls for proposals for grants or missions launched by institutions | | | | | | | | | | | |
| | Provision of services on a regular basis | | | X | | | XX | XX | | | | |

**Table 7** Repertoires of collective action of German SMOs

| Repertoire of collective action | Type of collective action | Associations | | | | | | | | | | | |
|---|---|---|---|---|---|---|---|---|---|---|---|---|---|
| | | AGA Rhein-Main | Amnesty international Deutschland | Arbeiter-wohlfahrt | Bayerischer Flüchtlingsrat | Caritas Deutschland | Diakonie | Flüchtlingsrat Berlin | Flüchtlingsrat Hamburg | Kanak Attak | Karawane | KMII | Pro Asyl |
| Protesting | Collective hunger-strike, collective occupation | X | | | | | | | | | X | X | |
| | Violent symbolic action | XX | | | X | | | X | X | X | X | XX | |
| | Demonstration | XX | X | | X | | | XX | XX | X | XX | XX | X |
| | Launching of a call or a petition | | XX | | X | X | X | X | X | X | X | XX | X |
| | Launching of a communiqué | X | X | X | X | X | X | X | XX | X | XX | X | XX |
| Pluralist | Juridical action | | X | | | X | X | | | | X | | XX |
| | Realization of an independent observation | | XX | | | | | | | | | | XX |

| | | | | | | | | | | | | | |
|---|---|---|---|---|---|---|---|---|---|---|---|---|---|
| | Organization of a conference, seminar, or information campaign | XX | X | X | XX | X | X | XX | XX | XX | XX | XX | XX |
| | Lobbying | | XX | XX | X | XX | XX | X | X | | | | XX |
| | Juridical help provided to asylum-seekers | | XX | XX | XX | XX | XX | XX | XX | | | X | XX |
| Corporatist | Answer to calls for proposals for grants or for missions launched by the institutions | | | | | X | X | | | | | | |
| | Provision of services on a regular basis | | | XX | | XX | XX | | | | | | |

leads them to a more contentious relation with power-holders and to form heterogeneous coalitions of associations.

The analysis shows first of all that *Forum Réfugiés*, *France Terre d'Asile* and the *Arbeiterwohlfahrt* are the only associations for whom the provision of services on behalf of the state constitutes the essential part of their activities. As a matter of fact, the activities for which a state convention has been signed represent the quasi-totality of their expenses. *Cimade*, *Caritas Deutschland*, and *Diakonie* have also signed up to a convention to provide services for the state (*Cimade*, for example, intervenes in detention centres and manages a *Centre d'Accueil pour Demandeurs d'Asile*). However, this does not represent an exclusive part of their repertoire as is the case for the three other organizations.

It is possible to distinguish these three associations from the rest of the SMOs because the dedication to these activities of service provision leads them to define a very specific repertoire of collective action. In fact, a common point of the interviews carried out in the associations that refused to sign a convention with public authorities was a strong criticism of their choice. A shared point of view was that an exclusive dedication to these activities would restrain their liberty to criticize the government's policy. The role of these associations would then be to implement states' policies. This is a constant source of conflict within the pro-asylum movements. In particular, the associations that refused to sign a state convention reproach those associations who do sign the state convention for intervening in detention centres for migrants and thus accepting *de facto* this practice. For example, in 2006, several demonstrations and (sometimes violent) protest actions were organized by militants close to the networks *Flüchtlingsrat Berlin*, *No Lager*, the *Karawane für die Rechte der Flüchtlinge und MigrantInnen* and *Kanak Attak* against the *Arbeiterwohlfahrt* as they discovered that it would be managing a new detention centre in Berlin.[31]

By extension, associations that do not rely on contentious types of collective actions can be distinguished from those that can – even occasionally – rely on protest. Three French associations (*Forum Réfugiés*, *France Terre d'Asile* and *Secours Catholique*) and three German associations (*Arbeiterwohlfahrt*, *Caritas Deutschland* and *Diakonie*) rarely launch petitions or participate in demonstrations, whereas these two forms of collective action represent an important part of the repertoire of all the other French and German associations. This distinction overlaps with the difference underlined in the discussion relating to the frames. It is indeed logical to observe that 'humanitarian' associations – having a non-critical discourse – do not rely on protest in order to represent their demands, whereas the more principle-oriented associations – having a more critical discourse against public authorities – often do. The definition of protest is already inscribed in the discourse of politicized associations whereas the humanitarian discourse leads to a focus almost exclusively on actions of relief towards asylum-seekers and refugees and to work in cooperation with public authorities.

More generally, this distinction corresponds to two different logics underlying the construction of a collective action. On the one hand, 'humanitarian' associations exclusively base their collective actions on a direct relation with power-holders. They establish a dialogue that principally involves two interlocutors: the representatives of public authorities and themselves. On the other hand, associations which have a more principle-oriented discourse can also construct a repertoire that privileges the addressing of power-holders through the mobilization of public opinion. The (more conflictive) dialogue that they establish involves a multiplicity of interlocutors. This statement is also related to the differences in terms of frames that have been analysed above. SMOs acting for the defence of human rights and for a more just society, and militant organizations have a discursive logic of 'politicization' of the asylum issue: they aim to present it as a general societal issue through the use of multiple frames in their discourse. Therefore, logically, politicized associations aim to construct collective actions that involve public opinion at large in a general debate on this issue. Conversely, humanitarian associations have a discursive logic of 'individualization' of the asylum issue: they present themselves as acting through concrete 'everyday actions' for the particular situation of individuals. The construction of a general society debate on the asylum issue through collective actions involving public opinion at large is therefore not a priority for humanitarian associations. The 'humanitarian' and 'political' (or principle-oriented) characterization of French and German associations is thus also related to their repertoire of collective action. Beside their discourse, French and German political associations are also political because they aim (through the form of their collective actions) to present the asylum issue as a question that concerns the whole of society: they aim to render it public. Humanitarian associations are also humanitarian because they privilege forms of collective actions that are not conflictive. Their 'politically-neutral' discourse also reflects a decision to focus on 'politically-neutral' types of activities (in the sense that they are less turned towards the discussion of political orientations). These empirical results resonate with the analysis presented by Dauvin and Siméant (2004). In their study of international NGOs and their humanitarian work, these authors have shown that the particular discourse presented by these organizations leads them inevitably to limit their repertoire to specific types of collective actions and to avoid protest.

Further analysis leads us to stress another line of difference, which distinguishes those associations having a wide repertoire of collective action from those relying on a more limited repertoire. On the one hand, humanitarian associations limit their repertoire to three main types of collective actions: the juridical help provided to asylum-seekers; the provision of services on a regular basis; and lobbying. On the other hand, SMOs acting for the defence of human rights and for a more just and egalitarian society, as well as militant organizations, rely on a more diversified repertoire: they implement various types of collective actions, which belong to the pluralist and protesting repertoires. Because of this difference, these two groups of associations will have different abilities to construct joint collective actions with other associations. Indeed, as they restrict their repertoire to a limited range of types of collective actions, the first group of associations can collaborate only sporadically with other associations: they can only participate in joint collective actions when these correspond to their own repertoire. These associations tend to work on their own. Conversely, those SMOs that have a wider repertoire of collective action can build coalitions more easily. They have the ability to form (or to be part of) heterogeneous coalitions. Thus, during the interviews with representatives of these associations, the activists underlined the fact that depending on the campaigns in which they are involved, the associations with whom they collaborate use different types of collective actions.[32]

Once again, this last remark allows us to link the analysis of the repertoires of collective action with that of the framing processes. I have underlined the fact that SMOs acting for the defence of human rights and for a more just and egalitarian society, and militant organizations, have more extensive framing processes than humanitarian associations. They are therefore able to establish ideological links with more diversified types of associations than humanitarian SMOs (who can only establish links with associations relying on the frame of the 'call for help'). The extensiveness of the frame-bridging process of an SMO is thus linked to the diversity of its repertoire of collective action: both are related to the ability of an association to construct inter-associative coalitions.

With regard to this last dimension, one must however point out that the French and German cases can be differentiated on one particular point. Among those SMOs who have a diversified repertoire of collective action, only two associations (*Pro Asyl* and *Amnesty International Deutschland*) are active at the national level in Germany. The others are exclusively active at the local level. In the French case, in contrast, all the associations having a diversified repertoire of collective action have a national scope of mobilization. Therefore, in Germany, the construction of heterogeneous coalitions of associations mainly takes place at the local level. In France, conversely, these coalitions are formed at the national level. As I will discuss further below, this remark is also linked to the question of the resources of these associations.

## Different organizational structures

The different relations with power-holders that have just been described are reflected in the organizational structures of French and German SMOs. The comparative analysis of their structures shows once again a difference between 'politicized' and 'humanitarian' associations. These two groups differ in terms of what can be defined as their associative culture: the set of cultural resources and practices on which their internal organization rely. This is particularly visible in the way in which they present themselves. On the one hand, humanitarian associations tend to define themselves as having centralized structures and being highly professionalized. On the other hand, politicized associations (and in particular militant organizations) tend to stress the role of their activist basis and to describe themselves as being less professionalized.

Thus, when *Forum Réfugiés* describes its organizational features, it highlights its mission as a 'service provider':

> With around hundred employees and an annual budget of 11 million euros for 2005, *Forum Réfugiés* offers a diversified range of services. First, the association offers services for asylum-seekers who do not benefit from housing in a reception centre: *Forum Réfugiés* offers juridical, administrative and social advices and it guarantees a service of postal domiciliation for thousands of persons who don't live in reception centres in order to facilitate their administrative procedures. The association also represents the secretariat of the admission commission of the Rhône department, which organizes weekly meetings under the supervision of the Prefect.[33]

In doing so, this association presents itself as being highly professionalized and hierarchically structured. It defines its own culture as being close to a culture of enterprise. The interaction between the people involved in the association tends to be formalized and the internal organization of the association is structured in a very centralized way: each of the individuals working in the association has a precise role, which is defined through a strict agenda.[34] Moreover, the association tends to stress the professionalization of the individuals who comprise it. Thus, it insists constantly on the fact that the association is composed of 'salaried' and 'volunteers', and not of 'activists', 'militants' or 'members'. In the case of *France Terre d'Asile*, this tendency is even more evident because it has an influence on the way the organization presents the individuals for whom they work. Thus, in the introduction of its 2004 annual report, the association is presented as a 'service provider' and the asylum-seekers and refugees are presented as 'users' (*usagers*):

> In 2004, *France Terre d'Asile* renewed itself and continued to extend its activities over the territory. The association handled with success the opening and management of reception centres for asylum-seekers, reception platforms, structures for the integration of refugees and it launched actions to shape and promote the asylum law. The creation of these structures shows our will to provide services that guarantee the rights of the users. [. . .] Members, volunteers and employees therefore dispose of a performing tool, which is based on the fundamental values of the organization: the respect of the dignity of everyone, users and employees. This supposes the mobilization of competences, savoir-faire and respect.[35]

The SMO therefore relies on a very formalized and hierarchical structure. This is underlined in the same report, where the functions of the 'central services' are presented:

> The central services are constituted by the general management, the management of human resources, the logistic sector, the training sector and the accounting management service. The general secretary is in charge of the relationships with the members, the administrative council, the ministers, the institutions, the media and the reception centres for asylum-seekers. The logistic sector is at the disposal of the centres and services of *France Terre d'Asile* in order to guarantee the pertinence and the homogeneity of the technical choices regarding equipment. The training sector offers training which is adapted to the asylum problematic faced by social workers active in the asylum field. The accounting management service follows the evolution of the expenses and incomings of each of the reception centres. Its director is responsible – under the supervision of the general director – for the implementation and monitoring of the budget procedures. All these sectors are under the responsibility of Pierre Henry, the general director.[36]

These degrees of professionalization and centralization are even more pronounced in the German case. Humanitarian SMOs have a similar size to large companies, and are organized through a 'federal' structure: they have representations throughout the German territory and a central office in Berlin. This is for example the case of *Diakonie*:

> *Diakonisches Werk der EKD* is made up of 22 regional delegations, 81 delegations specialized in a particular field of intervention and of German's evangelic church (EKD) and nine partner-churches. These members represent 26,800 structures and services of various sizes and legal forms. Today, 420,000 employees (full-time or part-time) work in *Diakonie*. [. . .]
>
> The highest body is the *Diakonie* conference (*Diakonische Konferenz*). The *Diakonie* council (*Diakonische Rat*) monitors the implementation of the decisions taken by the *Diakonie Konferenz* and it supports the management of the organization in its activities.[37]

In the same perspective, the self-presentation of the *Arbeiterwohlfahrt* underlines the fact that it is organized as an 'enterprise of service provision':

> The *Arbeiterwohlfahrt* has evolved from being an organization of members into an important service-providing company. It has thus become a central institution of the welfare state. The structure and the decisions are set by the bodies which are legitimized by the association. [. . .]
>
> Thanks to our provision of services, we are economically competitive. We understand this as a chance to test and to improve the quality of our work in the interests of the users. Our aim is to be a reliable partner for the users of the services we provide.[38]

In contrast with this analogy with private companies, politicized SMOs tend to stress the role of their activist basis. As a matter of fact, these SMOs have a lower degree of centralization and professionalization. Thus, when it presents its activities, *MRAP* highlights the idea of 'proximity anti-racism' and underlines the role of its 'member-activists':

> We are conscious that the fight against racism has to be more than a juridical fight. Therefore, *MRAP* focuses on preventive actions of 'education to citizenship' and it develops an 'anti-racism proximity'. [. . .] Every year, our member-activists answer thousands of requests for information, they participate in colloquiums and conferences organized by associations, trade unions, municipalities, cultural and social centres, press centres, etc.[39]

In the same perspective, *Amnesty International Section Française* writes that it is 'a movement of activists', in order to stress its difference from humanitarian associations:

> Amnesty is not a humanitarian association, nor an emergency NGO . . . It is a movement of activists in which mobilization is based on verified and reliable information.[40]

In the associative culture of these SMOs, individual interactions are less formalized. They underline the fact that internal deliberations are the result of debates that involve many activists. For example, when it describes its internal process of decision-making, the *Ligue des droits de l'Homme* insists on the autonomy of the local sections and on the principles of horizontal debate and vote:

> The LdH is open to everyone who accepts its goals and means.
>
> The LdH is both a unitary and decentralized association: the section is the basis for unity and the fundamental venue of mobilization for the members. It has full autonomy of expression and action, as long as it doesn't contradict the positions of the LdH congress. [. . .]
>
> The electoral principle is fundamental to the internal life of the LDH at all levels. The president and the bureau of each section are elected, every year, by the members after a debate in the general assembly. The important decisions of the LdH are taken at the national level, but these decisions emerge after discussions and debates in the national bodies: first of all in the congress, which is constituted by the representatives of the sections, and then in the central committee, which is elected by the congress. The national bureau and the president are elected every year by the central committee during the congress. They lead the association in a concrete way. The members of the central committee and of the national bureau are all volunteers. [. . .]
>
> Working groups are open to all (members and non-members) and they actively participate in the activities of the LdH. They are places of debate, of reflection and of proposition on precise questions related to human rights. On these questions, local groups can also be created and can contribute to the interactions with the national group.[41]

This horizontal organizational mode is even more fundamental in the organizations of activists. During an interview with a member of *No Lager*, the interactions within the network are described as being anti-hierarchical:

> As a movement of the anti-racist left, we don't want to reproduce – within our network – any kind of hierarchy that can be found in the system. This is true in terms of relationship between migrants and Germans, and this is true more generally. This is one of the reasons why we insist on the idea that our organization is a network and not a defined (and thus closed) structure. Even if there are members that are more active than the others, there is no bureau that would take decisions for the other members of the network. Decisions are taken through a discussion that is as wide as possible. Even if this often takes lots of time and lots of energy . . .[42]

As the cases of *Amnesty International* (in France and Germany), *Cimade* and *Pro Asyl* show, some human rights associations have developed a well-structured organizational form: they are formally divided into different sections with different tasks. It would be misleading, however, to consider that they have the same degree of professionalization and centralization as humanitarian associations. Indeed, unlike humanitarian organizations, their activist basis is involved in the work of the central offices. Thus, *Amnesty International Section Française* describes its internal organization through the idea of 'direct democracy':

> Direct democracy is fundamental within our movement. The local groups gather together in the national congress every two years and the general assembly is the most important body. The local groups decide upon the work orientations of the national section, they elect the executive bureau, vote on the budget, debate and reflect on the actions to be carried out.[43]

In sum, the comparative analysis leads us once again to distinguish humanitarian associations from those acting for the defence of human rights and for a more just and egalitarian society, as well as militant organizations. These empirical results corroborate the analysis proposed by della Porta and Diani (2006: 145–150), who suggest a distinction between 'professional movement organizations' (having strong professionalized leadership and being formalized) and 'participatory movement organizations' (having participatory orientations and a lower level of formal structuring). More generally, the analysis shows a strong correlation between SMOs' organizational structures and repertoires of collective actions. As the politicized associations define a repertoire that aims to involve public opinion, it is logical that they should give importance to their activist basis in their organizational structure. It is indeed through this basis that the construction of collective actions, such as petitions, symbolic actions and demonstrations, are made possible in practical terms. Moreover, as these SMOs have a diversified repertoire of collective action (which is thus not based on routinized activities), they tend to privilege a low degree of professionalization (in comparison with humanitarian associations): the activities of their members are not specialized in specific and strictly defined tasks. In contrast, humanitarian associations logically attribute less importance to their activist base in their organizational structure: their collective actions are based on the construction of concrete and routinized daily actions which are best implemented through a centralized structure. This is particularly true for the management of the reception centres for asylum-seekers (Valluy 2007). In this structure, the employees implement the decisions taken by the small group of individuals comprising the central offices: their activities are specialized and defined in the framework of a precise agenda.

These empirical results conform with Taylor's (1996) analysis of the feminist movement, where she has shown that associations constructing different types of collective actions tend to adopt different organizational structures: self-help groups tend to be structured in a less centralized way and to be less professionalized than groups providing services. They also echo the analysis of Piven and Cloward (1977), who observe an inverse correlation between these two elements. In their study of poor people's protest in the US, these authors have shown that the repertoire of collective action of an SMO is related to the evolution of its organizational structure: the more formalized and structured in a centralized way it is, the more it will tend to rely on non-protesting forms of collective actions.

The comparative analysis of the frames, repertoires and organizational structures of French and German SMOs has thus led us to distinguish three groups: humanitarian organizations; organizations acting for the defence of human rights and for a more just and egalitarian society; and militant organizations. This analysis has stressed moreover a fundamental distinction between the first group and the two other (more politicized) groups. In the last part of this chapter, I will relate this analysis to that presented in the preceding chapter and show that the three groups have comparable weight in the French pro-asylum movement, whereas the first group is clearly predominant in the German movement. I will show moreover that the distinctions separating the first group from the other two are more pronounced in France than in Germany. The comparison of their resources and the geographical scope of their mobilization will underline these facts.

## The position of humanitarian and politicized organizations in France and Germany: two different configurations

As discussed above, the empirical developments presented in this chapter are based on the idea that five elements compose the collective identity of SMOs: their discourse; their repertoire of collective action; their organizational structure; their resources; and the geographical scope of their mobilization. To a certain extent, all these elements are inter-related. I have thus underlined the correlations between the frames, repertoires of collective action and organizational structures of French and German SMOs (underlining the centrality of the framing processes). Going further, the comparative analysis shows that, of these five elements, two play a particular role: the resources and the geographical scope of their mobilization. While the three first elements highlighted the similarities between French and German pro-asylum movements, these two last elements serve to differentiate between them.

The definition of the geographical scope of mobilization is straightforward; however, that of the resources of an SMO needs to more explanation. Following Edwards and McCarthy (2004: 125–128), different types of resources can be distinguished:

- *Moral resources*: 'legitimacy, solidarity support, sympathetic support, and celebrity';
- *Cultural resources*: 'artefacts and cultural products such as conceptual tools and specialized knowledge that have become widely, though not necessarily universally, known. These include tacit knowledge about how to accomplish specific tasks like enacting a protest event, holding a news conference, running a meeting, forming an organization, initiating a festival, or surfing the web';
- *Social-organizational resources*: 'intentional and appropriable social organization. Intentional social organization is created specifically to further social movement goals. By contrast, appropriable social organization was created for non-movement purposes, but movement actors are able to gain access to other types of resources through it. Recruiting volunteers or disseminating information through work, congregation, civic, or neighbourhood connections are widely cited examples';
- *Human resources*: 'labour, experience, skills, and expertise'. Leadership is also included in this category because 'it involves a combination of other human resources included here';
- *Material resources*: 'what economists would call financial and physical capital, including monetary resources, property, office space, equipment and supplies'.

In the French case, the comparative analysis shows that humanitarian associations rely mainly on material and human resources whereas the two other groups of SMOs rely above all on non-material resources (moral, cultural and social-organizational resources). The analysis of the geographical scope of their mobilization shows that this dimension does not play a fundamental role. All these associations (with the exception of *Forum Réfugiés* which is mainly based in the Rhône-Alpes region) have similar territorial configurations: a centralized office in Paris and a network of contacts (or delegations) in various French cities. However, in the German case, these two dimensions are strongly interconnected, and they help us to distinguish two groups of SMOs. The first group of SMOs intervenes at the national and at the local level (though a centralized organization) and possesses a significant amount of diversified resources. The other group of SMOs intervenes mainly at the local level and has few resources. In contrast with the French case, this last line of difference does not overlap exactly with those presented above. If the second group of associations is exclusively composed of politicized associations, the first one is composed of the three humanitarian associations and of two more politicized associations (*Amnesty International Deutschland* and *Pro Asyl*).

In France, the budget dedicated to the immigration and/or asylum issues in each of these associations shows that humanitarian associations are much 'richer' than politicized associations. Thus, in 2004, *France Terre d'Asile* had a budget of around 27.5 million euros and *Forum Réfugiés* had a budget of around 9.5 million euros. In the same year, the *Secours Catholique* had a global budget of 121 million euros, the budget allocated to the 'migrants and asylum seekers' section representing around ten per cent of the total. In comparison, the budgets of the more politicized SMOs are much smaller. Thus the global budget of *Gisti* for the same year was around 620,000 euros. The *Ligue des droits de l'Homme* had a global budget of around 1.5 million euros (of which only a part is dedicated to its activities on immigration and asylum). The budget of *Amnesty International Section Française* is higher (around 13 million euros in 2004). However, as with the *LdH*, only a part of it is allocated to its work on immigration and asylum. Within the group of politicized SMOs, the association with the most important material resources is *Cimade*: its global budget was around 5 million euros in 2004. However, this represents only half of the budget of *Forum Réfugiés*, and only one fifth of the budget of *France Terre d'Asile*.

When examining the human resources of these two groups of associations, the distinction is less marked. A focus on the number of individuals employed by these associations may lead one to deduce that humanitarian associations have a more significant labour force globally than the politicized

SMOs. Thus, in 2004, 341 people worked for *France Terre d'Asile*, 100 for *Forum Réfugiés* and 957 for the *Secours Catholique*. In comparison, eight people were employed by *Gisti*, fifteen by the *Ligue des Droits de l'Homme* and seven by *Act Up Paris*. A higher number of individuals worked for *Amnesty International Section Française* in the same year (sixty); however, the activities of this association are divided into different sections, and only three people work full-time on the immigration and asylum issue. Within the group of political associations, *Cimade* seems to represent the exception, with around 100 individuals. It would, however, be misleading to limit the analysis of the human resources to this set of data. One should indeed underline that these SMOs also rely on a number of activists and volunteers. For example, *Cimade* has around 1,200 volunteers who provide regular help to the work of the association. The *Ligue des Droits de l'Homme* has around 7,500 activists, and *Gisti* around 200 (as well as around 50 volunteers). In this sense, one can consider that politicized associations, like humanitarian associations, dispose of an important human capital. There seems thus to be no obvious distinction between these two groups of associations as far as their human resources (in terms of human capital) is concerned. Further observation of their human resources shows moreover that politicized organizations (and in particular those acting for the defence of human rights and for a more just and egalitarian society) tend to have a high level of expertise. This is visible in the work of the French Coalition for Asylum Right (*CFDA*).[44] Most of its work and debates are led by the group of politicized associations (in particular *AISF*, *Cimade*, *Gisti* and *LDH*).[45] For example, these associations coordinate its annual 'national meetings for asylum rights'. Moreover, as the analysis of the repertoires of collective action has shown, they organize many seminars, colloquiums or conferences and thus show their ability to provide expertise. This observation was confirmed by the interviews with individuals from these associations. All of them insisted on the idea that, over the years, they have gained a capacity of analysis of immigration and asylum policies. *Gisti* represents the best example. This association was created by a small group of juridical experts and social workers, and among the members of this association, one finds many lawyers and academics. Conversely, the humanitarian associations tend to present themselves more as 'practicians' than as 'analysts'. They define their expertise mainly through their practical knowledge of the field, through their 'day-by-day' work with asylum-seekers and refugees.

Finally, the analysis shows that French politicized associations rely more on social-organizational resources than humanitarian associations do. SMOs like the *Ligue des droits de l'Homme*, *MRAP* or *Gisti* have constructed an important network of collaborators and allies. These range from partner-associations to trade unions and members of political parties. Thus, as was developed in the previous chapter, the example of the mobilizations of the *sans-papiers* in 1996–1997 shows that *CNSP* activists strategically managed to gain the support of an important network of allies: partner-associations, trade unions (such as the *CNT* or *SUD*), academics, figures from the media and from political and artistic fields, etc.

The differences surrounding the nature of resources are fundamental because they will lead these associations to privilege different ways of constructing their collective actions. Associations that privilege material and human resources will tend to work on their own. As was evoked above, *France Terre d'Asile*, *Forum Réfugiés* and the *Secours Catholique* rarely collaborate with other organizations. On the other hand, associations that have mainly non-material resources will tend to privilege communal work because the sharing of experience, expertise or specific savoir-faire is an absolute necessity for the construction of their collective action. More generally, these empirical results point in the direction of the analysis presented by Siméant and Dauvin (2004), who have shown that humanitarian NGOs tend to base their activities on a high amount of material and human resources. These results also echo the analysis of Piven and Cloward (1977), who have argued that associations privileging mass mobilization tend to rely on their ability to construct networks of activists and to communicate rather than on material and human capital. However, as I will develop here, an examination of the German case leads to more nuanced conclusions.

Unlike in the French case, an analysis of the German case shows a clear difference between associations disposing of important material and non-material resources, and SMOs that dispose almost exclusively of non-material resources and that have few (or almost none) material and human resources. In fact, even if this difference seems to be similar to that observed in the French case, it does not correspond to the same reality. While in France, this difference relates to the choice of the associations to privilege either material or non-material resources, in Germany, it is a distinction between a group of 'big' associations (that dispose of important and diversified resources) and a group of 'small' associations (that dispose of few – and almost exclusively non-material – resources). In the German case, only one association (the *Arbeiterwohlfahrt*) privileges almost exclusively material and human resources at the expense of non-material resources. If it is justified to talk about a difference between this association and the other SMOs (that rely on non-material resources), it would, however, be misleading to focus on this aspect. The difference that separates 'big' and 'small' associations seems indeed much more significant as it separates two groups of associations that have completely different resources.

On the one hand, the possession of important material and human resources does not necessarily entail the lack of non-material resources such as expertise or the ability to construct networks (social-organizational resources). *Caritas Deutschland*, for example, disposed in 2005 of a budget of around 190 million euros.[46] Around 480,000 employees work for this association, and the same number of volunteers offer their service. In total, 1,100 persons work for *Caritas Deutschland* in the frame of its activities on immigration and asylum. These massive material and human resources are associated with significant non-material resources such as experience and expertise. Its juridical office is thus recognized as having a precise knowledge of immigration and asylum legislation, and the association disposes of an important 'savoir-faire' of lobby techniques based on many years of experience. The *Diakonisches Werk der EKD* has a very similar profile: it disposes of similar proportions of material and human resources (with around 420,000 employees),[47] and it can also rely on a high level of expertise and experience. *Amnesty International Deutschland* and *Pro Asyl* do not have the same amount of material and human resources. They can, however, be considered 'big' associations: they have in general a high level of resources in comparison to organizations such as *Kanak Attak* or the *Karawane für die Rechte der Flüchtlinge und MigrantInnen*. In 2005, *Amnesty International Deutschland* had a global budget of around ten million euros, with nine persons working in the immigration and asylum section. *Pro Asyl* had a budget of around two million euros in 2005, and it employed fifty people. Both associations have a large number of members: around 90,000 for *Amnesty International Deutschland* and 13,000 for *Pro Asyl*. As is the case for *Caritas* and *Diakonie*, these two associations dispose of a high level of expertise and important experience of mobilization on immigration and asylum policies. Thus, these SMOs are central to the activities of the Information Coalition on Asylum (*Informationsverbund Asyl*): they lead the debates and they are in charge of most of the events organized by it.

In comparison, the other German SMOs are 'small' associations. They dispose of very few material and human resources, and – in contrast with the French case – they do not have much in the way of non-material resources. Refugee Councils are unusual in that they have an office and (few) employees. The other associations only dispose of the labour force of small groups of volunteers and have no office. Due to this lack of resources, these SMOs construct collective actions that have less amplitude than those of the 'big' organizations: the launching of important long-term campaigns such as the campaign for the right to remain ('Bleiberechtskampagne') is made much more difficult. They may participate in these campaigns, but would have more difficulty in initiating such collective actions.

This difference in terms of resources coincides with a fundamental difference relating to the geographical scope of their mobilization. 'Big' SMOs mobilize at the national and local levels: they all have a central office in Berlin and delegations in most German regions. On the contrary, the second group of associations mobilizes almost exclusively at the regional or local level. At the end of the 1990s, the *Kein Mensch Ist Illegal* network had the ambition to create a national movement; however, its main activities are now limited to two geographical zones: Brandenburg and Nordrhein-Westfalen. The network *Karawane für die Rechte der Flüchtlinge und MigrantInnen* has contacts in big German cities such as Munich and Hamburg, but its activities are very much concentrated in the region of Brandenburg, Sachsen and Sachsen-Anhalt. *Kanak Attak* is mainly active in Berlin and the *Aktionsbündnis Gegen Abschiebung Rhein-Main* mobilizes exclusively in the region of Frankfurt airport. Finally, the Refugee Councils mobilize exclusively at the level of the Länder in which they are based. In this configuration, two organizations play a particular role: *Amnesty International Deutschland* and *Pro Asyl*. They act as intermediaries between the other 'big' associations (all humanitarian) and the set of 'small' (politicized) associations. This is particularly true for *Pro Asyl*: this association is, on the one hand, part of the *Informationsverbund Asyl* (and collaborates intensively with the big humanitarian associations comprising it) and, on the other hand, coordinates the activities of all Refugee Councils at the regional level. For example, it provides financial supplies to groups of militants such as the network *No Lager*.

To conclude, the line of difference that divides French associations is above all qualitative (it is for example difficult to tell if *Forum Réfugiés* has more or less resources than an association like *Gisti*) whereas the line of difference that separates German associations is mainly quantitative (one can clearly distinguish associations which dispose of important resources from those having few resources). French politicized SMOs have compensated for their lack of material and human resources with a high level of expertise and social-organizational resources. This is, however, not the case in Germany, where most of the politicized organizations (with the exception of *Amnesty International* and *Pro Asyl*) lack both material and non-material resources. As the general conclusions of this chapter will show, the analysis of these organizational and geographical dimensions can be related to those presented in the preceding chapter.

## Conclusions. A cleavage between humanitarian and politicized SMOs

In this chapter, the comparative analysis has shown that French and German pro-asylum movements are composed of three different groups of SMOs.

The first SMOs (the humanitarian organizations) have a legitimized identity: they act for the relief of asylum-seekers and refugees, have a mainly corporatist repertoire, and highly professionalized structures. The second SMOs (those acting for the defence of human rights and for a more just and egalitarian society) have a principled identity: they mobilize on behalf of asylum-seekers and refugees, have a mainly pluralist repertoire, and structures which combine professionalization and horizontal dynamics. Finally, the third SMOs (militant organizations) have an oppositional identity: they act together with asylum-seekers and refugees, have a mainly protesting repertoire, and horizontal organizational structures.

This analysis has shown moreover that these fields are divided by the same lines of differences in both countries. 'Humanitarian' associations are separated from 'politicized' associations (those SMOs acting for the defence of human rights and for a more just and egalitarian society, and militant organizations) in terms of frames, repertoires of collective action and associative cultures. These (and in particular their framing processes) are the most important dimensions on which their collective identities are based. Put together, these differences lead to a cleavage between humanitarian and politicized associations in both countries. Indeed, their different identities prevent them from working together on a regular basis, and their ideological differences prevent them from producing common discourses, whereas their differentiated relations with power-holders and associative cultures impede the construction of joint collective actions. These two groups of associations are often in conflict. Activists belonging to one of these groups expressed systematically (and most of the time spontaneously) their distance from other types of associations. This distance was often articulated in an unappreciative way: activists argued that the work of the other group of associations was detrimental to the cause of asylum-seekers, refugees and migrants. It was sometimes presented as the result of a difference in terms of agenda of mobilization: they argued that other types of SMOs 'simply do not do what we are doing'.

The French and German cases are thus characterized by strong similarities: the line of cleavage between humanitarian and politicized SMOs is based on the same differences. Table 8 sums up the analysis relating to the frames, repertoires of collective action and organizational structures of these two groups of organizations.[48]

The two dimensions on which the French and German cases can be clearly distinguished are their resources and the geographical scope of their mobilization. In the French case, a difference exists between associations privileging material and human resources and those privileging non-material resources. In contrast, in the German case, there exists a difference between

**Table 8** Main features of the French and German SMOs mobilizing around the asylum issue

| **Types of associations** | **Associations** | **Principal dimensions of their collective identity** | |
|---|---|---|---|
| Humanitarian associations | Forum Réfugiés, France Terre d'Asile, Secours Catholique, *Arbeiterwohlfahrt, Caritas Deutschland, Diakonisches Werk der EKD* | Framing-process | Limited framing-process based on a de-politicized perception of the asylum issue |
| | | Repertoire of collective action | Non diversified and non-protesting |
| | | Organizational structure | Centralized and professionalized |
| Politicized associations | Act Up, Amnesty International Section Française, Cimade, CNSP, FASTI, Gisti, LDH, MRAP, *Aktionsbündnis Gegen Abschiebung Rhein-Main, Amnesty International Deutschland, Bayerischer Flüchtlingsrat, Flüchtlingsrat Berlin, Flüchtlingsrat Hamburg, Kanak Attak, Karawane für die Rechte der Flüchtlinge und MigrantInnen, Kein Mensch Ist Illegal, Pro Asyl* | Framing-process | Extended framing-process based on a politicized perception of the asylum issue |
| | | Repertoire of collective action | Diversified and including protest |
| | | Organizational structure | Low level of centralization and of professionalization |

associations disposing of significant resources (and mobilizing at the national and local level) and those disposing of a small amount of resources (and mobilizing exclusively at the local level). In France, this difference reinforces the distinction between politicized and humanitarian SMOs: politicized associations mainly base their activities on non-material resources whereas humanitarian associations mainly base their activities on material and human resources. This is not the case in Germany: looking at their resources and geographical scope of mobilization, politicized associations cannot be clearly differentiated from humanitarian associations.

As I have underlined in the preceding chapter, because of the low profile of the asylum issue in the public sphere, and to the federalized institutional system of the German state, German SMOs tend to organize through a method of geographical division. This explains why the territorial dimension is so important in the German case. I have also underlined the fact that, due to the absence of a cycle of protest since the beginning of the 1990s, the German pro-asylum movement has remained isolated (in the sense that it has lacked a diversified network of allies). Consequently, the German associations that do not rely on significant material and human resources have had difficulties in compensating for this through non-material resources such as social-organizational resources. This explains the difference between a group of 'big' associations who are active throughout the German territory and a group of 'small' associations who are active exclusively at the local level. In contrast, I have underlined the fact that, due to the high profile of the asylum issue in the political sphere, and to the centralized institutional system of the French state, French organizations have often coordinated their activities at the national level. Thus, the geographical dimension has not played such a strong role as in Germany.[49] I have also highlighted the fact that, due to the occurrence of a cycle of protest in France in the second half of the 1990s, the French pro-asylum movement has benefited from a diversified network of allies. Consequently, the associations that did not rely on significant material and human resources could counteract this through non-material resources such as social-organizational resources. This explains why it is not justified to talk about a cleavage between 'big' and 'small' associations in the French case.

To what extent and in what ways did these organizations Europeanize? How did their characteristics and history influence their degrees and paths of Europeanization? These are the questions that will be handled in the next chapters.

## Notes

1 The 'formal institutional structure' (the strength of the State); the 'dominant strategy' ('the informal premises of procedure, the shared implicit or explicit understandings which emerge from the political process, and which guide the actions of the authorities'); the 'facilitation' ('standing for any action by other groups that lowers the costs of collective action'); the 'repression' ('which includes any external action that increases such costs'); the 'success chances' ('which refer to the likelihood that collective action will contribute to the realization of a movements' goal'); the 'reform/threat' factor ('where reform stands for a situation in which collective benefits are expected even if no collective action is undertaken, and threat refers to a situation in which "bads" are expected if the movement does not act').

2 As discussed in the introduction, I analysed the documents published by these associations through a method of open-coding: a set of frames was defined in the beginning of the empirical analysis (on the basis of a few cases) and it was then constantly complemented and readjusted in the course of the process. In this part of the analysis, I selected the documents in which the SMOs present themselves

and put their mobilization in perspective. I have thus selected documents that are of particular importance in the history of these associations (for example those to which they regularly refer) and texts in which they disclose the reasons behind their mobilization to the public (for example, on websites). Around 200 documents were analysed. This analysis was complemented by the interviews: a series of questions referring to the 'sense given to their collective action' was formulated.

3 *CNSP* constitutes a particular case because, due mainly to internal dissensions, its process of frame-bridging became less intense after the period 1999–2000. An analysis of the discourses produced by *CNSP* since 1999–2000 shows that it justifies its collective action by using mainly three frames: the fight against precariousness, anti-racism and anti-discrimination, and the fight against repression. For more on this point, see the text writen by *Madjiguène Cissé*, 'A propos de la Coordination Nationale', 21 July 1999; see also Siméant (1998).

4 *Gisti, FASTI, Act Up-Paris*, 'Lettre ouverte à Lionel Jospin à propos de la future loi sur l'immigration et de son élaboration', 10 July 1997 (author's translation).

5 Ibid. (author's translation).

6 Ibid. (author's translation).

7 *Kein Mensch Ist Illegal*, Manifest, 1997 (author's translation).

8 Ibid. (author's translation).

9 *France Terre d'Asile*, 'Présentation de France Terre d'Asile' (author's translation).

10 *Diakonisches Werk der EKD*, 'Diakonie Perspektiven: Migration' (author's translation).

11 Master frames are more general and less context specific than collective action frames (Snow and Benford 1992).

12 *Secours Catholique*, website introduction (author's translation).

13 *Caritas Deutschland*, 'Die Position der Caritas zu Asyl- und Flüchtlingsfrage', September 1999 (author's translation).

14 This observation is characteristic of the humanitarian discourse more generally (Dauvin and Siméant 2004).

15 *MRAP*, 'Le MRAP appelle au soutien de la manifestation nationale du 3 mars 2001 pour la régularisation de tous les sans papiers', March 2001 (author's translation).

16 *Amnesty International Deutschland*, 'Flüchtlingsarbeit von Amnesty International' (author's translation).

17 *Les Sans-Papiers de Saint Bernard*, '18 mars 1996 – 18 mars 1999, Trois ans de luttes des sans-papiers', March 1999 (author's translation).

18 *Karawane für die Rechte der Flüchtlinge und MigrantInnen*, 'Wer und was ist die Karawane' (author's translation).

19 *Gisti*, '30 Ans!', Plein Droit N 53–54, March 2002 (author's translation).

20 *Karawane für die Rechte der Flüchtlinge und MigrantInnen*, 'Wer und was ist die Karawane' (author's translation).

21 The analysis presented above shows that this does not mean that some of these associations can present the asylum issue through multiple and diversified frames (this is where the distinction between the frame and the object of a discourse is important).

22 During the riots in the French suburbs (*banlieues*).

23 *Face aux lois d'exception, imposons 'l'urgence sociale'*, 8 December 2005 (author's translation).

24 *France Terre d'Asile*, 'Who we are – Objectives' (author's translation).
25 Ibid. (author's translation).
26 *Flüchtlingsrat Hamburg*, 'Kein Mensch ist Illegal' (author's translation).
27 *Ligue des droits de l'Homme*, 'Nos missions' (author's translation).
28 Kanak Attak, 'Speaking of Autonomy of Migration . . . Racism and Struggles of Migration', September 2004.
29 *No Lager*, 'For Freedom of Movement – Anti-Lager action Tour'.
30 *Karawane für die Rechte der Flüchtlinge und MigrantInnen*, 'The Caravan Self Description Paper'.
31 For more on the French case, see Valluy (2007).
32 These observations follow what has been developed in the preceding chapter. I have thus stressed the fact that since the beginning of the 1990s those associations who specialize in the provision of services for asylum-seekers and refugees tend to work on their own whereas the more politicized associations tend to build wider inter-associative networks.
33 *Forum Réfugiés*, self-presentation (author's translation).
34 In its annual reports, the association presents a complex organization chart describing the tasks of the various departments and sections.
35 *France Terre d'Asile*, 'Rapport d'activité 2004', p.3 (author's translation).
36 *France Terre d'Asile*, Ibid, p.12 (author's translation).
37 *Diakonisches Werk der EKD*, 'Organisation' (author's translation).
38 *Arbeiterwohlfahrt*, 'Dienstleistungsunternehmen' (author's translation).
39 www.mrap.asso.fr (author's translation).
40 www.amnesty.fr (author's translation).
41 www.ldh-france.org (author's translation).
42 Interview number one.
43 www.amnesty.fr (author's translation).
44 The French coalition that gathers together these associations (with the exception of *CNSP* and *FASTI*).
45 These four associations constitute the secretariat of this coalition.
46 One should however bear in mind that only part of this budget (around fifteen per cent) is devoted to its activities on immigration and asylum.
47 Although not all of these employees work in the field of immigration and asylum.
48 German associations are shown in italics.
49 Once again, this does not mean that associations acting at the local or regional level do not exist in France, but that, in comparison to the German case, these associations have played a more limited role.

Chapter 3

# The Europeanization of the Pro-asylum Movements

## Evidence from the Networks, Frames and Collective Actions

In October 2008, in order to protest against the European Union's Council of Ministers meeting in Paris to discuss the 'European pact on immigration and asylum', more than 300 associations from all over Europe organized a 'counter-summit and an alternative forum on migrations and development'. The call for this protest shows the ambition to create a 'very large-scale mobilisation' and to 'promote a different understanding of immigration'. It also presents a set of European collective actions:

> Concerned by the essentially security-orientated nature of the treatment of migration flows, by the treatment accorded to migrants, and by the economic choices adopted which maintain the African continent on the margins of development, we have decided to organise a European mobilisation in order to make the voices of French, European and African civil society heard.
>
> It is high time that the issue of migrations and development are genuinely re-thought in the light of mutual interests: those of the countries of origin, of the transit countries, of the receiving countries, and, above all, those of the migrants themselves. (. . .)
>
> We call for participation in a very large-scale European mobilisation during the week of 13th to 19th October in Paris, to promote a different understanding of immigration and a different relationship between the European Union, Africa and the rest of the world. We will organise at that time a counter-summit on the questions of migration and development, a big European demonstration for a different European politics, and a giant concert.[1]

This initiative was the first action of a newly created network against European immigration and asylum policies (*Des Ponts, Pas des Murs*, 'Bridges, not Walls'). It was followed by a 'European day of action for the rights of migrants' in May 2009, a call to European MPs during the European elections in 2009, and a participation in the World Social Forum in Dakar (2011). As this example illustrates, social movements for migrants' rights recognize the role of European institutions in the construction of immigration and asylum policies, they construct European networks in which they are able to define common perceptions of European institutions, and they launch collective actions that have a European dimension. In sum, social movement organizations are transforming from the inside; they progressively become European actors.

Chapters one and two presented the French and German pro-asylum movements in their national context. The next step is to analyse their evolution since the launching of the process of harmonization of asylum policies in Europe.

In the introduction, I defined this general process as being composed of three decisive (and intrinsically linked) steps:

- the Europeanization of SMOs networks: the progressive construction of inter-associative linkages across the borders of member-states;
- the Europeanization of their perception: the progressive definition of a common perception of the European Union as a target for collective action;
- the Europeanization of their collective action: the progressive construction of common collective actions addressing (directly or indirectly) power-holders involved in the EU integration process.

On this basis, I argued that SMOs can have different levels and different paths of Europeanization. More detail on these two dimensions can now be presented. In this chapter, I analyse the extent to which French and German SMOs Europeanize, and in the following one, I will focus on their different paths of Europeanization. Following the theoretical framework presented in the introduction, I present a dual comparative perspective. First, I identify whether associations with different profiles (humanitarian or politicized associations) tend to have different levels and paths of Europeanization. I will also observe whether associations from different national contexts of mobilization (France or Germany) tend to Europeanize to different degrees and through different modes. Most of the points presented in this chapter and in the following one will be developed in greater depth and put into perspective in chapter five. The aim of chapters three and four is to explore the possible relations between the characteristics and/or the national context of mobilization of an association and its process of Europeanization. I will however not explain in detail the correlation between these different elements. As

I will develop in chapter five, another type of analysis is needed for that, one that is not based on a conceptualization in terms of variables.

Considering the theoretical discussion in the introduction, one would expect that, depending on their characteristics, the associations mobilizing around the asylum issue in France and in Germany would tend to Europeanize to different degrees. According to the hypothesis of the 'NGOization' of associations that act at the European level, one might expect that humanitarian associations tend to Europeanize more than politicized associations. Associations which have a profile that is close to that of NGOs have a greater amount of material and human resources and they are thus able to Europeanize more easily than less institutionalized organizations. Moreover, their repertoire of collective action is better adapted to the one encouraged by European institutions. As I will develop in this chapter, however, this hypothesis is not confirmed by the empirical analysis: both groups tend to Europeanize to the same extent. It is not possible to draw a simple correlation between the profile of the collective identity of an association and its propensity to Europeanize. Moreover, the analysis shows that French and German associations tend to Europeanize to the same extent. Therefore, it is also impossible to draw a simple correlation between the features of the traditional context of mobilization of an association and its propensity to Europeanize. Indeed, it is not possible to say that associations coming from a context in which the pro-asylum movement is well organized and well embedded in society Europeanize more than those coming from a context in which this movement is more fragmented and isolated. The hypothesis of cross-national variations in the processes of Europeanization of SMOs (see the introduction) is thus not confirmed by the empirical analysis.

In this chapter, I will present successively the Europeanization of SMO networks, frames and collective actions. As I will show throughout, these three dimensions are correlated: as a consequence of their involvement in Europeanized networks, SMOs will progressively give more importance to the European dimensions of asylum policies and will thus Europeanize their perception of the asylum issue; they will moreover be involved in Europeanized collective actions organized through these networks. Therefore, the more an association is involved in Europeanized networks, the more it will tend to produce Europeanized frames and Europeanized collective actions.

## The construction of European networks

The network analysis shows that French and German SMOs are involved in different European social movement organizations (whether these are

European coalitions of associations, European delegations of international associations or European networks of activists). Tables 9 and 10 sum up the results of this empirical analysis. They show that eighteen European SMOs are active on immigration and asylum policies. These are European coalitions of associations like *ECRE* or *CCME*, European delegations of international associations like *Caritas Europa* or *Amnesty International European Office*, or European networks of activists like *Migreurop* or *No Border*. In these tables, one X represents a low degree of involvement in these networks (when an association is part of a European SMO but is not active in it); two Xs represent an intermediate degree of involvement (when it becomes involved in the activities of a European SMO but does not play a leading role in it); and three Xs represent a high degree of involvement (when it becomes involved in the activities of a European SMO and plays a leading role in it).[2]

These results show a clear tendency for French and German SMOs to Europeanize their networks. They participate in several European structures and often play a leading role in them. They also show, however, that their European networks are more or less extended and that they have different degrees of involvement in them.

First, some SMOs (the *Arbeiterwohlfahrt*, the *Bayerischer Flüchtlingsrat*, the *Flüchtlingsrat Berlin*, *France Terre d'Asile* and *Forum Réfugiés*) have rather limited European networks. Their process of Europeanization is limited to their involvement in one principal European coalition of associations (the *European Council on Refugees and Exiles*),[3] and in one national coalition of associations in which European issues are regularly handled (the *Coordination Française pour le Droit d'Asile* in France and the *Informationsverbund Asyl* in Germany).[4] Moreover, their involvement in these arenas has not been fundamental until recently: before the mid-2000s, they did not participate in the agenda-setting, for example, and their contact with member-associations or with the central office of the *ECRE* remained relatively minimal.[5]

Some organizations are involved in several European networks. *MRAP* is active in informal networks mobilizing for the regularization of undocumented migrants and in cross-issue networks such as the European Social Forums. It is also involved in the *European Coalition for Foreigners' Right to Family Life*, in the *European Network Against Racism*, and in the international network *Migrant Rights International*. The German network *Karawane für die Rechte der Flüchtlinge und MigrantInnen* is active in the informal networks mobilizing for the regularization of undocumented migrants, and has links with the networks *No Border* and *United*, as well as with cross-issue networks such as the *Euromayday*. Moreover, two of them (*Secours Catholique* and

**Table 9** The European networks of French SMOs

| | | European Social Movement Organizations | | | | | | | | | | | | | | | | | |
|---|---|---|---|---|---|---|---|---|---|---|---|---|---|---|---|---|---|---|---|
| | | European coalitions of SMOs | | | | | | European delegations of international associations | | | | | European networks of activists | | | | | | |
| | | ECRE | European Coalition for Foreigners' Right to Family Life | CCME | ENAR | PICUM | Migrants Rights International | Caritas Europa | German delegation of Caritas in Brussels | Eurodiaconia | AI-EU | EADH | Informations und Kooperations forum | Euromed Non-Governmental Platform | Migreurop | United | Informal networks for the regularization of undocumented migrants | No Border (and Frassanito since 2004) | Cross-issue networks (European Social Forums, Euromayday) |
| French associ-ations | Act Up | | | | | | | | | | | | | | XXX (since 2002) | | XX | XXX | XX |
| | Amnesty Interna-tional Section Française | XX (1994–2000) | | | | | X (since 2004) | | | | XXX (since end 1990s) | | | | | | | | X |
| | Cimade | X (since mid-1990s) | X (since mid 1990s) | XXX (since mid 1990s) | X (since mid 1990s) | X | X (since 2004) | | | | | | | | XXX (since 2002) | | XX | | XX |

| | | | | | | | | | | | | | | | | | | | |
|---|---|---|---|---|---|---|---|---|---|---|---|---|---|---|---|---|---|---|---|
| | CNSP | | | | | | | | | | | | | | | X | XXX (since end 1990s) | | XX |
| | FASTI | | | | | | | | | | | | | | | XX | XX | X | XX |
| | Forum Réfugiés | XX (since 1999) | X (since 2004) | | | | | | | | | | | | | | | | |
| | France Terre d'Asile | XX (since start 1990s) | | | | | | | | | | | | | | | | | |
| | Gisti | | X (since 1994) | | X | X (since 2004) | X (since 2004) | | | | | | | | XXX (since 2002) | | XX | | XX |
| | Ligue des droits de l'Homme | X (since 2005) | X | | X | | X (since 2004) | | | | | XXX (since 2000) | | XX (since 2005) | XXX (since 2005) | | XX | | XX |
| | MRAP | | X | | X | | X (since 2004) | | | | | | | | | | XX | | XX |
| | Secours Catholi-que | X | | X (since the 1970s) | | | | XX (since 1971) | | | | | | | | | | | |

**Table 10** The European networks of German SMOs

| | | European Social Movement Organizations | | | | | | | | | | | | | | | | | |
|---|---|---|---|---|---|---|---|---|---|---|---|---|---|---|---|---|---|---|---|
| | | European coalitions of SMOs | | | | | | European delegations of international associations | | | | | European networks of activists | | | | | | |
| | | ECRE | European Coalition for Foreigners' Right to Family Life | CCME | ENAR | PICUM | Migrants Rights International | Caritas Europa | German delegation of Caritas in Brussels | Eurodiaconia | AI-EU | EADH | Informations und Kooperations forum | Euromed Non-Governmental Platform | Migreurop | United | Informal networks for the regularization of undocumented migrants | No Border (and Frassanito since 2004) | Cross-issue networks (European Social Forums, Euromayday) |
| German associations | AGA Rhein Main | | | | | | | | | | | | | | | | X | XX | XX |
| | Amnesty International Deutschland | XX | | | | | | | | | XXX (since end 1990s) | | | | | | | | X |
| | Arbeiterwohlfahrt | X (since 2003) | X | | X | | | | | | | | | | | | | | |

| | | | | | | | | | | | | | | | | | | | |
|---|---|---|---|---|---|---|---|---|---|---|---|---|---|---|---|---|---|---|---|
| | Bayer-ishcer Flüchtlingsrat | X | | | | | | | | | | | XX (since 2004) | | | | | | X |
| | Caritas Deutschland | XX | | XXX (since the 1970s) | X | | | XXX (since 1971) | XXX (since end 1990s) | | | | | | | | | | |
| | Diakonie | XX | | XX (since the 1970s) | X | | | | | XX (since 1992) | | | | | | | | | |
| | Flüchtlingsrat Berlin | X | | | | | | | | | | | | | | X | | | X |
| | Flüchtlingsrat Hamburg | X | | | | X (since end 1990s) | | | | | | | | | XX (since 2005) | XX | XX | XX (since 2000) | XX |
| | Kanak Attak | | | | | | | | | | | | | | | | | XXX (since 2000) | XX |

**Table 10** (continued)

| | | European Social Movement Organizations | | | | | | | | | | | | | | | | | |
|---|---|---|---|---|---|---|---|---|---|---|---|---|---|---|---|---|---|---|---|
| | | **European coalitions of SMOs** | | | | | | **European delegations of international associations** | | | | | **European networks of activists** | | | | | | |
| | Karawane | | | | | | | | | | | | | | | X | XX | XX (since 2000) | X |
| | Kein Mensch Ist Illegal | | | | | | | | | | | | | | | XX | XX | XXX (since 2000) | XX |
| | Pro Asyl | XXX (member of the executive committee since 1995) | | | XX (since mid 1990s) | X (since end 1990s) | | | | | | | XXX (since 2004) | | X (since 2002) | XX | | X (since 2000) | XX |

*Diakonie*) were involved, as national sections of an international organization, in the creation of a delegation in Brussels (respectively *Caritas Europa* and *Eurodiaconia*). However, these two associations do not maintain such a regular contact with the delegation in Brussels as other groups. The relations between these two levels are mainly based on a method of task division: the *Secours Catholique* and *Diakonie* intervene on the European dimensions of the asylum issue only because of the position of their office in Brussels, and they are not as involved in the work of these offices.[6] Even if their cross-national networks are more developed than those of the preceding group, none of these SMOs (with the notable exception of *CNSP*) is a central actor in the European networks in which they are involved: they do not have a strong influence in terms of the agenda-setting or on the decision-making processes in these arenas.

Finally, some SMOs have extended European networks and play a central role in some of them. *Cimade*, for example, is involved in eight European coalitions of associations or European networks, and is also active in the informal networks mobilizing for the regularization of undocumented migrants as well as in European cross-issue networks. The *Ligue des droits de l'Homme* is involved in seven European coalitions and networks; it has worked for the creation of a delegation in Brussels (the *European Association for the Protection of Human Rights*); and it is also active in informal networks mobilizing for the regularization of undocumented migrants, as well as in European cross-issue networks (the European Social Forums in particular). In the German case, *Caritas Deutschland* is involved in five different European coalitions of associations or European social movement organizations, and it has created an office in Brussels (the German representation of *Caritas*). *Pro Asyl* is active in five European coalitions of associations or European networks, it has created its own network (*Informations- und Kooperationsforum – ICF*) and it is also involved in informal cross-issue networks such as the mobilizations related to the G8 counter-summit in Germany in 2007. As will be developed below, the involvement of most of these associations in the European coalitions of associations and European networks active in Brussels since the beginning of the 1990s (*ECRE* or *ENAR* for example) remains limited.[7] They participate actively in these structures only on the occasion of particular campaigns. However, most of these associations have created their own European networks. With regard to French associations, this is the case with the network *Migreurop* (by *Gisti, Cimade, Act Up* and the *Ligue des droits de l'Homme*); with *Amnesty International – European Office* (by *Amnesty International Section Française*); and with the *European Association for the Protection of Human Rights* (by the *Ligue des droits de l'Homme*). Moreover, all these associations are very active in the 'European group' of the *Coordination Française pour le Droit d'Asile*. With regard to German associations, this is the case with the representation of *Caritas Deutschland* in Brussels (beside *Caritas Europa*); with the *Informations- und Kooperationsforum* (*ICF*) (by *Pro Asyl*); the networks *No Border* and *No Lager* (by activists of *Kein Mensch Ist Illegal*); and with the *Frassanito* network (by *Kein Mensch Ist Illegal* and *Kanak Attak*). In the Europeanized networks that they have created, these associations are very active over time. Thus, *Gisti*, *Cimade* and the *LdH* are the most active associations in *Migreurop*. Another example is the leading role of *Pro Asyl* in the European network that it launched in 2004: *Informations- und Kooperationsforum* (*ICF*).

As this analysis shows, there is a clear Europeanization of French and German pro-asylum movements in terms of their networks: since the end of the 1990s, the majority of SMOs have multiplied their contacts across country borders and have constructed stable relations. This trend is confirmed by the analysis of their frames.

## The Europeanization of frames

The frame analysis shows that, together with their networks, French and German SMOs have Europeanized their discourse. As table 11 shows, between 1999 and 2007 they have produced an increasing number of documents with Europeanized diagnostic, prognostic and motivational frames.[8]

As the evolution over time shows, the more the process of harmonization of immigration and asylum policies has moved forward, the more SMOs have referred to it. It seems thus to confirm the idea that EU institutions become a point of reference when they gain more power (della Porta and Caiani 2009). Further analysis shows however that not all SMOs have Europeanized their frames to the same extent. For some organizations, the European dimension of immigration and asylum policies is significant and they refer to it frequently. For others, this dimension is less important and they rarely mention it. Logically, the more an SMO is involved in European networks, the more its framing of the asylum

**Table 11** The Europeanization of frames

| | | | | | | | | | | |
|---|---|---|---|---|---|---|---|---|---|---|
| Number of associative documents presenting a Europeanized framing of the asylum issue | France | 4 | 5 | 9 | 17 | 21 | 28 | 24 | 25 | 28 |
| | Germany | 2 | 1 | 6 | 9 | 13 | 26 | 18 | 29 | 21 |

issue will be Europeanized. As I will develop below, it is in the course of the construction of solidarities across borders that perceptions evolve and joint discourses are constructed.

First, the group of organizations which have a low degree of Europeanization of their networks also have a low degree of Europeanization of their frames: they produce very few discourses that concern the European dimension of immigration and asylum policy. Thus, in 2004, *Forum Réfugiés* was involved in the construction of four public documents (calls, communiqués or seminar for example) related to it, and only one of these documents was put together by the association alone. In the same year, *France Terre d'Asile* was involved in the construction of three public documents relating to this issue (and only one of these was drafted by the association alone). In 2004, the *Arbeiterwohlfahrt* was involved in the construction of one (joint) document, and the *Flüchtlingsrat Berlin* and the *Bayerischer Flüchtlingsrat* did not produce any document that relate to this issue. Moreover, the content of these documents shows that they do not consider the process of harmonization as being fundamental for the evolution of asylum policies. Thus, in a document published in 2006, *Forum Réfugiés* stresses the idea that the norms adopted at the European level are not compelling for member-states:

> The European Commission has played its role (even if it took longer than initially stated) and elaborated a set of proposition of texts (directives and regulations) on the asylum issue. These texts were the subject of intense negotiations by the fifteen member-states. Discussions were long and difficult before unanimity could be reached and the texts officially adopted. [. . .]
>
> One year after the first phase of harmonization, the result is disappointing for us: the instruments that have been adopted are texts of compromises, with very few constraints and which leave the essential competences to member-states. States can thus keep implementing their practices and they only have to respect minimal rules. In this context, it is rather difficult to talk about a real process of harmonization. The statement is rather that member-states refuse to modify their policies and their practices on the asylum issue, which is a very sensitive one.[9]

This particular example illustrates an important feature of the framing of these associations: they are characterized by a low level of Europeanization of their diagnostic frame (only the member-states are held individually responsible for the evolution of asylum policies over the last few years). Moreover, they have a low level of Europeanization in terms of identity: they refer very rarely to European social movements (partner-associations in other European countries or at the European level are rarely mentioned). Also, these associations do not express the need to construct a collective action that would target European institutions. Their prognostic frame remains thus exclusively at the national level.

The analysis shows then that a group of SMOs produces a higher number of documents on the Europeanization of immigration and asylum policies. Thus, in 2004, *FASTI* was involved in the production of seven public documents on this issue (and three were written by the association on its own); *MRAP* was involved in the production of seven documents; *CNSP* in four; and the *Secours Catholique* in three.[10] In the same year, the *Flüchtlingsrat Hamburg* was involved in the production of six documents related to the European asylum policies (and two of these were produced by the association on its own); the *Karawane für die Rechte der Flüchtlinge und MigrantInnen* and the *Aktionsbündnis Gegen Abschiebung* were involved in the production of five documents (the first association has published three on its own); and *Diakonie* in four.[11] Moreover, the content of these documents shows that they give greater importance to the European dimension of immigration and asylum policies than the first group of associations do. Thus, in the presentation of the 'European forum' that it organized in 2004, *FASTI* argues that:

> The recent evolutions of the laws related to immigration in the EU and within its member-states do not respect the minimal standards of the fundamental rights which have been recognized at the international level and even in the national laws. This is why it is more necessary than ever to gather together and discuss with associations and activists from diverse countries in order to deepen our reflections, to share experience and to consider common actions.
>
> This European forum wants to regroup the solidary and activist voices of organizations from different countries.[12]

As this example illustrates, these SMOs highlight the idea that the legislation elaborated at the European level and the national legislation would both go in the same direction: a restriction of fundamental human rights. It therefore presents a diagnostic frame that is Europeanized. Moreover, it insists on the need to construct European networks and European collective actions ('this European forum wants to regroup the solidary and activist voices of organizations from different countries'). It also presents Europeanized identities and prognostic frames. An important communiqué launched in 2004 by *CNSP* in France and by the *Aktionsbündnis Gegen Abschiebung* and the *Karawane für die Rechte der Flüchtlinge und MigrantInnen* in Germany is another example. This document is introduced as follows:

> Facing the development of Fortress Europe which denies the most fundamental rights of immigrant and refugee people (housing, healthcare, financial support, paid work, education, citizenship, freedom of movement and of settlement . . .), it has become essential to bring together the struggles of people who have no rights. Everywhere in Europe, victims of repressive European legislation are fighting for their basic rights and survival. The perspective of a network crossing national borders aims to create a collective, autonomous, mutually accountable force, led by the protagonists themselves, and capable of responding to the increased economic and political attacks in Europe that governments are promoting.
>
> The following text is the result of a series of meetings of various European collectives of *Sans-Papiers*, refugees and migrant people and supporters: first at the NoBorder Camp in Strasbourg in July 2002, then in Leiden (Peoples Global Action), Berlin (Caravan tour), Brussels, Florence (ESF 2002), and London (2003). This was continued by all organizations that attended the recent ESF in Paris-Saint-Denis. This document aims, among other things, to serve as a common platform to mobilize for the European Day of Action on 31 January 2004 agreed at the Forum.[13]

This document is emblematic because it presents a master-frame that is expressed in a very clear way: 'Fortress Europe'. It is based on a Europeanized diagnostic frame: the denial of 'the most fundamental rights of immigrant and refugee people' is due to the 'repressive European legislation'. The call presents Europeanized identities, prognostic and motivational frames. It concludes on the necessity of developing 'coordinated campaigns' across countries and constructing Europeanized collective actions with a set of specific demands:

> We, women, men and children who are *Sans-Papiers*, immigrants and refugees as well as all those concerned with human rights, are determined to strengthen and enlarge the global long term struggle against repression, detention centres, exploitation, sexism, racism and all other discrimination, violence and slavery.
>
> The development of coordinated campaigns such as the European Day of Action, on the 31st of January 2004, constitutes a crucial step towards this aim.

At the European level, we demand:

- freedom of movement and settlement;
- immediate closure of all detention camps in all European countries;
- an end to all deportations;
- the right to citizenship and permanent residency for all, in all European countries, including equal access to social, economic, cultural and political rights for all;
- implementation of a real right to asylum, including official recognition of rape and other forms of sexual violence as persecution and therefore grounds for asylum;
- an end to exploitation and neo-slavery, and the right to work based on the same entitlements as the workers in the country where we settle;
- unconditional regularization (right to stay) for all *Sans-Papiers*;
- for children; the right to live with their family in the community, receive free schooling and health care and to end deportations of unaccompanied children and young people.[14]

The analysis shows, however, that Europeanized frames are not central in the general discourse of these associations. One can for example observe that, apart from these documents, which are specifically focused on the European level, EU immigration and asylum policies are rarely evoked in their regular documents, which are traditionally focused on the national level. The production of Europeanized frames remains thus an exceptional occurrence for these associations.

This is different for the organizations which have the most Europeanized networks: for them, the reference to the European level is central. These organizations are the ones that produce the higher number of documents relating to the process of harmonization of immigration and asylum policies. Thus, in the French case, in 2004, *Gisti* participated in the production of sixteen documents relating to this process (and two of them were produced by the association on its own). In the same year, *Cimade* was involved in the construction of fourteen documents on this issue (and one of them on its own), the *Ligue des droits de l'Homme* in ten, and *Amnesty International Section Française* and *Act Up Paris* in nine. In the German case, in 2004, *Pro Asyl* participated in the production of twenty-seven documents related to this process (and seventeen of them were produced by the association on its own); the networks *Kein Mensch Ist Illegal* and *No*

*Lager* launched fifteen documents on this issue (and seven were launched by the networks on their own); *Amnesty International Deutschland* in eight (and three of them were launched by the association on its own); *Kanak Attak* in seven (and three on its own); and *Caritas Deutschland* in six.[15] Moreover, the content of these documents shows that they tend to construct a discourse that is very much Europeanized. They tend indeed to present the process of harmonization of the asylum issue as being fundamental for the evolution of asylum policies since the mid-1990s. And they tend to attribute more easily the responsibility of the problematic situation to European power-holders. Thus, in an inter-associative communiqué published by *Gisti* and *Cimade* (among other European and North-African association members of *Migreurop*), it is argued that the situation in Ceuta and Melilla in October 2005 is the direct result of the policy defined by the European Union:

> For several years, the European Union has engaged in a latent war against migrants. Now, a new step has been taken on the Southern borders: that of an open war. Within a few days, more than ten people were killed while they were intending to cross the border between Morocco and the Spanish territories of Ceuta and Melilla. Others have been seriously wounded and several hundred people were deported and abandoned, without water and food, in the middle of the desert of Sahara. [. . .]
>
> Bullets were shot by the Moroccan police, but it is the European Union which supplies the weapons. In the framework of the externalization of its migration policy, the task-sharing that is imposed by the EU consists in giving to its neighbours in the South the responsibility of its borders' protection. Migrants are the hostages of this process of subcontracting of violence. Member-states implement a selective opening of their borders, in the framework of the 'chosen' immigration needed by their economy. However, they are ready for any renunciation in order to avoid receiving those that they call 'non-chosen immigration': refugees and, more generally, all those escaping misery, environmental catastrophes and conflicts. They are for example ready to consider a country like Libya (in which arbitrary detention of migrants, mass expulsions and mistreatments are common practices) 'safe' in order to reject their entire charters of migrants who came by boat-people in Lampedusa. They are also ready to transform Morocco into a real barricade where thousands of Africans in transit are retained in infra-human conditions and have to face police repression.[16]

In this example, the Europeanized 'problematic situation' and responsibility described by these associations concerns all aspects related to immigration and asylum policies. With the use of the 'war of the EU against migrants' master-frame, they attribute to EU power-holders the responsibility for various problematic situations: the violence against migrants in Ceuta and Melilla and in Southern Mediterranean countries; the concept of 'selected migrations'; the deportations; the living conditions of migrants in Morocco, etc. The frame analysis shows moreover that they also tend to define their identity as being very much Europeanized. They often mention the existence of partner-associations or activists in other European countries, as well as the existence of European mobilizations. Some associations go further and evoke the emergence of a European social movement that is wider than the movement mobilized on asylum and migration issues. For example, the call for a European day of action that was signed by *Act Up*, *Gisti*, *Kanak Attak* and *Kein Mensch Ist Illegal* in 2005 (among hundreds of associations across Europe) relates the movement on immigration issues with the protest against the European constitutional treaty (which was submitted to a referendum in France in this period):

> Last year a European Day of Action against detention centers and for the legalization of undocumented migrants was launched during the European Social Forum in Paris. A call was subscribed to by many different networks and groups, and on the 31st of January 2004 demonstrations and actions were held in more than forty European cities. It was an important day in the development of a networking process among migrants, struggles and activists on a European level.
>
> This year we want to make a step forward. We propose to all European networks and social movements to join in the organization of a second day of action, to be held on April 2nd 2005, centered upon the claim for freedom of movement and the right to stay as an alternative to the European constitutional process. [. . .]
>
> We invite all groups, networks and social movements in Europe, not only the ones working on migration-related issues, to join this call and to mobilize for April 2nd 2005. On the second day of action we will emphasize the demands of the last year call.
>
> Demonstrations, actions and struggles must take place everywhere in Europe on that day![17]

Consequently, these associations also present clearly Europeanized prognostic and motivational frames. Thus, a communiqué published (among other associations from different European and North-African countries) by *Act Up*, *Amnesty International Section Française*, *Cimade*, *Gisti* and the *Ligue des droits de l'Homme* formulates precise claims addressed to all power-holders involved in the process of harmonization of immigration and asylum policies:

> The signatory organizations:
> - ask the EU member states to defer all decisions on European cooperation with Libya on matters of immigration, as well as with any other third country from which there is no clear commitment on fundamental rights protection. The ratification and the implementation of the international conventions guaranteeing human rights' protection, such as the Geneva Convention, and the access of governmental organizations and NGOs in charge of ascertaining the respect of fundamental rights, are, in this respect, an essential prerequisite;
> - invite the Commission, in order to ensure the conditions of a contradictory debate on the opportunity of a migratory cooperation, to make public the conclusions of the diplomatic missions it organized in Libya;
> - call the European Parliament to come soon to a decision about the advisability of a collaboration in this field with third countries where there is no insurance that the norms on human rights to which the EU is committed to are respected.[18]

One might also mention a document of the German association *Pro Asyl* in which the Europeanization of the diagnostic, prognostic and motivational frames is clearly present:

> In 1999, EU member-states committed themselves to agree on minimal standards relating to asylum law before May 2004. The regulations on which they have agreed are now valid for the ten new EU member-states. *Pro Asyl*, together with other human rights organizations, has monitored intensively the 'process of harmonization' because we have considered that the European norms could be the opportunity to create an asylum law that would no longer be torn between the individual interests of member-states. [. . .]
>
> In the EU, the number of asylum demands has been halved in the last ten years. In 2003, only 288,000 asylum demands were formulated. This is a result of the closure of the borders: Europe has

> closed almost all legal possibilities of entrance into its territory over the last years. [. . .]
>
> *Pro Asyl* has tried to inform and to mobilize against these developments through press communiqués, calls and a postcard action in the frame of the European elections in June 2004.[19]

This quotation is also emblematic because it shows that, in contrast to other associations, Europeanized references are central in the general discourse of these associations. *Pro Asyl* mentions in this text its efforts to inform public opinion about European developments. Moreover, it is notable that this quotation (and the whole section on EU asylum policies) is situated in the first pages of the association's annual report; an emphasis on EU asylum policies is thus made by the association. This is common to all associations that comprise this group. Another indicator of this is that EU policies are very often mentioned in documents that are not specifically focused on this issue, for example, in documents that describe a situation at the national level, in order to explain the evolution of member-states' legislations.

As this analysis shows, there is a clear Europeanization of the perceptions of the actors of the pro-asylum movement. In particular, even if to different degrees, SMOs recognize the EU as a new target and define their identities through references to their cross-national networks. This trend is translated in terms of collective action.

## The construction of European collective actions

The protest-event analysis shows that, together with their networks and frames, French and German SMOs have Europeanized their collective actions. Table 12 shows that, as the process of harmonization of immigration and asylum policies has developed over time, these organizations have constructed an increasing number of collective actions with a European dimension.

These results confirm that the Europeanization of networks, frames and collective actions are inter-related dynamics. Overall they show a move of

**Table 12** The Europeanization of collective actions

| | | 1999 | 2000 | 2001 | 2002 | 2003 | 2004 | 2005 | 2006 | 2007 |
|---|---|---|---|---|---|---|---|---|---|---|
| Number of Europeanized collective actions | France | 2 | 3 | 7 | 13 | 15 | 19 | 14 | 18 | 21 |
| | Germany | 1 | 1 | 4 | 9 | 11 | 15 | 19 | 23 | 17 |

French and German pro-asylum movements to the European Union level. However, further analysis shows that, as is the case with the networks and frames, not all organizations Europeanized their collective actions to the same extent. Logically, the organizations with a low degree of Europeanization of their networks and frames have rarely constructed Europeanized collective actions. Conversely, those which have a higher degree of Europeanization of their networks and frames have often constructed Europeanized collective actions.

First, the analysis shows that from 1999 to 2007, the associations which have a low degree of Europeanization of their networks and frames have been involved in the construction of a total of ten significant collective actions that have a European dimension. Among others, these were:

- the participation in the *European Council on Refugees and Exiles*'s 'Tampere parallel meeting being organized to promote a fair and human refugee policy throughout the European Union' (October 1999: *France Terre d'Asile* and *Forum Réfugiés*, among the other members of *ECRE*);
- the production of a 'Joint Statement from British and French NGOs on the situation in Sangatte' (September 2001) (*France Terre d'Asile* and *Forum Réfugiés*, together with a group of French and British associations);
- the joint lobbying campaign of European institutions (Commission and Parliament) for the abolition of the rule on the obligation of residence (*Residenzpflicht*) (2002: *Arbeiterwohlfahrt*, together with a group of German associations);
- the joint lobbying campaign of the German government against the inclusion of the concept of 'safe third-countries' in European directives (2004: *Arbeiterwohlfahrt*, together with a group of German associations);
- the involvement in *ECRE*'s campaign for the retreat of the directive on the procedures of examination of the statute of refugee (2004: *Forum Réfugiés* and the *Arbeiterwohlfahrt* together with other members of *ECRE*).

These associations have thus participated in a limited number of Europeanized collective actions since the end of the 1990s. Moreover, none of these actions was launched by one of these associations on its own. Their engagement at this level has always taken the form of participation in an action organized by a larger forum (the *European Council on Refugees and Exiles*, the *Coordination Française pour le Droit d'Asile*, or the German associations participating in the *Informationsverbund Asyl*). This aspect will be developed in more detail below, in the discussion about the relationship between these associations and the non-governmental actors which are directly involved at the European level.

The protest-event analysis shows then the existence of a group having a higher degree of Europeanization of its collective action. Thus, in the French case, *CNSP* has been involved in sixteen important European collective actions during the period under discussion, *MRAP* in seventeen, *FASTI* in fifteen, and the *Secours Catholique* in nine. In the German case, the *Aktionsbündnis Gegen Abschiebung Rhein-Main* has been involved in thirteen important European collective actions during the same period, *Diakonie* in ten, the *Karawane für die Rechte der Flüchtlinge und MigrantInnen* in fourteen; and the *Flüchtlingsrat Hamburg* in fifteen. These were, for example:

- the launching (by – among others – *CNSP*, *FASTI* the *Karawane für die Rechte der Flüchtlinge und MigrantInnen* and *MRAP*) of a call for a European demonstration for freedom of circulation (March 1999);
- the launching (by – among others – *CNSP*, *FASTI* and *MRAP*) of a European call for the ratification of the convention related to migrants' rights (December 2004);
- the participation (by – among others the *Flüchtlingsrat Hamburg*, the *Aktionsbündnis Gegen Abschiebung Rhein-Main*, and the *Karawane für die Rechte der Flüchtlinge und MigrantInnen*) in the 'European action-day' against the detention of migrants (January 2004);
- the participation of *Diakonie* in the joint lobbying campaign of the German government against the inclusion of the concept of 'safe third-countries' in European directives (2004);
- the participation (by – among others – the *Flüchtlingsrat Hamburg*, the *Aktionsbündnis Gegen Abschiebung Rhein-Main*, and the *Karawane für die Rechte der Flüchtlinge und MigrantInnen*) in the 'Euromayday Parade' in Berlin and Hamburg in May 2005;
- the participation of the *Secours Catholique* in the lobbying campaign against the European Commission's 'action plan for freedom, justice and security' (June 2005);
- the launching (by – among others – *CNSP*, *FASTI*, *MRAP* and the *Flüchtlingsrat Hamburg*) of several calls for demonstrations following the events in Ceuta and Melilla in September 2005 (October 2005).

This group of associations has thus been involved in a higher number of European collective actions. However, the analysis shows that none of these associations has played a central role in the phase of construction of these actions. Most of these actions have been initiated by large networks or coalitions in which these associations are involved but do not play a central role (as the analysis of their European networks has shown). Thus, their participation in these collective actions mainly takes the form of an involvement in the phase of implementation (signature of circulating calls or communiqués, or relay of a lobbying campaign at the national level, for example).

However, the last organizations (having a high degree of Europeanization of networks and frames) have constructed a high number of European collective actions and have been also involved in their phase of conception. Thus, from 1999 to 2007, *Act Up* was involved in twenty European collective actions, *Amnesty International Section Française* in twenty-five, *Cimade* in thirty-one, *Gisti* in thirty-five, and the *Ligue des droits de l'Homme* in twenty-five. In the German case, during the same period, *Amnesty International Deutschland* was involved in nineteen Europeanized actions, *Caritas Deutschland* in eighteen, *Kanak Attak* in twenty-three, *Kein Mensch Ist Illegal* in twenty-eight, and *Pro Asyl* in twenty-five. Some of the most significant Europeanized collective actions in which these SMOs have been involved were:

- the participation (of – among others – *Amnesty International Section Française, Amnesty International Deutschland, Cimade, Caritas Deutschland* and *Pro Asyl*) in *ECRE*'s 'Tampere parallel meeting being organized to promote a fair and human refugee policy throughout the European Union' (October 1999);
- the call (by – among others – *Kein Mensch Ist Illegal*) for an action-day against racism at the G8 summit in Genoa (July 2001);
- the launching (by – among others – *Act Up Paris, Gisti, Kein Mensch Ist Illegal* and the *LDH*) of a call for the regularization of undocumented migrants in Europe (September 2002);
- the organization (by – among others – *Act Up Paris* and *Kein Mensch Ist Illegal*) of the 'No Border Camp' in Strasbourg (July 2002);
- the organization (principally by *Cimade* and *Gisti*) of a seminar at the European Parliament on the externalization of immigration and asylum policies (June 2003);
- the launching (by *Cimade*) of a European petition against the joint return flights for immigrants (November 2003);
- the organization (by – among others – *Act Up Paris, Kanak Attak* and *Kein Mensch Ist Illegal*) of a 'European day of struggle for the regularization and for the closure of all detention centres for foreigners' (January 2004);
- the lodging (by – among others – *Cimade* and *Gisti*) of a complaint to the European Commission against the Italian government (February 2004);
- the launching (principally by *Act Up Paris, Cimade* and *Gisti*) of a European petition against the creation of camps for foreigners at the European borders (October 2004);

- the realization of several missions of observation on the situation of migrants in detention centres (in Malta by *Gisti* and the *LdH* in 2003, in Italy by *Gisti* in 2004, in several East European countries by *Pro Asyl* since 2004, and in Morocco by *AISF* and *Cimade* in 2004);
- the lobbying campaign (by *Pro Asyl*) of the Euro-deputies against the directive related to the procedures of examination of asylum claims (2005);
- the organization (by – among others – *Kein Mensch Ist Illegal* and *Kanak Attak*) of an action day on migrants' rights at the G8 counter summit in Heiligendamm (2007).

Further analysis shows that, due to their central position in the European networks in which they are involved, these SMOs have participated directly in the phase of construction of these mobilizations. Even if these actions take the form of a large coalition of actors across Europe, a limited number of associations or activists have initiated them. For example, the 'European day of struggle for the regularization and for the closure of all detention centres for foreigners' (2004) was initiated by a small group of activists from *Act Up*, *Kanak Attak* and *Kein Mensch Ist Illegal* (together with Spanish and Italian activists) that were active in the European network *Frassanito*. In the case of the 'European petition against the creation of camps for foreigners at the European borders', a few activists from *Act Up*, *Gisti* and *Cimade*, all involved in the European network *Migreurop*, initiated the process. The same observation leads us to claim that the German branch of *Caritas* is more Europeanized than its French counterpart (*Secours Catholique*). Indeed, even if these two organizations have the same representation in Brussels (*Caritas Europa*), the links between *Caritas Europa* and *Caritas Deutschland* are much more significant than those between the former and the *Secours Catholique*. Thus, the influence of *Caritas Deutschland* is so important that it has considered it necessary to create its own representation (the two individuals working in the German representation of *Caritas* in Brussels) besides *Caritas Europa*.

## Conclusions

This analysis of the levels of Europeanization of French and German associations mobilizing around the asylum issue shows that they increasingly recognize the EU as a new level of mobilization. Even if it is with different degrees, associations traditionally active in different countries create or participate in Europeanized networks, they produce discourses that concern

EU policies and they construct Europeanized collective actions. This process leads to the creation of new arenas of mobilization in which European policies are analysed and discussed, new identities are negotiated and new forms of collective actions are organized. This is obviously a sign that European institutions are increasingly recognized as fundamental power-holders. They favour the construction of what can be defined as a Europeanized 'imagined community' (Anderson 1983).[20] This process is, however, not consensual, as the dynamic of Europeanization of social movements shows. As will be developed further below, social movements therefore participate in the definition of a process of 'Europeanization from below'.

These results show that there is no clear correlation between the traditional context of mobilization of an association and its propensity to Europeanize: French and German SMOs Europeanize to the same extent. Neither can one observe a clear correlation between the profile of an association at the national level and its propensity to Europeanize: humanitarian and politicized SMOs Europeanize their networks, frames and collective actions to the same extent. These conclusions contradict the studies focusing on the groups active around European institutions and showing a 'NGOization' of the mobilizations against EU policies. It is thus generally argued that 'grass-roots associations' traditionally mobilizing at the national level tend not to address European institutions directly, but tend rather to delegate the construction of European mobilizations to a group of European SMOs exclusively active in Brussels. Moreover these studies show that this group of European SMOs is composed principally of associations from Northern Europe.

This remark leads one to say that further analysis is needed. As I have developed, the fact that more 'grass-roots associations' (or 'politicized associations' in the typology that I have defined) do not directly address European power-holders does not mean that they do not Europeanize: they can follow other paths of Europeanization which lead them to indirectly address European institutions. And the same can be said about the traditional context of mobilization of the organizations active in Brussels: the fact that French, Italian or Spanish associations are less present in Brussels than British, Dutch or German SMOs does not mean that they Europeanize less. One can indeed suggest that they have followed a path of Europeanization that leads them to construct European mobilizations without being present directly around the EU institutions in Brussels.

The following chapter will aim to analyse these questions. I will examine whether, depending on their profile and on the features of their traditional context of mobilization, French and German associations tend to follow different paths of Europeanization.

## Notes

1. 'First call for mobilization for a counter-summit and an alternative forum on 'Migrations and Development'. For a Europe of openness and solidarity', May 2008.
2. In the interests of readability, the networks of French and German associations are presented separately.
3. The *Arbeiterwohlfahrt* is also a member of the *European Coalition for Foreigners' Right to Family Life* and the *European Network Against Racism*. However, its participation in these arenas is almost non-existent.
4. The *Coordination Française pour le Droit d'Asile* has a monthly 'European group' meeting in order to exchange information on the evolution of European asylum policies.
5. This point will be discussed in greater depth below.
6. More developments on this point will be presented in the next chapter.
7. With the exception of *Cimade* and *Caritas Deutchland* who are very active in the *Churches' Commission for Migrants in Europe*, and *Pro Asyl* who is very active within the *European Council on Refuges and Exiles*.
8. As I developed in the introduction, I observed the Europeanization of their frames through the systematic analysis of the documents (communiqués, calls, petitions, internal literature such as annual reports, and website presentations), which they published between 1999 and 2007. This data was found in the websites of the associations and in their archives. In this table, I selected the documents that relate exclusively to the European dimension of immigration and asylum policies (I therefore excluded documents in which European developments were mentioned among other items). Moreover, I only selected those documents that were lengthy enough for analysis: short communiqués were excluded because they did not allow for the content analysis of the diagnostic, prognostic and motivational frames.
9. *Forum Réfugiés*, 'La politique d'asile européenne', April 2006 (author's translation).
10. The case of the *Secours Catholique* is however unusual because, as I will develop below, the documents and collective actions that relate to the European level are mainly published by its office in Brussels (*Caritas Europa*).
11. In the case of *Diakonie*, the same remark can be made as for the *Secours Catholique*: most of the documents and collective actions at the European level are published by its office in Brussels (*Eurodiaconia*).
12. Introduction to the 'European Forum' organized by *FASTI*, *Politiques européennes d'immigration. Politiques d'apartheid camouflées. Comment résister, élargir les droits acquis et conquérir de nouveaux droits?*, 29–31 May 2004 (author's translation).
13. 'Towards a convergence, a coming together of the struggles of *sans papiers*, refugees and migrants in Europe', January 2004.
14. Ibid.
15. As I will discuss below, the cases of *Amnesty International* (the French and German section), the *Ligue des droits de l'Homme* and *Caritas Deutschland* are not typical because most of the documents that concern the process of Europeanization of asylum policies are produced by their representation in Brussels.
16. 'Ceuta et Melilla. L'UE déclare la guerre aux migrants', October 2005 (author's translation).

17 'Call for a second European day of action for freedom of movement and the right to stay', March 2005.

18 'EU about to negotiate with Libya on immigration matters', April 2005.

19 *Pro Asyl*, 'Tätigkeitsbericht des Vorstandes des Fördervereins PRO ASYL, 2003/2004', June 2004, p.1–2 (author's translation).

20 As Benedict Anderson (1983) has shown in terms of the rise and spread of nationalism, institutions create 'imagined communities' which reproduce the values and symbols that are necessary for their rise and survival.

Chapter 4

# The Different Modes of Europeanization of the Pro-asylum Movements

In January 2009, the European network *Migreurop* launched a campaign for the 'right of access in detention centres for migrants'. Its objective was to protest against the detention of migrants across Europe and to criticize the institutionalization of this practice at the European level (in particular since the adoption of the 'return directive' in June 2008). More generally, it aimed to:

> Raise awareness on the situation and the detention conditions in these centers, report violations and protect migrants' rights in detention, inform on the consequences of detention and on situations leading to violations of migrants' rights.[1]

This campaign was based on a set of actions at the national and European levels, intended to address institutions and public opinion. Thus, it began with an audition at the European Parliament to present the campaign to the MEPs and with an action day around detention centres in several countries in order 'to give international media coverage to this event and to show the importance of an oversight by the civil society of detention centers'.[2]

A few months later, the No Border network organized a 'No Border Camp' in the Greek island of Lesbos. Activists from different European countries gathered together for a week and carried out a set of direct actions of protest (blockades or occupations) against EU border control policies and the Frontex agency. This event was part of the transnational campaign against Frontex and its objective was:

> to invite people and groups from outside and inside Europe to join the campaign against Frontex. Organise actions, events, debates. Monitor Frontex trainings and operations ashore, at sea and at airports, and to share the information. Act locally, regionally, transnationally.[3]

A year later, in March 2010, *Caritas*' European representation (*Caritas Europa*) wrote several position letters and launched a series of face-to-face meetings with the new members of the European Commission. The objective of this strategy was to 'firmly maintain its role monitoring the EU in order to push forward progressive legislation that would lead to a sustainable, welcoming and socially inclusive European Union'.[4] Thus, in its letter to Viviane Reding (EU Commissioner for Justice, Fundamental Rights and Citizenship), *Caritas* welcomes her intention to have 'a zero-tolerance policy as regards violations of the Charter of Fundamental Rights' and it argues that the EU Commission should develop new mechanisms of monitoring member-states policies in the field of immigration and asylum:

> We insist that this attitude be clearly reflected in the Commission's annual report to the Council on the implementation of the European Pact on Immigration and Asylum and the follow up given by the Commission to the violations observed in this area. We ask for your particular attention for the issues of detention and forced removal of undocumented migrants, including families with children, and measures regarding border control.[5]

As these examples illustrate, social movements Europeanize through different modes: their European mobilizations can take place at different levels, they can target different types of actors, through different forms of actions and different types of frames. The preceding chapter has analysed the extent to which the pro-asylum movements are Europeanizing. This chapter will now analyse how they Europeanize. As I developed in the introduction (see table 1), four different modes of Europeanization can be distinguished (depending on the types of networks, frames, repertoires and strategies).

**Domestication**: social movements attribute some responsibility for a problematic situation to the European Union, but they continue to mobilize at the national level. Their mobilizations target national institutions, but they have a European dimension because they are constructed in reaction to decisions taken at the European level. They aim thus to pressurize European institutions indirectly, through their national government (see also Balme and Chabanet 2002; della Porta and Caiani 2009). These mobilizations are mainly based on protest and they emerge through national networks.

**Externalization**: social movements traditionally active at the national level target European institutions in order to escape national obstacles and to put pressure on their own government indirectly. This strategy is similar to the 'boomerang effect' presented by Keck and Sikkink (1998). They also use opportunities offered at the European level (such as European funds) in order to ameliorate their situation at the national or local level (see also Balme and Chabanet 2002; della Porta 2003). In this mode of Europeanization, national social movement organizations are usually involved into supranational coalitions that represent them at the EU level, and collective actions are based on a corporatist repertoire or on a pluralist repertoire made up of lobbying strategies and juridical actions. European institutions are thus perceived as close allies that can be used against national governments, and European policies are considered as being more liberal than national policies.

The construction of **multilevel social movements**: national social movements become actively involved in networks which are coordinated by a centralized supranational structure (usually based in Brussels). Unlike the previous mode, however, European institutions are not considered as allies that can be used against national governments, and European policies are not considered as being more liberal than national policies. These networks aim indeed to pressurize both European and national institutions through the construction of multilevel campaigns: the European central structures target European institutions (mainly) through lobbying techniques whereas national social movement organizations target their own government through their traditional repertoire of collective action.

The construction of **transnational social movements**: movements target both European and national institutions through transnational protest. These transnational social movements are composed of national social movement organizations coordinated through formal structures (transnational groups) or loose networks (see also Tarrow 2001). Unlike the previous mode, this process leads social movements which are traditionally active at the national level to target directly European institutions and to define networks and collective actions addressing various polities (European or national) simultaneously (rather than through a multilevel framework). Also, again unlike the previous mode, protest is central in this process.

This empirical analysis reveals that associations mobilizing around the asylum issue have been following different modes of Europeanization. This is visible in the evolution of their networks, cognitive frames and collective actions (in terms of repertoires and strategies). A first group of SMOs has followed a process of externalization. Another group of SMOs has moved from a process of domestication to a process of construction of multilevel and transnational social movements. Throughout this chapter, I will show that these two modes of Europeanization are related to two different logics of Europeanization. SMOs following the first process tend to separate (in terms of networks, frames and collective action) their national mobilization from their European mobilization. In contrast, the organizations following the second path tend to view their European mobilization as the continuity (in terms of networks, frames and collective action) of their national mobilization.

Considering the hypotheses presented in the introduction and the general idea of an 'NGOization' of the mobilizations around EU policy issues, one would expect politicized associations to follow the first process and humanitarian SMOs to follow the second one. In comparison to humanitarian associations, politicized associations are indeed less well endowed in terms of the human and material resources necessary for the construction of transnational networks and collective actions. One would thus expect them to Europeanize through the participation in centralized coalitions that represent them in Brussels and to separate their mobilizations at the European and national levels. Conversely, humanitarian associations (which have more human and material resources) would be able to construct transnational networks and mobilizations that connect more the national and European levels. Moreover, considering these hypotheses, one could expect to observe cross-national differences. In their context of mobilization, French associations have access to more resources than do German associations (in particular, they have a more diversified network of allies). This would tend to facilitate their Europeanization through the second process. On the other hand, German associations (who have access to fewer resources in their traditional context of mobilization) would tend to Europeanize through the first process.

However, my empirical analysis has generated different results. Humanitarian associations tend to follow a mode of externalization that leads them to separate their European and national mobilizations, whereas politicized associations have been involved in the construction of multilevel movements (mainly SMOs acting for the defence of human rights and for a more just and egalitarian society) and transnational movements (mainly militant organizations). This leads them to connect more often their European and national mobilizations. The results show moreover that French and German SMOs cannot be clearly distinguished in terms of their modes of Europeanization. This is visible through the qualitative analysis of their networks, frames and collective actions. This chapter aims to present in detail these empirical results. In the first part, I will analyse the mode of Europeanization of French and German humanitarian associations. In the second part, I will analyse the modes of Europeanization of politicized associations.

## The Europeanization of humanitarian associations: a process of externalization

The lobbying action of *Caritas Europa* presented in the introduction is representative of the process of Europeanization followed by humanitarian SMOs. Since the end of the 1990s, all these SMOs have been Europeanizing their networks, frames and collective actions through a process of externalization. Thus, as is the case with *Caritas*, these associations Europeanize through participation in centralized structures based in Brussels. They tend to rely on non-protesting forms of collective action and to present European asylum policies as being guided by a different logic than that which applies to national asylum policies. This leads them to construct multilevel collective actions: they aim to change European policies through a mobilization that addresses national institutions and/or to change national policies through a mobilization that addresses European institutions. Thus, in the case presented above, *Caritas* urges the European Commission to monitor the policies of member-states. More generally, this process leads them to define a double-level configuration: the mobilizations at the European level are separated from those traditionally defined at the national level.

### The participation in centralized coalitions of associations based in Brussels

French and German humanitarian associations have Europeanized their networks through their inclusion into pre-existing European coalitions of associations. As tables 9 and 10 (in the previous chapter) show, all of these associations are indirectly represented in Brussels. This is made possible through their participation in *ECRE* (*European Council on Refugees and Exiles*) and/or through the presence of a European office (*Caritas Europa*, the European delegation of *Caritas Deutschland* and *Eurodiaconia*).

These European networks are very centralized. *ECRE* in particular has developed a significant secretariat based in London and Brussels. This bureau takes responsibility for the process of agenda-setting and decision-making, and it has progressively distanced itself from most of the member-associations. The organizational chart of this coalition shows that the national member-associations are not central in its daily activities: it is organized through a pyramidal structure in which member-associations represent the basis and in which decisions are taken by the secretariat. Member-associations gather together twice a year for plenary assemblies and most of them are hardly involved in the work of the central office.[6] The same remark can be made regarding the European offices of *Caritas* and *Diakonie*. It has been said during an interview with an employee of the European delegation of *Caritas Deutschland* that this office has an agenda that is disconnected from that of *Caritas'* section in Germany.[7] It has moreover been underlined that the mobilizations on European issues are organized centrally: the European delegation coordinates the interactions between national sections. Indeed, direct contact between national sections is relatively rare: the European central offices generally play the role of intermediary. This idea was confirmed in the interviews with personnel from other humanitarian associations. The interviewees agreed that the European networks to which their association belong are not transnational (in the sense that they would establish direct contacts across countries). They are rather described as centralized or pyramidal structures in which interactions have a 'top-down' dynamic.

In these structures, the function of member-associations is established in a stable way. They have a role of dual-representation which is defined in a multi-levelled configuration. They represent their national or local activities in the frame of the European coalition's structure, and they represent in turn the actions of the coalition in the frame of their national activities. This multilevel configuration is thus underlined in the way in which *Forum Réfugiés* describes its participation in *ECRE*:

> The European Council for Refugees and Exiles (*ECRE*) is a pan-European network of seventy-six NGOs and associations of help to refugees and asylum-seekers from thirty European countries. The ECRE is a resource centre (monitoring of asylum law, exchanges and diffusion of information, implementation of projects, actions of lobbying, etc . . .). The secretariat of the ECRE is based in London and it has an antenna in Brussels, which specializes in the lobbying actions addressed to the European Union authorities.
>
> *Forum Réfugiés* has been a member of the network since 1999 and it is a 'focal point' for France. *Forum Réfugiés* publishes for *ECRE* a yearly report on the development of the asylum system in France. It participates in the bi-annual meetings that bring together all the members of the network. And it participates in the lobbying activity by relaying to the French government the decisions which have been taken in the frame of the network and which concern the evolution of the European legislation on asylum.[8]

*Forum Réfugiés* describes itself as a 'focal point' for France. This shows that it works as a delegate of *ECRE*'s activities in France (it 'relays its positions') and as a representative of France at the European level (in particular through the regular writing of reports on the situation in France). The specificity and clearly defined character of this function was confirmed in the interviews. It was stressed that their activities are based on a 'clear distribution of roles' between the central secretariat and the 'national delegations'.[9] In the previous chapter, I stressed the fact that humanitarian associations can have different levels of Europeanization. As the analysis of their modes of Europeanization reveals, this is because the significance of their role of representation can vary. *Caritas Deutschland* is therefore a more important relay of *Caritas Europa* in Germany than the *Secours Catholique* in France.[10]

This specific mode of Europeanization of networks leads them to clearly separate their activities at the national and European levels. Their role in the European networks in which they are involved is indeed different from the one they traditionally have in their national networks. At the national level, they traditionally organize and coordinate their own mobilization, and they construct their networks around their own activities. They are themselves the 'central points' of their mobilization. Because of the way in which the European networks to which they belong are organized, they act on the contrary as 'focal points' of a movement that is coordinated at the European level. This is evident if one has a closer look at *ECRE*'s organization. Besides the secretariat, the *European Council on Refugees and Exiles* has an executive committee, whose function is presented in the following way:

> ECRE's goals and activities are decided by its member agencies through recommendations made at ECRE's twice yearly conferences.
>
> The members of the Executive Committee are elected by ECRE's membership at the autumn Biannual General Meeting. Ten members are elected to represent particular regions across Europe and the remaining members are individuals elected for the special contribution they can make at the European level.[11]

The mission of *ECRE*'s executive committee is thus to define the 'goals and activities' of the secretariat: it does not take the decisions but orientates the work of the coalition's central element. In this executive committee, national member-associations elect representatives; members of the executive committee are however elected in order to 'represent particular regions across Europe'.[12] The role of 'dual-representation' of member-associations is thus clearly stated. This observation can be extended to the other organizations composing the European advocacy coalition. For example, the executive committee of *Caritas Europa* is composed of members of each European state, suggesting thus a role of national representative. This role of 'focal point' or 'dual representation' is confirmed by the analysis of the Europeanization of their frames and collective actions.

## A process of frame-transformation

The analysis of the Europeanized frames produced by humanitarian SMOs shows that they tend to rely on new forms of discourses (in comparison to those they traditionally produce in their national context) when they refer to EU asylum policies. They follow a process of frame-transformation (the definition of new interpretive schemes; Snow et al. 1986). As I developed in chapter two, these associations base their discourse almost exclusively on the humanitarian frame at the national level – on the idea that the protection of refugees is a moral duty. In contrast, their Europeanized discourse is mainly focused on the frame of the defence of fundamental rights (the idea that states have to guarantee the asylum rights as a consequence of their existing fundamental laws and international commitments). Thus, when they move from a national to a European discursive context, these associations alter the general logic of their discourse. As I developed above, the humanitarian frame and that of the defence of fundamental rights are related to different discursive logics. The use of the humanitarian frame is part of the register of the 'call for help': to provide assistance and protection in a situation of emergency. Conversely, the frame of the defence of fundamental rights is part of the register of the 'call for reason': to argue that public authorities have gone beyond the limits set by the principles of democracy and individual freedoms and by their international engagements.

Associative documents that evoke successively both national and European frameworks provide a good illustration of this shift. Thus, in its 2006 annual report, *Forum Réfugiés* underlines the degradation of fundamental human rights relating to asylum in the context of European harmonization. For example, when it analyses the directive relating to asylum procedures, it quotes the *United Nations High Commissioner for Refugees* in order to underline the 'international standards' on asylum:

> The 'procedure' directive: a degradation of the standard on asylum.
>
> After the adoption of the 'procedure' directive, the HCR summed up the concerns of all organizations acting for the defence of asylum right. It declared that this directive could lead to a degradation of the standard on asylum, 'and even endanger the international standards of the refugee protection inside and beyond the European Union'.[13]

The association concludes its analysis by evoking 'a deteriorated asylum right at the end of the Tampere process' and 'a decline of asylum in Europe'.[14] This specific framing contrasts with the rest of the document, which is related to the situation in France. Indeed, if part of the text concerning France refers to asylum as a fundamental right, the large majority refers to the conditions of reception of asylum-seekers and refugees, presenting a typical humanitarian discourse. This difference of discourse was explicitly underlined during an interview with an employee of the *Secours Catholique*, who stressed the different logics of argumentation at the national and European levels:

> When we refer to European asylum policies (through *Caritas Europa*), we deal with directives and regulations. Whereas in France, we base our activities on concrete statements (statements of poverty and exclusion). We deal with concrete situations faced by individuals every day. At the European level, what we have to do is to anticipate these statements. We are situated upstream. We have thus a much more theoretical and technical discourse. We defend fundamental principles of rights which are defined in international treaties.[15]

As a matter of fact, through this discursive shift, these associations generally disconnect their framing of the European and national situations. The link between European asylum policies and French or German policies is thus rarely made. It is only through the question of the transposition of European directives at the national level that they establish this link. The lack of connection between these two discourses is explained by the fact that these SMOs perceive European policies as having a different logic to that of national policies. Thus, in its 2006 annual report, *Forum Réfugiés* presents the following introduction to the developments of EU asylum policy:

> After the end of the first phase of the Tampere program, the asylum right is weakened. Europe sees the damages of a process of harmonization that is guided by the principle of the lowest common denominator. It tries to decrease the strong differences between states as regards the application of the norms on international protection. This is a sign that Europe has missed its most important opportunity and that national approaches are still fundamental on the asylum issue. This is what the very controversial 'procedure' directive has shown. This directive is emblematic of the whole European process of harmonization on the asylum issue: it is the sum of the most restrictive measures of the member-states.[16]

This example is illustrative because it clearly expresses a difference between the 'European approach' and the 'national approaches' on asylum policies. It is thus argued that European asylum policies move in a restrictive direction because member-states keep control of the institutional process of harmonization. Consequently, member-states construct a common policy through the coordination of their more restrictive measures on asylum. In this discourse, it is implied that the 'European approach' on asylum policies is different (it is less restrictive) from the approaches of the member-states. In other words, it is argued that European asylum policies are restrictive because the policy-making process favours the Council of ministers (who is representative of the 'national approaches') rather than the European Commission and European Parliament (who are representative of the 'European approach'). This perception is common to all French and German humanitarian associations and is visible in the details of their discourses on EU policies. The analysis of the diagnosis frame (and more precisely the designation of the actors or institutions responsible for a problematic situation) shows that, for them, the member-states are responsible for the adoption of restrictive asylum policies. On the contrary, the European Commission and Parliament are perceived in a more positive way. Thus, in a communiqué published in April 2000, the German association *Diakonie* argues that, in comparison with the existing norms in European member-states (and in particular in Germany), the proposal of the EU Commission on family reunification is an improvement:

> The proposal of the EU Commission for a Council regulation related to family reunification also contains measures on the family reunification of refugees recognized by the Geneva Convention and refugees having a subsidiary protection. These proposals are very welcome and they should quickly find wide support. In comparison with the practices related to family reunification in Germany (and in other European countries), these proposals contain real improvements for refugees recognized by the Geneva Convention and they open the possibility of family reunification for refugees with a subsidiary protection.[17]

This general view on the process of harmonization of asylum policies was confirmed during the interviews with representatives of these associations. Thus, an employee of *Caritas Deutschland* described this process in the following way:

> When we follow the course of European negotiations, we see always more or less the same pattern. The Commission proposes a directive

> which we consider as positive in comparison to the asylum policies we have in Germany. But then, the proposal is examined by the Council. After these negotiations, the proposal is completely changed. It becomes a restrictive directive which is made of the worst measures of each member-state. This is how new concepts like the idea of a list of 'safe third-countries' determine European policies. Finally, the European Parliament is consulted but it is not heard.[18]

This interview shows thus once again that humanitarian associations present a clear distinction between the European and national approaches in terms of policy orientations. In conclusion, the shift in terms of framing processes that has been described above is more generally a shift in terms of perceptions: the European level is perceived as being from a different (more liberal) logic than the national level.

## The construction of multilevel collective actions

The tendency to separate the national and European levels of mobilization is finally confirmed by the analysis of their collective actions. Humanitarian organizations organize their actions on EU asylum policies through what Chabanet (2002) and della Porta (2003) defined as the process of externalization of collective action: 'the mobilization of national bodies targeting the EU in attempt to put pressure on their own government' (della Porta 2003: 12).

In the case of humanitarian organizations, the process of externalization is generally organized through what can be presented as a centralized model: their Europeanized collective actions are coordinated by the umbrella organizations which represent them in Brussels. They aim to change European policies through a mobilization that addresses simultaneously European institutions (at the EU level) and national institutions (at the national level). The organizations based in Brussels address EU institutions whereas member-associations address their national institutions in order to push for changes at the European level. This centralized model has been applied in the lobbying campaign coordinated by *Caritas Europa* during the 2004 European Parliament election campaign. The decision to organize this campaign was taken by the European bureau, which also supervised its implementation. The different national sections of *Caritas* then played the role of representatives at the national level. This is clear in the way *Caritas Europa* presents this campaign:

> The European Parliamentary elections are an important opportunity to meet new elected MEPs. *Caritas Europa* has put together a pack-

age, which member organizations can use as a resource while campaigning with their respective representatives. This package will also be used by *Caritas Europa* in its advocacy work with the European institutions. The resources provided cover *Caritas Europa*'s main work areas.[19]

This quotation is interesting as it shows the extent to which the European office of *Caritas* coordinates the work of the national delegations when it comes to constructing a European mobilization: it presents a 'package' which is then used as a 'resource' by the member organizations. Among other examples, this centralized model of mobilization has been also applied in the lobbying campaign of the German government against the inclusion of the concept of 'safe-third-countries' in European directives in 2004. This campaign was coordinated by *ECRE* at the European level: it addressed the European Commission and the secretariat of the Council whereas the German member-associations (such as the *Arbeiterwohlfahrt*) were exclusively mobilized at the national level. The same process can be observed in the campaign for the withdrawal of the directive on the procedures of examination of refugee statute (in which associations like *Forum Réfugiés* or the *Arbeiterwohlfahrt* were involved): member-associations relayed to their own country the position defined by the central office of *ECRE* at the EU level.

Further analysis of the Europeanized collective actions launched by humanitarian associations shows that they are also often constructed through a second model. This model corresponds to the strategy of the 'boomerang effect' (Keck and Sikkink 1998). This strategy has been illustrated by the case of British environmental organizations (Rootes 2002). In the 1990s, when these organizations saw that opportunities to influence their government directly at home were decreasing, they turned towards the European level in order to put pressure on their own governments indirectly. The European marches against unemployment, precariousness and exclusion in the late 1990s emerged following a similar strategy (Chabanet 2002).

The 'Joint Statement from British and French NGOs on the situation in Sangatte', launched in 2001 by a group of French and British associations (including *France Terre d'Asile* and *Forum Réfugiés*), is a good example of this process. In this communiqué, this group of associations asked European institutions to put pressure on French and British governments in order to come to a solution on the situation in the refugee camp. The European level was thus strategically targeted in order to change a situation that was perceived by these associations as local. Another example of this strategy was the 2002 lobbying campaign of the European institutions (Commission and Parliament) against the German law on the obligation of residence

('Residenzpflicht'). In this campaign, a group of German associations (including the *Arbeiterwohlfahrt*) demanded that the European directives that were negotiated at the moment should abolish this law.[20]

In sum, the Europeanized collective actions of humanitarian associations are based on a distinction and dissociation between the national and the European levels of mobilization. These associations follow the strategy of aiming to change national policies through the European level (whether through the coalitions active in Brussels or directly through the boomerang strategy). Their own collective actions do not address both levels at the same time. This confirms the idea that these SMOs act as 'focal points', representatives of a national situation when they Europeanize. This multilevelled configuration was evoked during the interviews, when the difficulties of coordinating the positions of associations originating from different countries were exposed. Thus, an employee of the *Arbeiterwohlfahrt* underlined the fact that European mobilizations have to take into account the particularities of the situations in each country:

> The European campaigns in which we are involved are very difficult to organize. The European coalitions in Brussels represent associations from more than twenty-five countries. And this means that more than twenty-five different situations have to be taken into account in order to arrive at common positions. In this framework, we (with other associations) represent the German situation. When we are consulted or when all member-associations gather together, we sometimes have to struggle so that the particularities of immigration and asylum policies in Germany are taken into account. In return, we have to relay the positions taken within these coalitions in Germany. This is not always easy to do . . .[21]

In explaining these difficulties, this employee shows clearly how he conceives the role of its association in the process of construction of European mobilizations: a dual-representation in a multilevelled space (where the different levels are rarely connected). More generally, the analysis of their European collective actions confirms that humanitarian SMOs perceive the European approach on asylum as being different from the national approach. Indeed, because of this perception, these actors address both levels separately, with distinct strategies. This also confirms the fact that these associations are involved in centralized European networks. The way in which European lobbying campaigns are organized shows that the secretariats of the groups that represent them in Brussels coordinate their European activities. As I will develop in more depth in the following chapter, humanitarian SMOs do not change the features of their repertoires of collective action (a mainly pluralist repertoire with a corporatist component) when they Europeanize. However, they have to adapt it to the specificities of the European polity. In particular, although they have traditionally been lobbying at the national level, they have to adapt to an EU lobbying which is based on a higher level of juridical expertise. They thus let the secretariats of the groups active in Brussels organize their European collective actions. This confirms again their choice to Europeanize through externalization.

More generally, the mode of Europeanization of these SMOs corresponds to that which has been described by various studies on EU activism. In his comparative analysis of the European networks *ECAS* and *CEDAG*, Weisbein (2002) has underlined the difficulties faced by national member-associations when they attempt to go beyond their role of national representatives. He has shown that this gap between the European secretariats and the national member-associations has prevented national associations from formulating common Europeanized claims and thus from defining a Europeanized mobilization. Rootes (2002) has also shown that when they mobilize around EU policy issues, British environmental groups act more as representatives of national interests than of European interests (for similar conclusions on the activities of trade unions at the European level, see also Branch 2002). This tendency to separate the work of the European structures from that of the national member-associations has been also observed by Geddes (2000) in his analysis of the European groups acting in Brussels for 'migrant inclusion in the European Union'. He highlighted the fact that these European 'umbrella' structures are characterized by 'hierarchy and discipline' (the contrary of horizontal coalitions) (Geddes 2000: 8).

## The Europeanization of politicized associations: from domestication to the construction of transnational and multilevel movements

During the 1990s, politicized SMOs followed a process of domestication of their collective actions: they recognized the European dimension of immigration and asylum policies and attempted to put pressure on their government in order to influence European policies. This was done mainly through communiqués, information campaigns and the inclusion of Europeanized claims in the calls for demonstration or petitions launched at the national level. Since the end of the 1990s, in contrast to humanitarian associations, politicized SMOs design Europeanized mobilization in which the national and European levels are more clearly connected. This is visible in terms of their networks, cognitive frames, strategies and repertoires of collective action. As is illustrated by the campaigns of *Migreurop* and *No Border* presented in the introduction, they construct horizontal and transnational networks and they perceive EU and national asylum policies as being guided by a similar logic. Their actions are addressed simultaneously at national and European institutions, and they tend to use contentious forms of protest at both levels. Some French and German politicized associations (those acting for the defence of human rights and for a more just and egalitarian society) combine these modes of Europeanization with those of humanitarian associations. This leads them to construct multilevelled social movements. The other SMOs (principally militant organizations) construct transnational social movements: they act independently of the sphere comprising the centralized groups based in Brussels.

## The creation of horizontal and transnational networks

The European networks in which French and German politicized associations are involved contrast with those of humanitarian associations. The network analysis (see tables 9 and 10 in chapter three) shows that they are involved in transnational networks which are not directly represented in Brussels. They participate in particular in the network *Migreurop*, in informal networks mobilizing for the regularization of undocumented migrants and against border controls, and in cross-issue networks such as the European Social Forums or Euromayday. These networks are thus less formalized and centralized than those of humanitarian organizations. Their organizational structure is horizontal: they work mostly thanks to the voluntary involvement of the member-associations. In 2005, *Migreurop* created a central office. The informal network that was created in 2002 (see below) was thus transformed into a more official structure. However, this process led to internal discussions that showed a willingness to define non-centralized types of networks. It was thus highlighted during an interview that activists were reluctant to create a secretariat that would be disconnected from the member-associations. They wanted to keep its 'grass-roots' nature (in the sense that member-associations determine their own agenda-setting and decision-making).[22] Consequently, *Migreurop* did not centralize the activities of the network with its central office. This is clear from the official statute of the individuals composing this bureau: they are employees of member-associations and work as volunteers for *Migreurop*.[23] Moreover, decisions are not taken by the bureau alone; they are taken after a deliberation (through exchanges on the mailing-list) of the member-associations.

The European networks mobilizing for the regularization of undocumented migrants and against border controls are also based on non-centralized organizational models. This was evoked during interviews with different activists involved in them. One activist from the *Frassanito* network insisted on this aspect:

> Some associations and activists are more active than others in the Frassanito network. I would say that there are around fifteen or twenty people who constitute sort of the hardcore of Frassanito. But we don't really have a structure. Our activities are based on the voluntary participation of the members. At some points, some are more active than others, but depending on what we do this can change. We are very flexible. And we try to take decisions unanimously, on the basis of the idea that whoever doesn't express a disagreement on a proposal approves it. Our mailing-list is a very effective tool for this. It permits the participation of everyone.[24]

Further analysis of these networks shows their transnational nature. In contrast with the networks of humanitarian associations, the distribution of roles between the central structure (when existing) and the member-organizations is not organized through the dynamic of dual-representation of national associations. Member-associations act as components of a transnational movement rather than as national 'focal-points'. Consequently, the national context of member-associations is not central. This was underlined as followed by an activist of *Migreurop*:

> We take our past and present experience at the national level into account of course. But we (*Gisti*) don't act as 'a French representative' in *Migreurop*. We try to construct a mobilization that goes beyond the national level. So at some point we have to forget that we are French, Italian or Spanish associations. In the way we organize in *Migreurop*, we try to find convergences across countries. When we write communiqués, we don't make a synthesis of different national situations. For example, we can write a communiqué about the situation in Lampedusa or Sangatte because we think that it is representative of the general logic of European policies. So when *Migreurop* writes about these situations, it doesn't do it because there are Italian or French associations in it that are worried about national measures. It does it because it believes that these are European situations.[25]

The willingness to go beyond national situations is thus fundamental to the way in which these networks are constructed. In this interview, this activist argues that *Migreurop* does not try to 'make a synthesis of different national situations'. It rather uses the term 'convergence' in order to describe the organization of the network. The same term is also used by the *No Border* network in its website presentation:

> The no border network is born of the convergence of campaigns in various European countries at the moment when undocumented foreigners had started to get self-organized to get together and become visible to all (occupations, especially of churches, actions, demonstrations), to take their struggle in their own hands, in short to be autonomous. Freedom of movement, documents for all, abolish racist laws, no deportations were the main slogans of these *sans-papiers*.[26]

The choice of the term 'convergence' is significant because it shows that these European networks are not based on a multilevelled dynamic. The term 'convergence' suggests indeed that a European mobilization is created through a transnational configuration. In other words, the European mobilization is not situated above national mobilizations; it is situated in their continuity, in the sense that there is no separation between the national and European level in the organization of these networks. This analysis shows that these networks are created through direct linkages between national associations: there are no central structures that play the role of coordinator and of intermediary between member-associations. The form of these networks suggests thus the idea of continuity: they are an extension of their mobilization beyond national boundaries and across countries.

However, we have to specify that some of the politicized associations have combined two different modes of Europeanization of their networks. Human rights associations like *Amnesty International, Pro Asyl, Cimade* or the *Ligue des droits de l'Homme* are involved in transnational networks as well as in more centralized coalitions based in Brussels. These associations are all part of the *European Council on Refugees and Exiles* or of *European Network Against Racism*. Moreover, *Amnesty International* and the *Ligue des droits de l'Homme* have each created a European delegation in Brussels: *Amnesty International European Office* and the *European Association for the Defence of Human Rights*.[27]

## A process of frame-extension and frame-bridging

The frame analysis reveals that politicized SMOs follow two processes when they Europeanize their discourse: frame-extension ('the extension of the boundaries of a framework so as to encompass interests or points of view that are incidental to the primary objectives but of considerable salience to potential adherents'; Snow et al. 1986) and frame-bridging ('the linkage of two or more ideologically congruent but structurally unconnected frames regarding a particular issue, problem or set of events'; Snow et al. 1986). This leads them to rely on similar framing-processes when they refer to the national context and to EU asylum policies.

First, one can refer to the annual reports published by these associations in order to illustrate these similarities. Thus, in the 2004–2005 report of *Pro Asyl*, the evolution of European asylum policies is directly linked with that of the German policy:

> In 2004, the Refugees' day was organized under the slogan 'Europe fortifies itself'. *Pro Asyl* criticized the fact that Germany plays a leading role in the race to be the most efficient country in terms of refugee expulsions. In particular, the minister of the Interior Schily is responsible for the rigid policy towards refugees in Germany and for the attempt to make the EU a continent without refugees through the externalization of asylum policies.[28]

Moreover, in this quotation and in the rest of the report, similar frames are used in order to present the German and the European situations: the defence of fundamental rights, anti-racism and anti-discrimination, the promotion of new fundamental rights, and the humanitarian frame. The continuity between the national and Europeanized discourses is also visible in the communiqués, calls and petitions produced by these associations. The link between national and European policies is often evoked, and both policies are presented through the same framing-processes. Thus, the petition that was launched by *Cimade* in 2003 (and signed by numerous politicized associations across Europe) uses as its point of departure a decision taken by the Council of the European Union:

> The council of the European Union has just reached a political agreement on a text organizing joint chartered flights for the removal of migrants.[29]

It then links this decision – 'taken at the European level' – with the policies implemented at the national level by most of the European countries 'for twenty years':

> Furthermore, expulsions by chartered flights are the symbol and incarnation of a European policy centred on repressive measures. It is now time to assert and to explain to public opinion that a policy centred on 'more and more controls' characterizes a dead-end and a threat to democracies.
>
> A dead-end because, while the economic and democratic gap between our countries remain, it is an illusion to think that security measures will be able to discourage and prevent candidates for emigration or asylum to seek a better life or refuge.
>
> A threat because this false belief in the efficiency of police controls can only – as it can be seen in the past twenty years with the continuous hardening of the European legislations – weaken fundamental freedom and the constituent principles of rule of law and leads to the constitution of a repressive regime at the European level.[30]

The text then goes further by saying that the policies implemented by the EU and by 'Northern countries' are – in 'collective memories' – in continuity with the policies of colonialism and of slavery that have been practised for centuries:

> Such a haughty indifference of the rich countries in treating persons from countries directly hit by conflicts and poverty recalls and revives memories of a collective perception of centuries of domination, exploitation and humiliation.[31]

The explicit comparison between current European immigration and asylum policies on one hand and the periods of colonialism and slavery on the other has to be put into context: this comparison is not rare but it is not systematically made by these associations. One finds it in particular in documents relating to deportation policies. As it comes from a French association, one should recall that this petition was launched at a moment when French history of colonialism and slavery was being widely debated in the public sphere.[32] However, this example is illustrative because it shows that in their discourses these associations establish a continuity between the 'national approach' and the 'European approach' on immigration and asylum issues. This continuity is established on the basis of their perception of the history of 'Northern countries', immigration and asylum policies and the history of the relationships between 'Northern' and 'Southern' countries and populations. This idea was clearly expressed during an interview with an activist of the *No Lager* (*Kein Mensch Ist Illegal*) network in Germany:

> We are a Left anti-racist association. This means that we fight against the racist policies of exploitation of migrants by Northern liberal states. In this perspective, our action has since its beginnings had an international dimension. The policy implemented by the German state today is of course the one we fight concretely, but this policy is not specifically German. It is more generally the policy that is implemented by European and Northern states towards states and populations from the South. This is the sense of the motto: 'we are here because you destroy our countries'.[33]

Following these arguments, it is because these associations have a politicized discourse that they establish a continuity between the national and the European approaches. The features of their discourse lead them to develop arguments that go beyond the national level. More generally, one can recall that – in contrast with humanitarian associations – their framing-processes are not based on the statement of concrete individual situations. I have underlined the fact that the frames of politicized associations are more principle-oriented: they relate to general principles (anti-racism, the defence of fundamental rights, etc.) rather than to particular situations. This discourse is therefore less entrenched in the local context. Consequently, the construction of a process of frame-extension is easier for politicized SMOs than for humanitarian associations. This dynamic can clearly be seen in the communiqué launched by the *Coordination Nationale des Sans-Papiers* in 1999:

> Three years ago, we were some hundreds of people occupying the Saint-Ambroise church. In doing so, we presented to the French, European and international public the question of the administrative situation of the political refugees and migrants coming to live in Europe. [. . .] Today, thousands of people are still living in Europe without having any rights.[34]

In this document, a particular situation ('some hundreds of people') is presented in order to put forward general principles (the defence of fundamental rights, framed through the denunciation of 'the total absence of rights'), and this general principle is then extended beyond national boundaries ('several thousands of people in Europe'). In the same communiqué, a direct link is made between the prognostic frame (the definition of what should be done in order to resolve the problematic situation) and the situation in France and in Europe:

> The 18th of March is an important day for us and for all the democrats that support us in our fight for equality of rights. Beyond the symbol, the 18th of March is a day of reunion, of fight and of renewal. The 18th of March stays in our minds as an important day that we will celebrate through the unity of our movement in a big demonstration. In the perspective of the European meeting on the 27th March in Paris, we will walk together in order to celebrate the third birthday of the fight of the *sans-papiers*.[35]

These examples show that French and German politicized associations present similar types of frames when they refer to national and European levels. They justify their mobilization on EU policies as providing a continuity with their mobilization at the national level.

This process of frame-extension is often coupled with a process of frame-bridging. While the process of frame-extension is related to the targets and strategies of action, frame-bridging is mainly related to the construction of identities and the definition of a cause. Indeed, in the course of their interactions with SMOs mobilizing around other issues (during events such as the European Social Forums in particular), they tend to establish links with other causes and to participate in the definition of general master frames such as the 'global justice movement' (della Porta et al. 2006). This is visible in the 'Call for a second European day of action for freedom of movement and the right to stay' (signed by several hundreds of SMOs across Europe), in which the situation of migrants is linked to the situation of the 'whole workforce':

> Camps are the dark symbol of a migration politics which is not simply aimed at keeping refugees and migrants out of Europe, but rather at promoting a process of selective inclusion, also through illegalization, of the migrants. This process corresponds to the production of a hierarchy of rights as well as of legal and political positions, that lies at the core of the material transformations of citizenship in Europe and which is far from regarding only the migrants. And it corresponds to a new model of labour force management centred upon precarization and exploitation. The migrants are the subjects who experience in advance life and labour conditions that the whole workforce, certainly with different degrees, is beginning to experi-

> ence in Europe. But on the other hand, their practices of mobility express a set of claims and demands which at the level of everyday life point to a different Europe. That is why we want to bring these interconnections and twenty-three demands inside the Euro-May Day process and therefore call for a strong participation to the 1st of May 2005.[36]

This process of frame-bridging is important as it points to the fact that European social movements participate in the creation of new forms of identities through the construction of joint demands. This evolution is above all visible in the German case, where, for historical reasons, the cause of asylum-seekers and refugees is more isolated than in France. Thus, the anti-G8 protests in Rostock in 2007 were seen by many pro-asylum SMOs active in Germany as a way to 'reinforce the strategy of alliances' with other social movements (interview 14). As is illustrated by the call for participation in an action-day on immigration at these protests, this strategy is related to a presentation of the struggle for the rights of migrants as being part of a more general struggle:

> We seek connections to other social movements, progressive groups in trade unions and other institutions, who wish to join us in this struggle against social and political inequality and marginalization. For this reason, we will participate in the actions against the G8 summit. We aim for a strategy based on commonality, as we are struggling against the same apartheid and migration regime and for global social justice.[37]

As I will now show, the analysis of the Europeanization of collective action of politicized associations shows that there is also a connection between their collective actions at the national and European levels.

## The construction of transnational and multilevel actions

The analysis of the Europeanized protest events carried out by politicized SMOs shows that they construct particular types of actions: they target both national and European polities simultaneously through a mobilization at the transnational level. These actions have several fundamental features. First, they are 'multi-target' and 'multi-strategy': they address national and European polities at the same time in order to demand changes in EU and national policies. These changes are demanded directly (addressing the EU in order to demand changes in EU policies for example) or indirectly (addressing the EU level in order to demand changes in national policies, or the reverse). Secondly, these actions take place neither exclusively at the EU level, nor exclusively at the national level: they are at the transnational level. They are the result of the convergence of the mobilizations across borders. At the transnational level, there is therefore no real distinction between the European and the national spaces of mobilization. These collective actions address – be they at the local, national or European level – symbols of power related to immigration and asylum policies – be they national or European symbols of power.

This can be seen in the claims put forward in the course of the mobilizations. As an example, one can cite one of the first Europeanized collective actions carried out by a group of politicized associations (the 'European demonstration for an open Europe' in March 1999):

> The progressive harmonization of the European migration policies will be implemented in an essentially repressive way if EU and non EU citizens living in Europe do not undertake to define their common demands and fight together for their approval. Yet, the European Parliament in its resolution of the 17 February 1998 urges 'all Members States to proceed to the legalization of the undocumented immigrants in consideration of human rights and international conventions'. The States ignored this resolution, thus encouraging the permanence of an overexploited illegal labour.
>
> The defence of foreigners' rights does participate in the overall fight for a true EU wide social policy, respectful of all women and men.
>
> This is why the under-signing associations of the EU countries call for a European march on Saturday 27 March 1999 in Paris, followed on the 28th by a working meeting that will give representatives of the various countries an opportunity to inform all participants both about the situation in their respective countries as well as the actions presently undertaken. Against the States' logic of closed borders and repression, enshrined in the Schengen agreements, our organizations together will thus start to impose together on their governments their common concerns about the immigrants' rights and freedom.
>
> Call for a European march
> for the rights and freedom of foreigners
> on Saturday 27 March 1999 in Paris (Place d'Italie)
>
> * for the respect of freedom of movement
> * for an open Europe, respectful of the rights and freedom of foreigners

* for the legalization of the undocumented immigrants
* for the banning of foreigners' deportations and the return to Europe of the deported
* for the closing of retention centres in the countries they exist
* for the abolition of the 'double penalty/jeopardy' where it exists.[38]

This example shows that such collective action is 'multi-target'. The activists address the member-state to demand the regularization of undocumented migrants; and they address the EU to demand a 'true EU wide social policy, respectful of all women and men'. These demands show, moreover, the 'multi-strategic' characteristic of the protest. The activists want to change both European and national policies directly ('our organizations together will thus start to impose together on their governments their common concerns about the immigrants' rights and freedom') and indirectly (when they refer to the resolution of the European Parliament in order to put pressure on member-states).

The way in which these actions are constructed and implemented suggests that they are situated in a transnational configuration: links are established between the local, national and European levels. The 'European action-day for the freedom of movement and the right to stay (here)' which was held in 2005 in most European countries, and the 'European appeal against the creation of camps at European borders' launched by the network *Migreurop* in 2004, are illustrative examples of these forms of protest. They encompass the local, national and European spaces of mobilization. The 'European day of action' was thus carried out simultaneously by numerous associations and networks of activists all over Europe. They protested around the symbols of power relating to immigration and asylum policies that were present at the local or national level (in particular, detention centres and borders). They gave a European dimension to these actions by stressing that these symbols were common to all European countries and by presenting these actions as the result of a convergence of movements in Europe. The 'European appeal against the creation of camps at European borders' was circulated through the Internet, and many associations from most European countries (be they mobilized around the immigration and asylum issue or not) relayed it to their own networks of activists.[39]

The transnational convergence of the mobilizations around immigration and asylum is thus expressed in the demands and in the way in which Europeanized protest events are organized. Collective actions relating to EU policies are conceived and organized as being in the continuity of the collective actions that traditionally take place at the local or national level. As has been stated, this is because politicized associations perceive the European and national approaches on the immigration and asylum issues as being similar and because they create transnational networks. These empirical results converge with those presented in recent studies analysing the processes of Europeanization 'from below'. In his analysis of the marches against unemployment, precariousness and exclusion, Chabanet (2002) has shown how SMOs and activists from different countries were able to create direct transnational links (without the intermediary of European SMOs based in Brussels) and to organize Europeanized protests which addressed both European and national institutions during various European counter-summits. During the course of these mobilizations, demands linking national and European policies were formulated: the denouncing of social inequalities, the need to guarantee the rights of people living in precarious conditions and the rights of the unemployed, and the need to reduce working hours (Chabanet 2002: 462). This dynamic was also observed by della Porta et al. (2006) in their analysis of the first European Social Forum in Florence in 2002. The authors have shown how activists from all over Europe could interact directly, organize Europeanized mobilizations and formulate claims for 'another Europe', for social justice and for 'democracy from below', thereby establishing a continuity between their mobilization at the national and European level.

The analyses of the European marches against unemployment, precariousness and exclusion and of the European Social Forums show however that, due to their heterogeneity – Chabanet (2002: 476) evokes a 'fragile and problematic cohesion' – these movements were only able to coordinate on the occasion of important events such as the European counter-summits and European Social Forums. In their study of the European mobilizations against the closing of a Renault factory in Vilvorde in 1997, Lefébure and Lagneau (2002) arrive at similar conclusions: they show that this movement of protest was only a 'moment' in the European public space. In contradiction to these studies, my observation of the pro-asylum movements shows that SMOs were able to construct durable and stable movements at the transnational level. As a matter of fact, the transnational pro-asylum movement is characterized by more homogeneity and associations are thus able to coordinate on a more regular basis. More developments on this aspect will be presented in the next chapter.

To conclude, one must however specify that some politicized associations have been combining two modes of Europeanization of their collective action. Logically, the group of SMOs which has been also involved (in parallel to the construction of transnational networks) in the centralized coalitions based in Brussels have been also following a process of construction of multilevelled collective actions. One can cite for example the participation of *Pro Asyl* in the lobbying campaign against the directive related to the procedures of examination of asylum demands. Moreover, due to the increasing power of the European parliament since the mid-2000s, groups which exclusively followed a process of construction of transnational movements move increasingly towards the European institutions and construct some forms of multilevelled collective actions. More details about the strategies of Europeanization of these associations will be offered in the next chapter, where this will be analysed in greater depth.

## Conclusions

I have shown in this chapter that, depending on their profile, French and German SMOs mobilizing around the asylum issue have followed two distinct paths of Europeanization. Humanitarian associations have Europeanized through the separation of their national and European networks, frames and collective actions. In contrast, politicized associations have Europeanized through the construction of movements based on a more transnational configuration.[40]

In the introduction, I underlined the fact that European protests could take place in different spaces of mobilization: the European political space, the national political space or the transnational space.[41] I provide a visualization of this idea with figure 2.

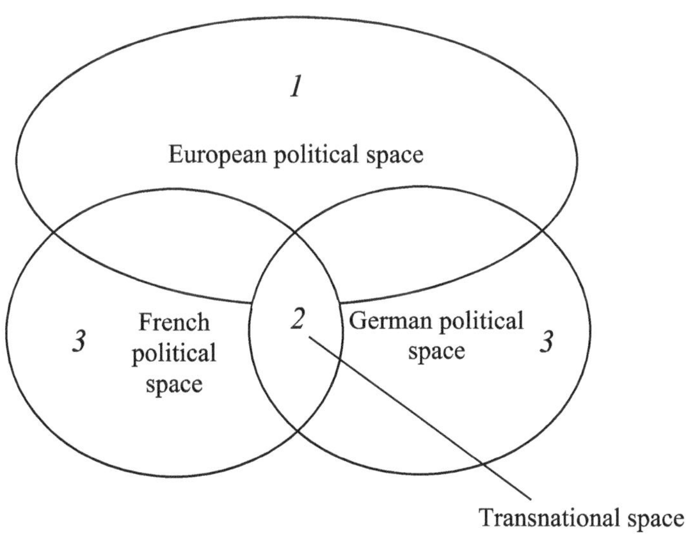


**Figure 2.** The spaces of mobilization around a European policy issue

The empirical results presented in this chapter can be related to this concept of the space of mobilization. I have indeed underlined that, in a multilevelled configuration, European mobilizations take place in the European political space (exclusively around the European institutions in Brussels) and in the national political spaces. Both spaces are however separated in this configuration: the mobilizations address the European and national political spaces separately. Conversely, European mobilizations can take place in a transnational space which establishes links between the national and European political spaces. Thus, referring to the figure, European mobilizations defined through a multilevelled configuration take place in the zones marked as *1* and *3* whereas those defined through a transnational configuration take place in the zone marked as *2*.

More generally, this analysis allows us to appreciate why the literature related to the activities of the lobby groups active in Brussels (Greenwood 1997; Mazzey and Richardson 2002; Favell 2000) remains generally disconnected from that related to the Europeanization of more politicized associations (della Porta et al. 2003; Agrikoliansky and Sommier 2005; della Porta and Caiani 2009). These two streams have different objectives: the first focuses on the European political space whereas the second focuses on the transnational space. Keeping this reflection in mind, we can say that the empirical results presented in this chapter concord with the analysis of Guiraudon (2001). In the conclusion of the previous chapter, I underlined the fact that humanitarian and politicized associations have similar levels of Europeanization. This result could thus not explain the fact that politicized SMOs (more 'grass-roots' groups) are less active in the European political space, and so do not directly address European institutions. My results show that these SMOs are less active in the European political space because they Europeanize through another path which leads them to become involved at the transnational level. In the next chapter, I will explain that this is mainly due to the fact that they criticize EU policies in a more fundamental way than more institutionalized organizations do. I will also show that, in the transnational space, French and German politicized associations address European power-holders indirectly (unlike associations mobilizing in the European political space).

This analysis shows then that there is no general difference distinguishing the modes of Europeanization of French and German SMOs: political associations from both countries have been following the same mode of Europeanization, and the same can be said of humanitarian SMOs. Bearing in mind that the same conclusion was drawn for the degree to which French and German associations Europeanize, one can conclude that the processes of Europeanization of SMOs is not fundamentally determined by the features of the national contexts of mobilization from which they originate. As I will develop below, this means that the dynamics of Europeanization from below (around EU asylum policies) overcome traditional national specificities of protest: the European (or transnational) context of mobilization prevails over national contexts of mobilization.

## Notes

1 *Migreurop*, 'Presentation of the campaign "Right of access in detention centres for migrants"', January 2009.
2 Ibid.
3 No Border, 'Lesvos call against Frontex', August 2009.
4 *Caritas Europa*, 'Caritas tells new Commissioners about its priorities', March 2010.
5 *Caritas Europa*, 'Letter to Commissioner Viviane Reding', March 2010.
6 See this organizational chart on the website www.ecre.org.
7 Interview number 16.
8 www.forumrefugies.org (author's translation).
9 Interview number 16.
10 Interview number 10.
11 www.ecre.org.
12 The 'remaining members' evoked in this abstract represent two of the twelve members of the executive committee.
13 *Forum Réfugiés*, 'L'Asile en France et en Europe. Etat des lieux 2006', June 2006, p.27 (author's translation).
14 Ibid., p.26.
15 Interview number 10.
16 *Forum Réfugiés*, 'L'Asile en France et en Europe. Etat des lieux 2006', June 2006, p.1 (author's translation).
17 *Diakonisches Werk der EKD*, 'Stellungnahme des Diakonischen Werkes der EKD zum Richtlinienentwurf der EU über das Recht auf Familienzusammenführung', April 2000 (author's translation).
18 Interview number 16.
19 www.caritas-europa.org.
20 The fact that humanitarian associations apply this type of strategy does not imply that other types of (more politicized) associations are not involved in these mobilizations. As a matter of fact, associations with different profiles participated in the construction of the collective actions mentioned above as examples. This means that humanitarian associations do not rely on other types of strategies.
21 Interview number 29.
22 Interview number 21.
23 A few years later, however, two people were recruited to work full-time for the bureau.
24 Interview number 19.
25 Interview number 21.
26 www.noborder.org.

27 Further analysis of the strategies of Europeanization of these associations will be presented in the next chapter. I will thus have the opportunity to discuss in greater depth their participation in these European networks.
28 *Pro Asyl*, Tätigkeitsbericht des Vorstandes des Fördervereins PRO ASYL 2004/2005, p.8 (author's translation).
29 *Cimade*, 'Appeal Against Humiliating Chartered Flights', November 2003.
30 Ibid.
31 Ibid.
32 During this period, a group of MPs proposed a law amendment which stipulated that the 'positive role played by France in its former colonies' should be put forward in history instruction manuals.
33 Interview number 1.
34 *CNSP*, '18 MARS 1996–18 MARS 1999. 3 ans de lutte des *sans-papiers*', March 1999 (author's translation).
35 Ibid., March 1999 (author's translation).
36 '2/4: For freedom of movement and the right to stay. Call for a second European day of action For freedom of movement and the right to stay', April 2005.
37 Call for an action-day 'escape and migration', June 2007.
38 'For an open Europe', European demonstration in Paris on 27 March 1999.
39 More details about these collective actions will be presented in the next chapter.
40 Some of the politicized associations have however combined these two modes of Europeanization in terms of networks and collective action.
41 The definition of these different spaces of mobilization has been provided in the course of this chapter.

Chapter 5

# The Europeanization of Social Movements

## A Process of Inclusion into, and Exclusion from, a Particular Field

In 2011, during the wave of protest in Southern Mediterranean countries (known as the 'Arab Spring'), many migrants tried to reach Europe by boat in order to escape the political instability in the region. This was the case in particular in Libya where the protest took the form of a violent conflict between the government and its opponents: according to the *International Office for Migration*, one million people left the country between February and June 2011. However, as much evidence has shown, many of these immigrants could not reach the European territory: most were trapped in refugee camps in Tunisia,[1] and many others (2,000 according to the UNHCR) died in their attempt to cross the Mediterranean by boat.[2] This situation has led to different types of mobilizations on the part of European pro-asylum movements. Thus, in June 2011, a group of organizations including *ECRE*, *Caritas Europa* and *Jesuit Refugee Service* launched a lobbying campaign targeting EU member-states and demanding their intervention for the protection of refugees. In a 'Joint letter to the European Council', the organizations urged 'the Heads of State and Government to give a strong signal of compassion with people in need of international protection and solidarity with the countries in the region'.[3] This campaign points in particular to the question of border controls. The letter to the European Council highlights the 'lack of assistance' to migrant boats that aim to reach Europe. Consequently, the organizations demanded that EU member-states comply with their European and international obligations: they urged 'EU Member states, and in particular the Southern EU Member States directly affected by the new arrivals, to continue to ensure access to the territory and to a fair asylum procedure to those arriving in the EU in line with the EU acquis, Article 18 of the EU Charter of Fundamental Rights and their obligations under international refugee and human rights law'.[4]

During the same period, *Migreurop* and a network of organizations across Europe launched a call in which they denounced the role of member-states as well as of the European Commission: 'Meanwhile, the Commission sent patrols on its sea borders, via Frontex, to prevent potential refugees, considered as irregular migrants, from crossing the Mediterranean Sea!'[5] This call was followed by a series of protest actions involving public opinion at large. The most significant of these actions was the Boats4People initiative: a 'ships of solidarity' rally with the aim of undertaking 'maritime surveillance so that assistance is finally provided to people in danger'.[6] More generally, the objective was to

> create a network of people working on behalf of exiles (members of associations, activists, politicians, journalists, sailors, amateur yachtspeople, artists, inhabitants of the Mediterranean, etc.) and to establish links with exiles themselves in order to initiate new actions, to establish a more permanent observation of events taking place on the borders of the European Union and to fight together against the anti-migratory policy implemented by the majority of Mediterranean governments.[7]

Along the route of the ship from Italy to Tunisia, a series of collective actions and press conferences was organized: activists participated in an anti-racist camp in Cecina (Italy), they organized a protest against detention in Sicily, they attended a preparatory meeting of the 2013 World Social Forum in Tunisia, and they organized a symbolic protest in Lampedusa. Actions aiming at increasing the awareness of this campaign were also organized in Calais, Paris, Frankfurt or Amsterdam.

As this example illustrates, European social movements can mobilize on the same specific issue but with different strategies and through different channels. Thus, in the campaign coordinated by *ECRE* and other groups active in Brussels, the European Commission was more an ally than a target. However, the organizations mobilizing in the second campaign addressed European immigration and asylum policies more generally. Whereas the first campaign was based on a series of direct contacts with representatives from EU institutions, the second campaign placed greater emphasis on raising awareness in public opinion and on developing transnational networks. More generally, this example shows that these movements can have different objectives and mobilize separately. It is thus interesting to note that, although these two campaigns related to the same specific issue, activists did not link them and did not even refer to one another in their communication.

In this chapter I aim to develop an in-depth contextual analysis on the Europeanization of pro-asylum movements. In doing so, I will put into context the results presented in the two preceding chapters. The dynamic of

Europeanization of an SMO is a complex process in which different factors intervene. I will underline in particular that it is composed of two fundamental phases (or steps). These can be briefly presented as follows.

First, the Europeanization of SMOs is determined by the possibility of finding partners across Europe. The process of construction of (or inclusion into) a coalition of actors across borders is the first decisive step through which an association moves to the EU level. It is through this process that common Europeanized frames are activated and that Europeanized collective actions are constructed. As I will develop below, this process can be described as a permanent quest for the best possible coalition. The adequation (or compatibility) of the characteristics of the associations is a fundamental factor that determines the construction of a coalition in a multileveled environment. This leads to the formation of different (and sometimes competing) European coalitions and networks. In this perspective, particular attention will be paid to the relations between the national associations and the set of Brussels-based organizations (international non-governmental organizations and lobby groups) that gravitate around European institutions.

Secondly, the process of Europeanization of an SMO is determined by the possibility of mobilizing adequate resources once it is involved in a coalition. This question is fundamental because it is through the mobilization of specific resources that an association will define its role at the European level. Thus, an association that is able to mobilize the appropriate resources will play a central role in the network in which it is involved; it will participate actively in the construction of common Europeanized frames and collective actions. In contrast, an association that is not able to mobilize the appropriate resources will be less actively involved. It will follow a dynamic of 'passive inclusion' within a particular coalition or network. I will show that, depending on the European coalitions in which they get involved, different types of resources are needed by the associations that are part of them.

As is shown by Favell (2000), the set of agents that interact around the harmonization of immigration and asylum policies constitute a specific 'public policy field'. Following Bourdieu (1987; 1992; 2000), a field is composed of individuals who interact around a particular issue through specific 'cultural practices' and 'values'. In a particular field, elites are in competition for 'social power' through the mobilization of the specific resources (or 'capital') that are attached to the cultural practices and values which are predominant in it. The elites that are established within a specific field are thus distinct from those constituted in other fields because they hold the monopoly of these resources. For example, the elites of the political field are distinct from the elites of the cultural or economic field. Using this reflection for my case of study, I argue that as they are based on new 'cultural practices' and 'values', the interactions between the actors in the European political space are of a different type than those taking place at the national level: they are regulated by (and they reproduce) different 'rules of the games'. The process of Europeanization of immigration and asylum policies has been launched and used by national elites. In particular, the European ministers 'responsible for law and order' saw this process as an opportunity to implement measures that were blocked at the national level (Guiraudon 2000; 2003). However, as policy-making at the EU level requires other forms of 'savoir-faire', new sources of 'social power' have been created and new (Europeanized) elites have progressively emerged. These new elites are distinct from the national elites which launched the process of Europeanization of immigration and asylum policies. In particular, they have distinct formations: they are mainly lawyers and experts in EU policy-making which have been formed in international arenas such as the *College of Europe*. They have distinct cultural practices which are based on the use of several languages and on a knowledge of the European 'jargon'. They also have distinct circles of socialization which are based in Brussels (Favell 2000). Therefore, the process of construction of a European policy corresponds to the construction of a 'new public policy field':

> The existence of a European dimension is a challenge for established national hierarchies. Even if it is a resource that is principally used by – and for – elites, 'Europe' (as an idea and as a set of cultural practices) offers a range of practices and of values which are slightly different from those on which elites rely in national political cultures. (Favell 2000: 4; author's translation)

These perspectives are important and lead us to use the Bourdieusian theory of fields for the study of social movements (for more on this theoretical perspective, see Crossley 2002 and Mathieu 2007). I define the public policy field related to European immigration and asylum policy in a wide sense: it includes all actors that are in regular interaction at the European level in order to participate in the construction of common immigration and asylum policies. This field therefore includes more than institutional actors: associative actors can be part of it. However, not all types of association are included in this field. Following this definition, the associations that are part of it base their activities on regular and close links with European institutions, typically through lobbying techniques. From a theoretical point of view, the use of the concept of field for the analysis of European mobilizations has advantages. It highlights the fact that, because of their specific characteristics, the actors (institutional and non-institutional) interacting on a regular basis in a particular venue do it through specific 'rules of the game': their interactions are based on a set of practices and values that are different from those in other arenas. In other words (and this will be shown empirically), the institutional and non-institutional actors interacting at the European level have different characteristics than those interacting traditionally at the national level. This concept therefore allows us to observe precisely the particularities of a specific European public policy field (the dynamics of interaction within it) and to understand why certain non-institutional actors are involved while others are excluded. In Bourdieu's (1992, 2000) analysis, the definition of particular 'rules of the game' on the part of elites has as a primary function the exclusion of other actors (who do not dispose of specific practices, values and resources) from the competition for 'social power'. In brief, what the concept of field brings to the analysis of the Europeanization of social movements is a sociological understanding of their 'access to Europe'.

In order to understand the Europeanization of the pro-asylum movements, it is first of all necessary to analyse in detail the characteristics of the organizations (international NGOs and lobby groups) that mobilize in Brussels for the integration of these policies. This is the aim of the first part of this chapter. In the subsequent sections, I will analyse in greater depth the dynamic of the Europeanization of humanitarian and politicized associations. I will develop the idea that their Europeanization can be understood as a process of inclusion into, or (auto)exclusion from, the coalition formed by the non-governmental actors gravitating around European institutions since the beginning of the 1990s. I will then show how alternative European coalitions and networks have progressively been formed since the end of the 1990s.

## The organizations active at the EU level since the beginning of the 1990s: a closed European advocacy coalition

Since the beginning of the 1990s, a set of non-governmental actors has been mobilizing around immigration and asylum issue exclusively at the EU level. These are lobby groups like the *Migration Policy Group*, or the *Meijers Committee* as well as European coalitions of associations like the *European Council on Refugees and Exiles* (*ECRE*), the *European Coordination for Foreigners' Right to Family Life*, the *Churches' Commission for Migrants in Europe* (*CCME*), the *European Network Against Racism* (*ENAR*), or the

*Platform for International Cooperation on Undocumented Migrants* (*PICUM*). These are also European offices of international NGOs: *Jesuit Refugee Service*, *Caritas Europa*, *Amnesty International – European Office* (since the end of the 1990s), *Human Rights Watch* (since the beginnings of the 2000s) or the *European Association for the Protection of Human Rights* (since 2000). Their activities started very early, before the Tampere program. For example, *ECRE* was created in 1974, the *European Coordination for Foreigners' Right to Family Life* in 1994, and the *European Platform on EU Migration and Asylum Policy* in 1994. These organizations are in constant interaction with each other: they form a European advocacy coalition. In particular, they meet regularly in the frame of the *Brussels NGOs Platform on EU Migration and Asylum Policy*. Moreover, they have constructed very close links with the institutional actors responsible for the harmonization of immigration and asylum policies: institutional and non-institutional actors are in a relationship of interdependence at the EU level. Indeed, these organizations can be considered as being part of the European field related to the definition of common immigration and asylum policies. They try to exercise influence through their inclusion in this public policy field.

As I now discuss, these actors share very similar characteristics (in terms of discourses, repertoires of collective action, resources and organizational structures). I will argue that it is on this particular aspect that the concept of field can be linked with the study of social movements. It is because they share common characteristics that these actors can interact on a regular basis, and that they can progressively define new practices, new values and a specific 'savoir faire'. Through the definition of these elements, these actors distinguish themselves from other actors, and so are able to enter the public policy field on EU immigration and asylum policies. At the basis of the definition of a specific field (and of the 'social power' that it includes), it is thus necessary to study the characteristics of the agents that are interacting within it. This is what I will underline in the first part of this chapter.[8] Various studies have provided in-depth analyses of the role of these organizations (see, in particular, Favell 2000; Geddes 1998, 2000; Geddes and Guiraudon 2004; Guiraudon 2001; and Ruzza 2004). In the following, I will often relate my own empirical results to the results that they present.

## Framing asylum as a European issue: the promotion of European integration for the defence of refugees' rights

In his analysis of the organizations lobbying 'for migrant inclusion in the European Union', Geddes (2000) has underlined the very technical discourse (in juridical terms) of the groups active in Brussels. Favell (2000) and

Guiraudon (2001) have also stressed this fact. These authors highlighted moreover that this discourse is generally turned towards the promotion of 'more Europe':

> The ECRE, like other prominent pro-migrant organizations, views the supranationalization of immigration and asylum as a favourable development, as more progressive, and as a positive restraining force on member state actions that have tenuous regard for international legal standards. (Geddes 2000: 640)

The application of a frame-analysis to the documents produced by these actors confirms these ideas. This analysis reveals in particular two major characteristics. First, their discourse is based on a similar perception of the asylum issue: it is presented as being separate from other issues, as being fragmented in sub-issues, and it is introduced through a very technical framing formulated in juridical terms. Secondly, their discourse is not turned towards the formulation of general principles: rather, it is policy-oriented, in the sense that it aims to promote EU policy-building. These observations do not imply that these actors produce a homogeneous discourse. As I will develop below, they rely on different cognitive frames and elaborate different forms of argumentations. However, their discourses have common underlying logics. In particular, their features show that they are guided by a logic of inclusion into the European public policy field.

These actors share a similar definition of the scope of the asylum issue. All of them consider asylum as a particular issue, conceptually separated from other fields. They establish a clear distinction, for example, between the asylum issue and the migration issue or the issue of the fight against discrimination. Some of these actors can mobilize on several issues, but they rarely produce a transversal discourse. Thus, in a paper presenting an overview of the measures adopted by EU institutions between 1999 and 2004, *Migration Policy Group* writes:

> Nowadays, migration and asylum are shared responsibilities of national justice and internal affairs ministries and the Commission's Directorate General for Justice and Home Affairs. The Union's mandate to act on these related but distinct issues stems from the 1997 Amsterdam Treaty which sets out the legislative agenda for the creation of an area of freedom, justice and security. [. . .] This paper gives an overview of the developing EU policies in these areas and takes stock of the measures proposed and adopted at European level since the Amsterdam Treaty came into force in 1999.[9]

In this presentation, the immigration issue is clearly separated from the asylum issue: it evokes 'related but distinct issues' and a plurality of 'agendas'. More generally, this document is illustrative because it shows one major feature of the type of discourse that is produced by these actors: its structure follows the agenda of European negotiations. It follows the negotiations on each of the directives in these domains, one separately from the other. It is for this reason that they establish a distinction between asylum and other issues. Because EU institutions develop their competences in these fields following clearly separated agendas,[10] actors interacting on a regular basis with them follow the same logic of fragmentation. Moreover, the asylum issue is separated into various sub-issues, each of them corresponding to a specific directive: the directive on the reception conditions for asylum-seekers, on the definition of the refugee status, on common asylum determination procedures, etc. Consequently, these actors adopt a very technical discourse, following quasi day-by-day (and word-by-word) the evolution of each of these directives, each one separately from the other. Moreover, each of these actors tends to specialize in one particular issue and/or sub-issue in the asylum domain. For example, the *European Coordination for Foreigners' Right to Family Life* tends to specialize in negotiations related to family reunification, *ECRE* follows the agenda related to asylum procedures, *PICUM* has focused on the health conditions of migrants for several years, and *MPG* follows in greater depth the agendas related to anti-racism and anti-discrimination policies. Thus, in an interview with a representative of *Caritas* at the European level, it was argued that:

> The sharing of tasks is something that works very well between our group of organizations in Brussels. For example, in this moment we are working with the *CCME* on the question of the resettlement. We are very much focused on this issue at this moment. The network of the organizations based in Brussels is very efficient and very useful in order to find the adequate alliances depending on the issues that are in the agenda. [. . .] Our natural partners in Brussels are the Christian groups (*CCME, Diakonie, JRS*). It is with these organizations that we work the most because we are logically interested in the same topics. But we actually have a very good coordination with all the organizations that are present in Brussels on these agendas. We can have some differences of point of view of course. But there are no ideological tensions. In fact, in Brussels, every one of us has its speciality, and we act as experts, as technicians, and not as politicized associations.[11]

As it is clear from this interview, the specialization in specific sub-issues logically reinforces the tendency to frame the asylum issue as being separated from other issues. It is moreover revealed in these lines that these organizations present a very technical view of the asylum issue. This is the second major feature of their discourse.

These actors tend to rely on non-reactive types of frames (in the sense that they are not turned towards past or present policy orientations but towards future policy orientations). When they present the purpose of their collective action, one fundamental idea is that the European asylum policy has to be constructed. Thus, the themes of 'policy-building' and 'capacity-building' are central in their discourse. There is the underlying idea that European asylum policies still have to be constructed. Thus, in its introduction, *ECRE* defines its activities in the following way:

> Aim:
> To promote the protection and integration of refugees in Europe based on the values of human dignity, human rights, and an ethic of solidarity.
> Methods:
> ECRE seeks to achieve this aim by:
> 1. Advocating a humane and generous European asylum policy and by promoting the development of a comprehensive and coherent response by the international community to refugee movements.
> 2. Strengthening networking between refugee-assisting non-governmental organizations in Europe.
> 3. Developing the institutional capacity of refugee-assisting non-governmental organizations in Europe.[12]

In the same perspective, *Migration Policy Group* presents its activities with a strong emphasis on its mission of 'policy development' at the European level:

> MPG's mission is policy development on migration and anti-discrimination, with a view to generating innovative and effective responses to the challenges and opportunities of migration and diversity.
> In order to achieve this mission, MPG operates on two parallel fronts: stimulating policy debates and promoting stakeholder co-operation.[13]

As these examples illustrate, these organizations base their activities on the idea that everything has to be done in the domain of asylum policy at the

European level. Consequently, this discourse does not include strong criticism of past and present orientations of power-holders (as it is the case in the discourse of the majority of associations in France or in Germany). On the contrary, the idea of a necessary collaboration with European power-holders is central. Behind the central concept of 'policy-building', there is the idea that they should try to influence the work of the European power-holders through an extensive collaboration.[14] In its introduction, *ECRE* talks for example about the objective to 'provide wide-ranging guidance for decision makers'.[15] Indeed, their inclusion in the public policy field on asylum is already justified through their discourse. They justify their mobilization by arguing that their objectives ('the promotion of the protection of refugees', for example) have to be attained through the construction of an EU policy.

Further analysis of their frames shows that the human rights frame (the idea that EU member-states have to guarantee the asylum right as a consequence of their existing international engagement) is central for them. In the case of *ECRE*, the human rights frame is linked with the humanitarian frame. In the case of *ENAR*, it is bridged with the frame of the fight against racism. Finally, in the case of religious groups like *CCME* or *Caritas*, it is bridged with the humanitarian frame and with that of international solidarity. However, the human rights frame is by far the most central in the discourse of all these organizations. As I developed in chapter two, French and German associations use the human rights frame through what has been defined as a 'principle-oriented' discourse. For them, human rights constitute principles that are above political choices: immigration and asylum policies should conform to these principles. When it is used by the actors of the European advocacy coalition, the sense of the human rights frame is distinct. Unlike the 'principle-oriented' discourse, their framing is 'policy-oriented'. In their perspective, the objective of the respect of human rights is something that has to be achieved through the construction of European policies rather than a principle that is placed above political choices. Therefore, the objective to 'create' a European policy through a concrete and technical process of norm-construction is the first justification of their activity; the idea is to 'promote' or to 'advocate' a respect for human rights. This is for example visible in their objective to define 'best practices' in the domain of the protection and integration of refugees. Consequently, these actors tend to rely on a discourse that is 'politically neutral'. Thus, the *Brussels NGO Platform on EU Migration and Asylum Policy* presents its activities as follows:

> The NGOs Platform on EU Asylum and Migration Policy is an informal group of European non-governmental organizations and networks which works to contribute to the debate on asylum, refu-

> gee and migration policy development in the European Union. The Platform was created in 1994 at the initiative of UNHCR. Meeting regularly to share information and coordinate advocacy strategies, the group is politically neutral and independent. Its participants have an extensive knowledge and expertise on asylum and migration matters.[16]

Once again, it would be misleading to conclude that this group of organizations presents a homogeneous discourse. However, as this presentation of the Platform illustrates, their framing is determined by a common underlying logic. Indeed, by arguing that it 'works to contribute to the debate on asylum, refugee and migration policy development in the European Union', the Platform underlines that it wants to include the public policy field related to EU immigration and asylum policies. As I will develop now, this idea is confirmed by the analysis of their repertoire of collective action, organizational structures and resources.

## A relationship of interdependence with EU power-holders: the principles of 'corridor activism'

All studies which analyse the actors mobilizing around EU immigration and asylum policies have highlighted the fact that their repertoire of collective action is almost entirely based on lobbying techniques. They aim to influence EU policies through the construction of routinized relationships of cooperation with key institutional actors (Ruzza 2004). This leads to the creation of a relationship of interdependence with European institutions:

> The activities of the NGOs in the European circles were intensified when the Commission and the Parliament turned towards 'political' and 'democratic' questions in order to legitimate their competences, so that they could find an alternative to the logic of the European Union (which was above all economical). The NGOs have been inspired by the powerful organizations of lobbying which were long established in Brussels and which managed to obtain the legislation they wanted through their cooperation with the Commission. (Favell 2000: 8; author's translation)

My analysis of their repertoires confirms this analysis. Table 13 sums up the empirical results of this analysis. It represents the repertoire of collective action of the most important actors of this European advocacy coalition.[17] In this table, two Xs represent a type of collective action that is central in the

**Table 13** Repertoires of collective action of the organizations active around the asylum issue in Brussels

| Repertoire of collective action | Type of collective action | Caritas Europa | CCME | ECRE | European Coalition for Foreigners' Right to Family Life | ENAR | Jesuit Refugee Service | Migration Policy Group | PICUM |
|---|---|---|---|---|---|---|---|---|---|
| Protesting | Collective hunger-strike, collective occupation | | | | | | | | |
| | Violent symbolic action | | | | | | | | |
| | Demonstration | | | | | | | | |
| | Presentation of a call or a petition | | | | | | | | |
| | Presentation of a communiqué | X | X | X | X | XX | X | | X |
| Pluralist | Juridical action | | | | X | | | | |
| | Realization of an independent observation | XX | X | X | | XX | XX | X | XX |
| | Organization of a conference or a seminar | X | X | X | X | X | X | | XX |
| | Lobbying | XX | XX | XX | XX | XX | XX | XX | XX |
| | Juridical help provided to asylum-seekers | | | | | | XX | | |
| Corporatist | Application to calls for proposals for grants or missions launched by the institutions | XX | XX | XX | XX | XX | XX | XX | XX |
| | Provision of services on a regular basis | | | | | | | | |

repertoire of an organization (those which are the most frequent in the list of collective actions that they have constructed since the beginning of the 1990s); one X represents a type of collective action that can be carried out by an organization but that remains less frequent.

The analysis shows that their repertoire is clearly non-protesting. In 2004, *ECRE*, *Amnesty International – European Office* and *Human Rights Watch* initiated a call addressed to European institutions (relayed by many associations across Europe) for the withdrawal of the directive proposal on the minimal procedures of examination of the refugee statute.[18] This type of collective action remains however an exception. Four types of collective action are central in their repertoire of collective action: the launching of communiqués, the lobbying work, the realization of independent observations, and the application to call for proposals for grants or missions launched by the EU institutions.

Not surprisingly, the work of lobbying constitutes the most important part of their activities. This is visible in the way in which these organizations present themselves. Thus, the *Brussels NGOs Platform on EU Migration and Asylum Policy* presents its main objectives as follows:

> The primary purpose of the Platform is to discuss developments and issues of common concern within the EU asylum and migration area. In addition, it aims where appropriate to coordinate lobbying approaches and information on key questions for decision at EU level. The aim of this exchange is to achieve better co-ordination between its members and establish common approaches, which can in turn better inform the institutions and Member States which benefit from its contribution.[19]

Mention should also be made of a series of papers published by *ECRE* in 2006. According to the presentation that it gives, its collective action is entirely oriented towards advocacy and the promotion of policy orientations:

> Last year ECRE issued a series of five papers entitled *Europe's Role in the Global Refugee Protection System. The Way Forward: An Agenda for Change.* These proposals provide constructive recommendations on a number of topical refugee policy issues to positively influence the European debate on: improving refugee protection in regions of origin; developing European resettlement activities; creating fairer and more efficient asylum systems in Europe; improving refugee integration; the return of asylum seekers whose applications have been rejected.[20]

This example shows clearly that the main objective of these organizations is to 'provide constructive recommendations [. . .] to influence the European debates'. Among the important lobbying campaigns that they carried out, one can mention *Caritas Europa*'s campaign against human trafficking in 2004 or *PICUM*'s campaign for the access to health care for undocumented migrants in 2005–2006. These campaigns are particularly illustrative because they follow the same typical construction (common to most of the collective actions constructed by these actors). *PICUM*'s campaign started with a research project on the conditions of access to health services for undocumented migrants across Europe. With the expertise gained during this work, the organization was then able to organize a series of informal face-to-face meetings with the relevant institutional actors (principally within the European Commission). It then elaborated a position paper (a series of recommendations) that was circulated more widely in the European institutions (Commission, European Parliament, offices of the Council, etc.). Finally, it built an ad-hoc network of associations across European countries in order to address authorities at the national level (through the centralized model presented in chapter four).

In their framing of the asylum issue, these organizations tend to define different sub-issues or agendas. Logically, this is also the case for their agenda of mobilization. Each of them tends to specialize in one sub-issue and to construct its own advocacy campaign on it. This method of task-sharing leads to the construction of simultaneous campaigns on different questions. However, adequate coalitions are formed around particular campaigns when they feel that more pressure has to be put on European power-holders. This was, for example, the case with the campaign for the withdrawal of the directive proposal on the minimal procedures of examination of the refugee status in 2004. As was illustrated by the example presented in the introduction, it was also the case with the campaign for the protection of migrants coming from Libya in 2011. However, due to their technical and fragmented perception of the asylum issue, there are few global collective actions which address European asylum policies as a whole.

The fact that organizations active around the European institutions (whether on asylum or other issues) concentrate their activities mainly on lobbying has been observed by numerous studies (see in particular Mazzey and Richardson 2002; Greenwood 1997; Clays, Gobin, Smets and Winand 1998; and Chabanet 2001). In his study of the repertoires of environmental groups active in Brussels, Rucht (2002) has shown that lobbying largely prevails over more contentious forms of collective actions: protest on this issue almost never occurred in Brussels in the 1990s. The same findings have been presented by Weisbein (2002) in his comparison of two 'public interest groups' (*CEDAG* and *ECAS*). He has shown that even if they have different strategies of representation, these organizations limit their repertoire of collective action to lobbying techniques and to the provision of expertise to European institutions.

The significance of the last type of collective action (the application to calls for proposals for grants or missions launched by EU institutions) reveals that these actors also rely on a corporatist repertoire. These collective actions are similar to the provision of services to public authorities on a regular basis: they allow the associations constructing them to become involved in the process of elaboration of a public policy (through, for example, the carrying out of studies commissioned and funded by public authorities) and in its process of implementation (though, for example, the management of local projects of reception of asylum-seekers funded by public authorities). They can however be distinguished from the regular provision of services (in which an organization tends to have a monopolist representation in a specific field) as, due to the fact that they are based on calls for grants, they imply a more regular competition between different organizations. Moreover, they generally consist of more specific and short-term projects. Considering what has been developed above, one can however argue that these collective actions belong to the corporatist (or 'neo-corporatist' – Marques-Pereira 1998) repertoire. I have highlighted that each of the European organizations mobilizing around the immigration and asylum issue specializes in a particular agenda: each of them tends to focus on a specific sub-issue. The principal consequence of this is that each of them tends to have a long-term monopolistic representation in the specific domain in which they are specialized: they apply to the calls for grants that correspond to this domain and establish a regular provision of services. Moreover, they have gained the expertise that allows them to match the criteria defined by the European Commission (Guiraudon 2001). The most illustrative example is that of the *Migration Policy Group*. Thus, in his analysis, Favell (2000) stressed that: 'MPG has become a partner (often in its role of secretariat of projects) of the Commission, of the Parliament and of the Council when they wanted to finance research or seminars on immigration' (Favell 2000: 10; author's translation).

The European Commission launches a significant number of calls for proposals for grants, and the European Refugee Fund is the main channel through which it funds studies and projects carried out by non-governmental actors. In 2004, *ECRE* was funded through the European Refugee Fund for a project on 'Refugee stories in a developing common European asylum system'; *CCME* was funded for a project entitled 'Understanding resettlement in practice: capacity building for action'; and *Jesuit Refugee Service* was funded for a mission on the 'training of individuals attending the needs of asylum seekers and refugees in reception and detention centres'.[21] Moreover, the European Commission supports research and action plans that are more limited in time. This is for example the case with the annual 'Anti Discrimination Country Report' carried out by *MPG*; with the 'Book of Solidarity, Providing Assistance to Undocumented Migrants' published by *PICUM* in 2003; and with the project 'Christian Action and Networking Against Trafficking in Women' organized by *Caritas Europa* and *CCME* in 2007. Finally, and most importantly, these groups work as channels to enable member-associations (at the national level) to gain access to projects (in particular, local projects of reception of asylum-seekers) funded by the European Refugee Fund (Valluy 2007).[22]

## The professionalization of collective action

Previous studies have underlined the fact that the groups active in Brussels are highly professionalized. They have also shown that their activities are essentially based on a high level of expertise and on their capacity to build networks of contacts within European institutions. Indeed, they all rely on the same types of resources and they are structured through similar organizational models. Consequently, access to the EU public policy field is limited to a small number of organizations (Favell 2000; Geddes 1998; Guiraudon 2001).

My empirical observation has led me to the same conclusions. Considering the resources of the group of actors mobilizing at the European level, one is aware of strong similarities between the various groups. They are based on a high level of expertise, an important network of contacts with relevant European institutional and non-institutional actors, and financial resources originating from European institutions. Thus, they present themselves as highly qualified specialists and technicians on the immigration and asylum issue. For example, to the question of what it has to offer members of the European Parliament, the *Brussels NGOs Platform on EU Migration and Asylum Policy* answers:

> The Platform can offer a wealth of experience on asylum and immigration law, policy and practice at the European and Member State level. Its members have dealt with asylum questions for many years and understand and can provide expert advice, research and statistics on asylum and refugee rights. They have expertise in legal and political issues that concerns matters on asylum and migration, which will be particularly important

as the EU moves into the second phase of establishment of its asylum system.[23]

A look at the profile of the individuals active in these organizations confirms this idea. There is indeed a significant representation of highly qualified legal experts: many of them have undertaken international training in the field of human rights law or international and European law (*Migration Policy Group* being maybe the most illustrative example). Beside their high level of expertise, all these actors dispose of important social-organizational resources (the ability to construct social networks). During an interview, an employee of *PICUM* stressed that the organization was created by a small group of individuals who had a 'good address-book including relevant people inside and outside European institutions'.[24] These actors have privileged contacts within European institutions (in particular within the European Commission and European Parliament). Individuals within this group of associations and within European institutions are in constant communication, all of them being in a relationship of interdependence. The *Odysseus* network is a perfect illustration of this. This network has been created and is funded by the European Commission and it gathers together members of the Commission as well as members of several European associations, and academics. Its goal is to create a network of experts in order to provide legal expertise and analysis on European asylum policies. In doing so, this network establishes the conditions for the construction of a relationship of dense cooperation, which obviously facilitates the work of lobbying done by these associations. In his analysis of these groups, Geddes (2000) highlighted the fact that most of them are in a situation of financial dependence towards EU institutions. He described this as a process of 'interest co-option' (Geddes 2000: 639). This is confirmed by the analysis of their financial resources. *ECRE* is thus almost entirely financed by funds from the European Union and member-states. In 2004, more than half of its total income (around 1,000,000 GB pounds) came from EU funds (including the European Refugee Fund). The rest of its income came mainly from European governments (or foundations financed by European governments). The same can be said of *ENAR*. Thus, in 2005, from a total income of around 930,000 euros, around 817,000 euros came from European Union support.

An observation of their interactions shows that these organizations constitute a dense network. There is an intense cooperation between them, whether it is formal as in the frame of the *Brussels NGOs Platform on EU Migration and Asylum Policy*, or less formal on a daily basis. To cite one example, we can refer to the creation of the *Anti-Racism and Diversity Intergroup* (*ARDI*) by *PICUM* and *ENAR*. Due to this intense common work, these actors are able to exchange information and expertise very regularly. One can moreover highlight the European dimension of these networks. Each of these associations has an extensive network of partners all over Europe. For example, *ECRE* gathers together around seventy member associations. Moreover, it disposes of the *ELENA* (*European Legal Network on Asylum*) which brings together over 2000 lawyers specialized on the asylum right in Europe, and it coordinates the activities of the *ERAD* (*European Refugee Advocacy Organization*). *PICUM* represents over 200 ordinary and affiliated members, and *ENAR* gathers together over 600 ordinary and affiliated members. The extensiveness of their network is a great advantage for these organizations as it enables them to stress their legitimacy when they address EU institutions. This is clear in the way in which *ECRE* introduces itself: 'With some 70 Member organizations in 30 countries, *ECRE* aims to influence the European agenda to promote the protection and integration of all individuals who seek refuge and protection within Europe'.[25]

Finally, according to the empirical analysis, their organizational models show strong similarities. Each of these organizations has developed an important secretariat (based in Brussels – or in London, as in *ECRE*'s case) that has become relatively autonomous from the member-associations. The day-to-day activities of these organizations is thus based on the work of a small group of professionals (fourteen in *ECRE*'s case, four in *PICUM*'s case, and seven in *ENAR*'s case) with a formalized structure: each of the members of the secretariat has a precise task that is defined in a hierarchical logic. Moreover, these organizations have developed similar centralized structures that are based on the work of the secretariat, the executive committee, the general assemblies (usually bi-annual), and several 'working-groups' related to specific questions.[26] As a consequence of this highly professionalized associative culture, none of these organizations present their activities as a 'mobilization' or as a 'struggle'; rather, they define these activities as 'work'. In this sense, the *Migration Policy Group* represents probably the best example. Thus, when it presents its activities, it employs a managerial vocabulary: 'MPG is a small organization with a highly committed team. We strongly believe in the value of partnership and co-operation, maximizing outcome and impact and reducing costs'.[27]

This high level of professionalization is confirmed by the profile of the individuals active in these groups. As has been evoked above, many of them have undergone similar training. One can moreover underline the fact that most of them entered these arenas at a relatively young age (not long after the end of their training). Their activity in these specific arenas is thus generally not based on experience in the field of social movements. Thus, recruitment in the office of *ECRE* or *PICUM* is carried out through public job offers in which an activist's experience is considered as an advantage and not as a condition (the knowledge of European policy-making and of human rights law, and the demonstration of good communication skills in an international environment are highly valued).

In order to relate these developments to the other dimensions of their profile (their frames and repertoires of collective action), one can refer to the literature on interest mediation at the European level. This literature shows in particular that the constraints on the resources of these associations (their limited human and material resources) explain their dedication to lobbying techniques and their non-critical discourse (Clays, Gobin, Smets and Winand 1998; Weisbein 2001, 2002; Chabanet 2001; Magnette 2000). Indeed, because these organizations do not have the resources to construct transnational collective actions based on the 'call of the number' (Offerlé 1998), they tend to focus on expertise and consequently to privilege lobbying (Greenwood 1997; Ruzza 2004). Moreover, the fact that they largely depend on funding from the European institutions tends to 'diminish their critical sense' (Weisbein 2002: 97). This leads to a risk of 'vassalization' of the groups active in Brussels (Magnette 2000). My empirical results seem to confirm these analyses. They lead however to revise some of these conclusions (at least as regards the groups active around the asylum issue). An analysis of their resources shows that their 'small size' (the fact that they have few human and material resources) is relative. Indeed, even if their activities depend on the work of a small group of individuals, they are able to construct wide networks of associations across Europe. Moreover, these associations dispose of important material resources (through the European Refugee Fund in particular). Therefore, as will be developed below, one can argue that it is their perception of EU asylum policies (the fact that they consider this process as something that should be encouraged and accompanied rather than criticized) and of what is an effective collective action at this level which leads them to privilege a specific profile.

To sum up, the actors mobilizing at the European level since the beginning of the 1990s have similar characteristics. Due to the similarities in their profiles, these actors have defined a strong inter-organizational cohesion made up of mutual recognition and exchanges of information, and they have organized their collective actions through a method of task-sharing. Consequently, they have become the privileged – and almost exclusive – interlocutors of European institutions representing civil society. This analysis leads us to draw some conclusions about the logics that are inherent to this specific field. Some observations, which have been mentioned above, can now be brought together.

First, specific cultural practices and values are attached to this field. I have shown that the actors comprising this advocacy coalition have the same cultural practices as their interlocutors within European institutions (in particular the European Commission). As has been cited, they have followed similar training and base their interactions on a knowledge of different languages and EU jargon and codes. In Brussels, they spend time at the same places and have similar daily activities, thereby developing a common 'habitus' (for more on this dimension, see Favell and Guiraudon 2009). These actors share similar values such as the belief that the rights of asylum-seekers and refugees have to be guaranteed through a process of norm-construction at the European level. In other words, these cultural practices and values are very Europeanized (or, more precisely, 'Brussels-based'): they have developed over time around the activities of the European institutions in Brussels. The 'social power' monopolized by these elites (the fact that they are the exclusive non-governmental interlocutors of European institutions) is the result of their very specific immaterial resources. They organize their activities through their high level of expertise and their direct contacts within European institutions. This allows them to be included in the public policy field related to EU immigration asylum policies and to gain in return exclusive access to European funds. More generally, the analysis reveals that this field is regulated through specific 'rules of the game'. In particular, the interactions between the agents present in it are determined by a depoliticized handling of the asylum issue (in the sense that it is turned towards the technicality of EU norm-making) and by a separation of it from other public policy fields (in the sense that they promote a perception of the asylum issue as being disconnected from other issues). Another important 'rule of the game' is that the interactions between the actors involved in it take place in a field that is distant from public opinion (in the sense that these actors rarely involve public opinion – through the media or through public meetings for example – in their activities). Finally, this field is euro-centric (in the sense that only actors from European countries are present).[28]

As I will develop in the following sections, the particular characteristics of these actors determine the confines of the public policy field in which they are involved. This has influenced in a fundamental way the processes of Europeanization of the pro-asylum movements traditionally mobilized at the national level. Depending on the features of their own identity, associations active at the national level will consider whether or not their demands can be represented by the actors of this advocacy coalition. National associations that share similar characteristics with these actors will feel that they can represent their demands. They will thus consider integration into existing European coalitions as a natural channel of Europeanization. Moreover, the actors constituting the European advocacy coalition will logically privilege collaboration with national associations that share similar features with their own. On the contrary, national associations that do not have a similar identity to the actors of this European advocacy coalition will feel that their demands cannot be represented by them. They will not participate in existing European coalitions of associations and they will thus choose (at least initially) to remain excluded from this particular field.

## Why and how humanitarian organizations were included into this field

French and German humanitarian associations have followed a process of inclusion into the European advocacy coalition established in Brussels since the beginning of the 1990s. These associations have a profile that is relatively close to these actors, and they could therefore easily find allies at the EU level. This has favoured their inclusion into the European public policy field related to immigration and asylum. These associations share with the group of EU organizations a perception of the asylum issue as being more policy-oriented than principle-oriented. Their similarities are even more evident when their repertoires of collective action are compared. They rely on a repertoire that is limited to non-protesting forms of collective action. And they tend to construct corporatist types of relationships with power-holders. Finally, the high level of professionalization that characterizes their associative culture is also an important similarity.

Due to these similarities, French and German humanitarian associations consider their integration into the existing European advocacy coalition as a natural channel of Europeanization: they perceive the organizations active in Brussels as natural partner-associations. Thus, the associations devoted almost exclusively to the provision of services (*Forum Réfugiés* and *France Terre d'Asile* in France and the *Arbeiterwohlfahrt* in Germany) have all integrated into the *European Council on Refugees and Exiles* (which defines itself as 'a pan-European network of refugee-assisting non-governmental organizations').[29] Through their participation in *ECRE*, these associations pursue two major objectives. This is explicit in the presentation of *Forum Réfugiés*'s involvement in this structure:

> Since 1999, *Forum Réfugiés* is a member of the European network *ECRE* (European Council on Refugees and Exiles) and it therefore participates in various works on questions relating to asylum law at the European level. The joint positions on the agenda of European

> authorities are adopted in the framework of this network. Privileged relationships are created with the seventy-six member-associations, which are based in the European Union and in the countries of central and Eastern Europe. We relay the adopted positions through different means at the national level – in particular through meetings with the ministers concerned – and we also publish press communiqués.
>
> *Forum Réfugiés* is also involved in European programs which support the actions of reception and integration of refugees in member-states of the European Union.
>
> Thus, in the framework of the European Refugee Fund, *Forum Réfugiés* has benefitted since 2000 from European co-financing in order to implement several projects.[30]

The first aim of these SMOs is the adoption of common positions through the creation of 'privileged relationship' with partner-associations over Europe. *ECRE* allows associations from different European states to gather together, so that they can share experiences and information; indeed, this was its *raison d'être* when it was created in 1974. Moreover, participation in this structure allows them to access information and analyses that are hard to come by for national associations not in direct contact with the European institutions. The second aim is the access to the finances offered by the European institutions (the European Refugee Fund or the EQUAL program, for example). *ECRE* works as a channel that allows indirect access to these funds. It offers its member-associations the cultural savoir-faire and connections which are necessary to answer the calls for proposals for grants that are launched by the European Commission (Guiraudon 2001).

The humanitarian SMOs with a religious background (*Secours Catholique* in France, *Caritas* and *Diakonie* in Germany) have logically integrated into the group of European religious coalitions (the *Churches' Commission for Migrants in Europe*, in particular). They have also integrated into *ECRE* or *ENAR*. Moreover, *Caritas* and *Diakonie* have created their own offices in Brussels (*Caritas Europa* and *Eurodiakonia*). The significance and the role of these European networks were highlighted during an interview:

> The Christian network is logically our first network at the European level. Traditionally, it is with the Christian associations that we have worked the most, and it is thus with them that we have more contacts. This network works very well as far as the asylum issue is concerned. Within the *CCME* (*Churches' Commission for Migrants*

> *in Europe*) in particular, we have a good coalition and we manage to take common positions easily even if every one of us comes from different countries and from different traditions. This network is moreover very helpful in a more practical sense as it permits us to exchange information and practices that can improve our day-to-day work with asylum-seekers and refugees. In a context of harmonization of the asylum procedures, this is something that is very helpful. This is something that we also do through our participation in other networks like *ECRE* in particular.[31]

As is explained in this interview, humanitarian associations with a religious identity have followed (like associations that are devoted almost exclusively to the provision of services) a process of inclusion into the pre-existing European advocacy coalition. Several reasons have led them to follow such a process. It permits them to define common positions at the European level and to exchange practical information related to the work of solidarity with asylum-seekers and refugees. We should remind ourselves that these organizations are also service-providers. Thus, this process also allows them to benefit from the financial programs launched by the European Commission (in particular the European Refugee Fund).

However, with their inclusion in this particular field, humanitarian associations have to adapt to some of its specificities. This is particularly the case in terms of their framing. Their frames have some fundamental features in common with those of the groups active at the EU level. In particular, they are non-reactive and politically neutral: the definition of diagnostic and responsibility frames is not fundamental in their discourse and they are generally formulated in a non-politicized way. However, they are also characterized by some differences: humanitarian associations rely almost exclusively on the humanitarian frame whereas the organizations active in Brussels tend to rely on the human rights frame. This leads humanitarian associations to transform their frames (the process of frame-transformation) when they produce a discourse that is related to the EU level. As I analysed in chapter four, this frame-transformation is one of the main factors that leads humanitarian associations to construct a multileveled configuration when they mobilize around EU asylum policies. Relating this to the analysis of their mode of Europeanization, it is because the field of lobbying on EU asylum policies is homogeneous that humanitarian associations are led to a multilevel configuration. The organizations active in this field represent their natural partner-organizations; however, they have to adapt to their characteristics. This adaptation is also related to the question of their resources. Indeed, a knowledge of European policy-making and the socialization processes around European institutions are by definition new for associations that have traditionally acted at the national level. This idea was stressed during an interview:

> Our activity is almost entirely geared towards the day-to-day work with asylum-seekers and migrants. We therefore have a different profile from the experts that are in Brussels. We simply don't act with the same tools. In the *Secours Catholique*, at the national level, we have major difficulties in following what is going on within the European institutions. It is something that is very technical and that is constantly changing. So many decisions are taken that it is very difficult to see which are the important ones. Moreover, it takes lots of time to follow all this. So I think that it is very important that there are these non-governmental experts in Brussels that can dedicate all of their time to European negotiations. They have been following these issues for many years now, and they have thus gained the necessary experience in order to be efficient at this level.[32]

As this interview illustrates, the adaptation to the features of the European field leads these organizations to separate their activities at the national and EU levels: they belong to different logics. Consequently, their Europeanization can be analysed as a process of delegation of competences based upon the agenda of the EU umbrella group. Humanitarian organizations therefore participate in the centralized structure of *ECRE*, assuming the role of focal point between the EU and the national level.

However, some of the humanitarian associations have adapted more easily to the 'ways of doing' established at the EU level, and they have therefore been playing a more important role directly at this level. This is the case in particular of *Caritas* and *Diakonie*, which have a high level of expertise and important social-organizational resources at the national level (see chapter two). This is particularly true for *Caritas Deutschland*: its presence has been notable in this arena since the mid-1990s. It is very active within the *Caritas Europa* coalition, and it has also created its own delegation in Brussels, where it employs two people. For example, *Caritas* uses the variety of its resources in order to play a central role in European lobbying campaigns to combat and prevent human trafficking. In particular, it has based its participation in this campaign on the knowledge of the European policy-making that it has acquired and on the personal contacts that it has created in this arena over time.[33] It also played a central role (through *Caritas Europa*) in an advocacy campaign during the European parliamentary elections in 2004. *Caritas* was the key organization that launched the creation, in January 2007, of the European network *ERSO* (*European Reintegration Support Organisations*), which is co-financed by the European Commission. This network is described in the following way by two *Caritas* sections that participate in its activities:

> Caritas Belgium – 'ERSO is: a gathering of Skill, Knowledge and Will'.
>
> Caritas Essen – 'ERSO – A network of voluntary return counsellors, putting their resources together to support refugees on their way back home'.[34]

One notices in this quotation how the question of resources (and in particularly the level of expertise) is emphasized by the member-associations. This shows that it is through the mobilization of the adequate resources that associations like *Diakonie* and *Caritas* can be included in the European advocacy coalition to a greater extent than other organizations. Although they have a lower level of Europeanization, associations that do not initially have the specific resources necessary in this particular field can progressively gain access to them through their involvement with this coalition. This is the case with *FTDA* and *Forum Réfugiés*, which have enjoyed increasing importance within *ECRE* since the mid-2000s.[35] Thus, since 2005, *Forum Réfugiés* has employed a person that actively follows the work of *ECRE*. Through this more constant presence, it has gained a higher expertise in the field of European asylum policies and can develop its contacts in Brussels. *Forum Réfugiés* has therefore become *ECRE*'s most important contact (or focal point) in France, and is able to access significant European projects. In particular, the association has benefitted from European funds in order to develop its activities in Morocco (Valluy 2007).

This question of resources leads to a more general conclusion on the use of the concept of field to analyse social movements at the EU level. Indeed, this dimension is fundamental in Bourdieu's theory of fields. According to him, the position of an agent within a particular field is largely determined by its ability to mobilize the adequate resources (or 'capital'). Indeed, elites are constituted by the agents who dispose of these resources to a large extent and who manage to monopolize them. Consequently, the question of the resources largely determines the 'rules of the game' within a particular field. In this case, the analysis shows that the specificity of the resources used at the EU level leads to the centralized and multilevel nature of the mobilizations constructed by the European advocacy coalition.

## Why politicized organizations remain excluded from this field

In contrast to humanitarian associations, politicized associations remain relatively distant from the advocacy coalition which has been active around the field of EU immigration and asylum policies since the beginning of the 1990s. Most of them have no regular contact with them. Some of these associations have followed a process of inclusion into this field; however, this inclusion has been limited to temporary periods of involvement for their own purposes. Politicized SMOs have a critical view of these actors. In particular, one important point that was raised during the interviews is that they could not represent their demands. For them, their perception of the Tampere process, and their 'way of doing things' in general, do not correspond to their own collective identity. This idea was developed in an interview:

> *ECRE* and this type of organization have been created by the European Commission. We have problems working with them. We have very divergent points of view regarding the role of associations towards authorities. I personally went to some of the meetings organized by this network in Brussels . . . And it simply doesn't correspond to the way in which we work. In the *LDH*, we do technical work when we act on asylum policies. This is inevitable because this is a very complex issue in terms of laws and procedures. But at the end, we don't act as technicians. We have a politicized action because somehow we believe that things can only be changed if we denounce the general political orientations that lie behind the technical measures. There are evident political orientations that guide the general tendency towards restrictive asylum laws. This is true in France; this is true in other European countries; and this is true at the European level. We have to work to denounce these orientations at all these levels. [. . .]. And I think that this is not what organizations like *ECRE* or *ENAR* are doing because they act as technicians.[36]

In particular, as is made clear in this interview, the technicality of the discourse that is produced by the European advocacy coalition is a strong point of criticism. Too technical a discourse would not allow them to present the Tampere program in a general and political way. For this reason, an adaptation to this type of discourse would lead them to contradict their political perception of the asylum issue. Moreover, this would lead to a strong disconnection in the associations between the 'technicians' of the European asylum policy and their activist basis.

More generally, politicized organizations argue that the profile of the groups active in Brussels comes in contradiction with their own profile. Thus, an adaptation to their non-protesting repertoire of collective action would lead them to contradict their own traditional repertoire by abandoning the actions that are based on the 'call to number'. And the same can be said regarding their associative culture, which is different from the professionalized culture of the organizations active in Brussels (with the exception of some associations like *Pro Asyl* or *Amnesty International*). Finally, another point of criticism concerns the financial dependence of these organizations on European institutions. This was underlined in the following interview:

> We are quite different from the group of organizations that does lobbying around the European institutions. They don't have our history and we don't have the same kind of relationship towards power-holders. As you know, these are structures that are entirely financed by the European Commission. And this causes us some problems in Amnesty because we believe that – in the end – you behave differently with authorities if they are the ones that finance you. In Amnesty, we strongly believe that the independence of our action and of our discourse can only be guaranteed if we maintain monetary independence.[37]

Thus, unlike the case with humanitarian associations, Europeanization through this channel would lead to too many contradictions for politicized associations. Their involvement in the European advocacy coalition remains at a low level. Most of them do not participate at all in their activities. Some of them are part of *ECRE* or *ENAR* (this is the case with *Cimade*, *Pro Asyl*, the French and German sections of *Amnesty International*, and the *Ligue des droits de l'Homme*).[38] However, they do not participate in their everyday agenda-setting and decision-making processes.[39] *Cimade* or *Amnesty International*, for example, are members of the *European Council on Refugees and Exiles*, but they no longer participate in the bi-annual conferences organized by this body.

However, for limited periods of time, some politicized associations are very active in some of the campaigns that are carried out by these European structures. In particular, associations that have a high level of expertise and dispose of important social-organizational resources (such as *Amnesty International*, *Gisti*, *Cimade*, *Pro Asyl* or the *Ligue des droits de l'Homme*) are able at times to influence the work of these groups. For instance, in 2004,

*Gisti* coordinated the campaign carried out by the *European Coordination for Foreigners' Right to Family Life* for the retreat of the directive on family reunification. It wrote the juridical argument that was used for the action at the European Court of Justice. Another example is the leading role played by *Cimade* in the inter-organizational communiqué on the conditions of return of undocumented migrants and rejected asylum-seekers in 2005.[40]

Although, the involvement of these SMOs in this field is limited, these associations remain part of these structures for two main reasons. The first reason is that it gives them access to information that would otherwise be inaccessible. This explains why the *European Association for the Protection of Human Rights* decided to get involved in *ECRE* in 2005. The second reason is that it gives them access to European networks that are already constituted and that they can use on a temporary basis for their own purposes. *Cimade*, for example, used the network of *ECRE* and *CCME* to launch its petition against the return charter flights for migrants in 2003. In the same way, it could rely on the networks constituted by these structures when it participated (with the other associations of *Migreurop*) in the elaboration of a 'map of foreigners' camps in Europe' in 2003 (see below). In the first example, the involvement of *Cimade* in these structures helped the association to give a European dimension to the petition that it launched. *ECRE* or *CCME* represented already existing European-wide platforms of SMOs that could be easily contacted and informed. In the second example, its involvement helped the association to access more easily information provided by partner-associations across Europe. In a similar way, *Pro Asyl* used its involvement in *ECRE* to constitute its own European network in Eastern Europe in 2004 (*Cross-border Asylum Network*).[41]

In conclusion, unlike humanitarian associations, politicized associations have not considered the inclusion within the field on European immigration and asylum policies as a natural channel of Europeanization. The cleavage between humanitarian and politicized associations that was observed in France and Germany is thus reproduced at the European level. Moreover, the hypothesis of the 'NGOization' of associations that follow a process of Europeanization (i.e. the idea that when they move to the European level, SMOs adapt to the forms of mobilization that are the most commonly used at this level – advocacy and lobbying) is contradicted by these results. This analysis shows that when they move to the European level, politicized associations are reluctant to transform their identity in order to adapt to the ways of functioning of an existing field. On the contrary, politicized associations rapidly developed the idea that it was necessary to construct their own European structures in order to represent directly their demands at the European level. The following section aims at an analysis of this process.

# Towards the construction of alternative coalitions: how politicized associations become European

As I will now develop, two main ideas have to be mentioned when analysing the Europeanization of SMOs which rely traditionally on politicized mobilization. First, since the beginning of the 2000s these associations have constructed (or have been involved in the construction of) new coalitions at the European level. These coalitions represent alternatives to the European advocacy coalition active around EU institutions since the beginning of the 1990s because they are based on different types of identities. Secondly, these SMOs have used different resources (in comparison to those used within the existing European public policy field) in order to Europeanize. These are the associations that rely on the most diversified resources which play a leading role in these alternative coalitions.

## Different processes of Europeanization corresponding to distinct strategies

The process of Europeanization of French and German politicized associations has taken two different forms:

- The creation of European transnational networks through a process of *construction of alternative coalitions*. These are mainly the network *Migreurop* and the networks of activists for the regularization of undocumented migrants' and against border controls. In terms of modes of Europeanization, this corresponds to the construction of transnational movements (chapter four).

  The SMOs that follow this process construct transnational links in order to create a mobilization that is different from that traditionally constructed within the existing European public policy field. In doing this, they follow a particular strategy. They aim to create new fields of contention around the asylum issue which are based on alternative forms of frames, repertoires of collective action, resources and organizational structures.
- The creation of the European delegation of international social movement organizations through a process of *pro-active inclusion* in the existing European public policy field. These are the European offices of *Amnesty International* (*Amnesty International – European Office*) and the *Ligue des droits de l'Homme* (*European Association for the Protection of Human Rights*). In terms of modes of Europeanization,

this corresponds to the construction of multilevel social movements (chapter four).

The SMOs that follow this process will become involved in the European field related to the asylum issue in order to mobilize directly at the EU level. They will represent their interests with a mobilization that is different from that traditionally carried out within this field. In doing this, they follow a particular strategy. They aim at changing the 'rules of the games' that prevail within this European field by including alternative frames and repertoires of collective action.

These two processes of Europeanization are guided by the same logic. They aim to make possible the emergence of a politicized mobilization on European immigration and asylum policies. They are moreover based on the same four strategies:

- The strategy of *politicization*, through which associations will present as a general and contentious issue a public policy that is traditionally defined in a technical and fragmented way by the European institutions and non-governmental actors gravitating around them.
- The strategy of *making public*, through which associations will involve public opinion in European mobilizations.
- The strategy of *globalization*, through which associations will involve non-European SMOs in a debate that has remained European-centred.
- The strategy of *construction of linkages with other movements*, through which associations that specialize in a specific issue (the immigration and asylum issue in this case) will construct links with movements specialized in other issues and formulate common claims with them. In doing this, these associations participate in the construction of cross-issue networks.

### *The Migreurop network*

The creation of the *Migreurop* network by activists of *Gisti*, *Cimade* and *Act Up* (among other European associations), following the first European Social Forum in 2002, is the result of a strategy of creation of new fields of contention. It emerged because this group of SMOs judged it necessary to work together in order to make public a phenomenon (the detention of migrants in 'camps' in Europe and on its borders) that was generally not taken into account by the groups already active around EU institutions. Thus, the presentation given on the network's website underlines the fact that it aims to understand, present and mobilize on a reality that remains unknown:

> To many activists for foreigners' rights the mediatization of the refugee camp of Sangatte during the year 2000 appeared as a perfect illustration of the absurdity of EU migration policies. The effects of obstacles to freedom of movement and the refusal of receiving migrants and refugees became fully visible. While usually invisible because dispersed along borders or because hidden, they instantly became visible because of their concentration in the only (non)-place where they were tolerated.
>
> It shortly appeared that far from being an exception, the Sangatte camp was only a cog in the wheels of a European policy leaving foreigners aside. The necessity of sharing opinions and experiences led to the holding of a workshop devoted to 'the Europe of camps' at the European Social Forum of Florence in November 2002. *Migreurop* was born, a network of activists and scholars aimed at spreading knowledge about the generalization of retention for undocumented foreigners as well as the increasing number of camps, the latter being at the centre of EU migration policy.[42]

This network was created to facilitate cooperation between a small group of French, Belgian, Spanish and Italian SMOs. This cooperation was needed in order to collect information on this specific phenomenon, so that public opinion and their representatives (the European MPs in particular) would become aware of it. The first actions of the network were the organization of a seminar to which activists and researchers were invited (and which took place in the European parliament),[43] and the realization of a 'map of camps for foreigners in Europe' which has been largely circulated via the Internet, in public meetings (like the European Social Forum) and in alternative media.[44] The next steps of this cooperation were the progressive construction of a common discourse (framing), and the organization of common collective actions.

Therefore, *Migreurop* emerged in order to place new items on the agenda of the mobilizations related to European immigration and asylum policies. This group felt that the issues of the detention of migrants and externalization of migration and asylum policies had been neglected by the actors that were already mobilizing at the EU level. The idea of these associations was thus to become themselves European actors in order to transform this agenda of mobilization. In doing this, the aim was to contest the common definition of the interest (the reason actors are interacting within a particular field) on which the existing European advocacy coalition agreed. As I have discussed, these actors agreed on the idea that the construction of a common European policy on immigration and asylum was limited to the frame of the institutional negotiations for the definition of common norms. However,

*Migreurop* stressed that this process had to be analysed not only through the evolution of the European and national legislations, but also through the set of practices, policies, and discourses that European states have in common (the question of the detention of foreigners being the most spectacular in this regard). This network contests the specific 'rules of the game' on which the non-governmental actors of the European public policy field agreed. They put forward the idea that the process of harmonization had to be considered not exclusively as a normative process, but as a more general political process.

*Migreurop* defines itself as a European advocacy coalition that provided an alternative to the one active at the European level since the beginning of the 1990s. It can be considered as alternative because it presents a different form of identity. This is visible in terms of its discourses. The frames put forward by these actors are indeed very reactive and critical towards the European power-holders. In contrast to the policy-oriented discourse formulated by the existing European advocacy coalition, *Migreurop* presents a discourse that is more 'principle-oriented'. Referring to the eight cognitive frames that justify a mobilization on the asylum issue,[45] the analysis shows that the discourse of *Migreurop* relies on five fundamental frames: the fight against repression; the defence of fundamental rights; international solidarity; the broader opening of borders; and anti-racism and anti-discrimination. The articulation of these five frames is visible in the 'petition against the creation of camps for foreigners at European borders':

> The idea of creating asylum-processing centres outside European borders, put on hold at the European Summit of Thessalonica in 2003, seems to have gained support at the European Union Interior Ministers' meeting on the 1 October 2004.
>
> Diplomatically called 'assistance centres', the aim is in fact to create camps in countries bordering the European Union. Foreigners who attempt to reach Europe to claim asylum or for other motives, seeking protection or a better life, would be detained or sent to these centres. A significant amount of funding appears to have been approved in principle.
>
> According to European Union leaders, this procedure of offshore processing is in response to humanitarian concerns: in order to save the lives of people who every week try to reach the European coasts, it is preferable detaining them in camps on the other side of the Mediterranean.
>
> If this proposal becomes reality, it would endorse an unprecedented regression in the way in which Europe intends to assume its responsibilities towards those who are fleeing conflicts, human

> rights abuses and poverty. It is the extension of a cynical logic, which far from addressing the root causes of forced migration, has sought to protect Europe over the past ten years from these victims of world disorder. It is taking the risk of creating refugee camps, which will bring back dark memories of those dating back to the 1930s, or more recently during the war in Bosnia. [. . .]
>
> The Europe we want must put an end to this senseless approach in the treatment of asylum seekers and migrants.[46]

This example illustrates moreover that, in contrast to the discourse of the more established European actors, the asylum issue is not separate from the migration issue. This petition evokes for example the 'responsibilities (of the European Union) towards the populations that escape the conflicts, the violations of human rights and poverty', or 'the insane drift of Europe in regard to migrants and refugees'.

*Migreurop* must then be considered as an alternative European advocacy coalition because it presents new forms of collective action. In contrast to *ECRE* or *MPG*, for example, it relies on a more contentious repertoire of collective action. Thus, in an interview carried out with an activist from this network, it was argued that:

> When we mobilize on issues that are defined at the European level, we are in a logic of alert. Our aim is to alert public opinion about the dangers of the European policy towards migrants and refugees. We realized rapidly that it was impossible to influence the course of the European policy through a work of lobbying for example. We have less and less direct contacts in Brussels; this is useless. We try thus to confront this policy through a mobilization of the consciousness of the public opinion. The petition against the camps is a good example of it.[47]

Another form of collective action that has been put forward by *Migreurop* is a juridical action that targets the European power-holders responsible for the harmonizations of the asylum policies. Thus, in February 2004, the associations comprising the network *Migreurop* lodged a complaint with the European Commission against the Italian government in order to protest against the deportation of migrants from Lampedusa to Libya.

Finally, *Migreurop* has to be considered as an alternative European advocacy coalition as it relies on new forms of organizational structures. It defines itself as a grass-roots network and therefore relies on a horizontal and non-professionalized structure (in contrast to the centralized European coalitions of associations). The participation of the activists involved in the network is thus on a volunteer basis.[48] This has permitted it to include actors with different profiles. Thus, in contrast with the experts involved in groups such as *ECRE* or *CCME*, *Migreurop* involves a large number of researchers and individuals that can produce a political discourse on the asylum issue. Through the involvement of these actors, *Migreurop* is able to present forms of 'savoir-faire' and practices that contrast with those that prevail within the European public policy field. It is for instance able to organize seminars that can address a public who is not expert on the asylum issue (at the European Social Forums or more recently at the World Social Forums, for example).

Moreover, the network is turning increasingly towards those associations active in migrants' countries of origins, and in particular towards North-African associations; associations based in Morocco and Tunisia have become important actors in it and they participate in the strategy of politicization. In an interview, it was argued that the involvement of these associations permitted them to present the consequences of EU policies in concrete terms, and so to denounce the general orientations taken by European leaders:

> *Migreurop* is less and less euro-centred. Associations from the South get more and more involved in the network, and I think that this is something that is very important. We mobilize on something that remains relatively invisible if we stay in Europe. Logically, it is not concrete to talk about detention of migrants and about externalization of immigration and asylum policies if we stay between European associations. We are not in touch with what happens concretely and it is thus difficult to denounce these processes in politicized terms. With the involvement of the associations from the South, we get concrete information about the consequences of these policies. We are able to say that – as a direct consequence of European policies – fifty migrants were deported in the desert in Morocco last week or that hundreds of persons have been stranded in the forests next to Ceuta and Melilla for months. I think that this speaks more to public opinion than saying that such disposition in such directive is contrary to such article of the Geneva Convention . . .[49]

This process of globalization was actualized by the launching of a 'Euro-African Non-Governmental Manifesto on Migrations, Fundamental Rights and Freedom of Movement' in 2006. This call is particularly significant as it shows that through this dynamic of globalization, *Migreurop* is following a strategy of creation of links with other causes. Since the mid-2000s, it has participated in the creation of global cross-issue movements. This call is thus addressed to European as well as to African governments and it links demands relating to freedom of circulation or the closing of detention centres with demands relating to the cancellation of the debt of Southern countries, for example:

> As actors in the civil societies of Subsaharan Africa, North Africa and Europe, we met in Rabat in a Euro-African non-governmental conference on the 30th of June and 1st of July 2006.
>
> We share indignation about the war that is increasingly being waged along the Mediterranean and Atlantic coastlines. We refuse the division of humanity between some who may freely move about the planet and some who may not. We also refuse to live in a world where borders are more and more militarized, dividing our continents and trying to transform every group of countries into a fortress. [. . .]
>
> We demand:
>
> - that governments abandon the securitarian and repressive ideology which currently inspires migration policies, in particular the 'externalization' of asylum and border controls, the criminalization of migrations, as well as all racist, xenophobic or discriminatory laws; [. . .]
> - that any Euro-African negotiation be based on the principle of equality between partners, and that African leaders, who have been so deficient in the defence of their peoples' interests, take on their responsibilities, particularly by challenging the Euro-African partnership agreements;
> - the setting up of mechanisms ensuring food sovereignty, and the cancellation of agreements which endanger the future of African agriculture;
> - the suppression of conditions imposed on African countries in international negotiations, more particularly that providing for the subcontracting of the anti-migrations fight;
> - the unconditional cancellation of the debt of Southern countries, and the repatriation of their assets placed in foreign banks.[50]

These strategies may evolve over time, depending on political developments at the EU level. Thus, since the Den Haag Program in 2004, the European Commission and European Parliament have seen their power increasing in the domains of immigration and asylum. These policies are now defined through the co-decision procedure. As the power of the European Parliament increases, so new potential allies have emerged within European institutions for networks such as *Migreurop*. Indeed, some European MPs have opposed the policies negotiated by the member-states and the European Commission. Most of these MPs were already active on immigration issues at the national level and close to the associative field. Pro-asylum groups could thus benefit from the presence of contacts with whom they were already working at the national level, and so move closer to the European institutions. For example, during the negotiations relating to the directive on the return of undocumented migrants (adopted in 2008), several European MPs created an opposition group and worked in close cooperation with *Migreurop* activists. Together, they created a website, launched a petition, and organized several demonstrations and conferences in Brussels. Following the adoption of the directive, these initiatives were followed by the 'campaign for a right of access inside detention centres for migrants' (see above). Thus, in recent years, because of the arrival of new actors in the European negotiations, networks such as *Migreurop* have increasingly combined a process of construction of European movements with a process of externalization.

### *The movements for the regularization of undocumented migrants and against border controls*

The will to see the emergence of new fields of contentions also resulted in the construction of European networks of militants mobilizing for the regularization of undocumented migrants and against border controls. These two movements have been constructed separately. The European network for the regularization of undocumented migrants emerged as an extension of the movement of *sans-papiers* in France after 1996–1997. Figures of this movement have created links in different European countries and the experience of activists in France has served as a great incentive for other movements to work together. Its first significant collective action was the 'European demonstration for freedom of circulation' in Paris in 1999 (during the European electoral campaign). Associations from France (*CNSP*, *FASTI*, *MRAP*, etc.) and from Germany (*Karawane*, *Kein Mensch Ist Illegal*, etc.) are active in this network, as well as associations from other European countries. The creation of European movements against border controls was an initiative of German militants (involved in *Kein Mensch Ist Illegal* or in the *Aktionsbündnis Gegen Abschiebung Rhein-Main*) who created the *No Border* network in 2000. Its most significant collective action has been the 'No Border Camp' in Strasbourg in 2002. Since 2004, the European *No Border* network as such has been inactive. Activists involved in the network have, however, created local groups which communicate on a regular basis and other platforms in which they coordinate their mobilization. The most active since the mid-2000s is probably the *Frassanito* network. Associations from Germany (*Kein Mensch Ist Illegal*, *Aktionsbündnis Gegen Abschiebung Rhein-Main*, *No Lager*,

*Flüchtlingsrat Hamburg*) and from France (*Act Up*) are active in this network, as well as associations from other European countries. Even if they have been constructed separately, these two movements have strong connections with each other. They are involved in the construction of the same mobilizations and the same activists are often engaged in these two networks.

As is the case with the network *Migreurop*, these (more informal) networks represent alternatives to the mobilizations constructed around EU institutions. In particular, they present a very critical discourse that targets the European power-holders. Thus, in the call for a European demonstration for the regularization of undocumented migrants, we find the following:

> We refuse a xenophobic and securitarian Europe. Yesterday, Europe colonized, enslaved, deported and assassinated. Today, it sets up barbed-wires around itself, it constructs internment camps, it files and it expulses . . . All this in order to repress a population whose only fault is to have another nationality.
>
> Because being a refugee or a foreigner is a crime for European authorities. Ten years after the fall of the Berlin wall, the German police does not hesitate to open fire in order to prevent refugees crossing the Polish-German border. Hundreds of migrants drown in their attempt to cross the strait of Gibraltar. In Trieste, in Italy, and in the Adriatic sea, those who escape from war, massacres and misery are driven back by the Italian police. In France and in Belgium, special prisons called 'zones d'attente', 'centres de rétention' or 'centres fermés' deprive thousands of persons of one fundamental liberty: that to circulate and to settle. [. . .]
>
> If one accepts the kind of Europe that is conceived by European states and governments (being right-wing or left-wing), one accepts the vision of a world where inequalities and misery rule whereas a minority monopolizes all world resources and protects itself through all means. [. . .] If one tolerates this situation, one accepts apartheid at the global level.[51]

As is shown in this example, their discourse is based on an intense process of frame-bridging. The frames of the fight against repression and persecution and of the fight against precariousness and social inequalities are particularly central. This gives to their discourse a very oppositional orientation, which strongly contrasts with the 'politically-neutral' discourse of the advocacy coalition present in Brussels.

This contrast must also be highlighted for the types of collective actions that they implement. Their repertoire is based on disruptive and symbolic forms of collective actions (the dismantling of detention centres or the protest against the Frontex agency, for example) and on transnational public campaigns (see for example the regular diffusion of the 'transnational newsletter – Crossing Borders' by *Frassanito* activists). And, finally, the same can be said about their organizational structure. They have developed a type of organization that is completely different from that of the groups active in Brussels. They describe themselves as 'grass-root networks' which are not centralized and not professionalized. This is stated in the website presentation of the *No Border* network:

> The *No Border* network is a tool for all groups and grass root organizations who work on the questions of migrants and asylum seekers in order to struggle alongside them for freedom of movement, for the freedom for all to stay in the place which they have chosen, against repression and the many controls which multiply the borders everywhere in all countries. This network is different from lobbying groups and NGOs because it is based on groups of grass root activists and intends to remain so.
>
> The coordination between the groups is done through two meetings every year and a working list on e-mail.[52]

An analysis of their discourse, collective action and organizational structures shows that the networks for the regularization of undocumented migrants and against border controls follow a strategy of making such controls public. A good illustration of this is the network's attempt to present the European Union policies through a visualization that emphasizes border controls. As the following examples illustrate, this is evident in the posters they diffused during the course of their collective actions (figures 3, 4 and 5).

**Figure 3.** Poster for the No Border camp in Strasbourg, July 2002

**Figure 4.** Poster for the 'Europeanwide Action Day for the Right to Stay and Freedom of Movement'

**Figure 5.** Poster for the No Border camp in Calais, June 2009

These examples show how these networks attempt to make European immigration and asylum policies public by making them as visible as possible (here symbolically through their visual presentation). They also illustrate the strategy of politicization that leads them to focus their discourse on the concrete consequences of these policies (here the activation of the frame of the fight against repression through a visualization of the politics of control represented by symbols such as the barbed wire or helicopter). In this regard, a parallel can be drawn with the strategy followed by *Migreurop*. With the elaboration of a 'map of the camps for foreigners in Europe', *Migreurop* also attempted to present a concrete visualization of what is presented as the consequence of European immigration and asylum policies (see Figure 6).

This specific example shows moreover that through the use of the term 'camp', *Migreurop* also aims to present a politicized discourse on this issue. Thus, in an article that justifies the use of this term, *Migreurop* underlines the fact that it aims to denounce what it perceives as a general political logic:

> Since the denunciation of the denials of rights (and in particular the right to demand asylum . . .) and of the living conditions of the refugees in Sangatte, we have chosen to use the word camp. This is for two reasons:
>
> The euphemistic use of terms like 'centre' doesn't begin to describe the reality of human gatherings which are not chosen by the exiles but are due to the systematic policy of hindrance of circulation and settling of persons escaping war, persecutions or misery. The word camp is used in order to describe, in periods that can be anterior to totalitarian experiences, the factual imprisonment (and thus the deprivation of rights) of populations for political reasons.[53]

There have been many other attempts to render this issue public through a visualization of European policies. One such is the 'aviation campaign'[54] which was launched by activists of *No Border* in the early 2000s. In the same way, Kanak Attak designed a series of maps on the 'governing of migration' (MigMap) in 2006. This 'virtual cartography of European migration policies' consists of four different maps: 'Key Players', 'Discourses', 'Europeanization' and 'Places + Practices'. Each of these maps aims to illustrate European immigration policies (i.e., whether in terms of actors, discourses, processes, locations or practices).

As is the case with *Migreurop*, the networks for the regularization of undocumented migrants and against border controls follow a strategy of globalization. Thus, the 'Call for a 3rd Day of Migration-Related Actions on 7 October 2006, all over Europe and beyond . . .' underlines the need to create links beyond Europe:

> Taking into account specific regional and national conditions and the circumstances of various struggles, our Day of Action aims

> for resistance at European and even transcontinental levels. Our mobilization will make the first moves towards Europe-wide central activities in order to develop the idea of a common demonstration in 2007, either in Brussels or at another place of public interest. Our aim is to address Europe as a whole and not only national governments.
>
> In addition the chosen date in October is a reminder of the events in Ceuta and Melilla in 2005. We will make a particular effort to build cooperation with initiatives in Africa. A simultaneous day of actions in European and African cities in October would help to promote an axis on migration in the next World Social Forum, which will take place in Nairobi (Kenya) in January 2007. [. . .]
>
> Above all, we are determined to stress the global dimension of migrant struggles today. Thus, we intend to connect our Day of Action with the initiatives and ongoing mass mobilizations of the American migrants movement in the next future.[55]

The globalization of these networks has resulted in a series of collective actions involving actors from Europe and Africa. Thus, an 'international day of solidarity with migrants' was organized at the World Social Forum in Nairobi in 2007. In 2008, these networks launched a 'Transnational chain of migration related actions' that involved activists from both continents and that included protests in several symbolic places in Europe and Africa. Interestingly, this chain of actions was presented through the title 'Fighting the border regime! Transnationalization now!' It therefore explicitly linked the demands made by the network (the opening of borders) with its transnational nature.

Finally, an analysis of their frames and collective actions shows that these networks also follow a strategy of creation of links with other movements. As is the case with *Migreurop*, they participate in the creation of cross-issue networks. In an interview, it was underlined that the networks against border controls have strong links with the *EuroMayday* network (the European network against precariousness):

> I think that most of the activists that are present in the *Frassanito* network are also activists of the *Euromayday*. I thus participated in the organization of the last *Euromayday* parade in Paris. I think that both movements are very active and very innovative. Moreover, we all strongly believe that the fight against actual migration policies is part of a more general fight against all policies that lead to precarity in general.[56]

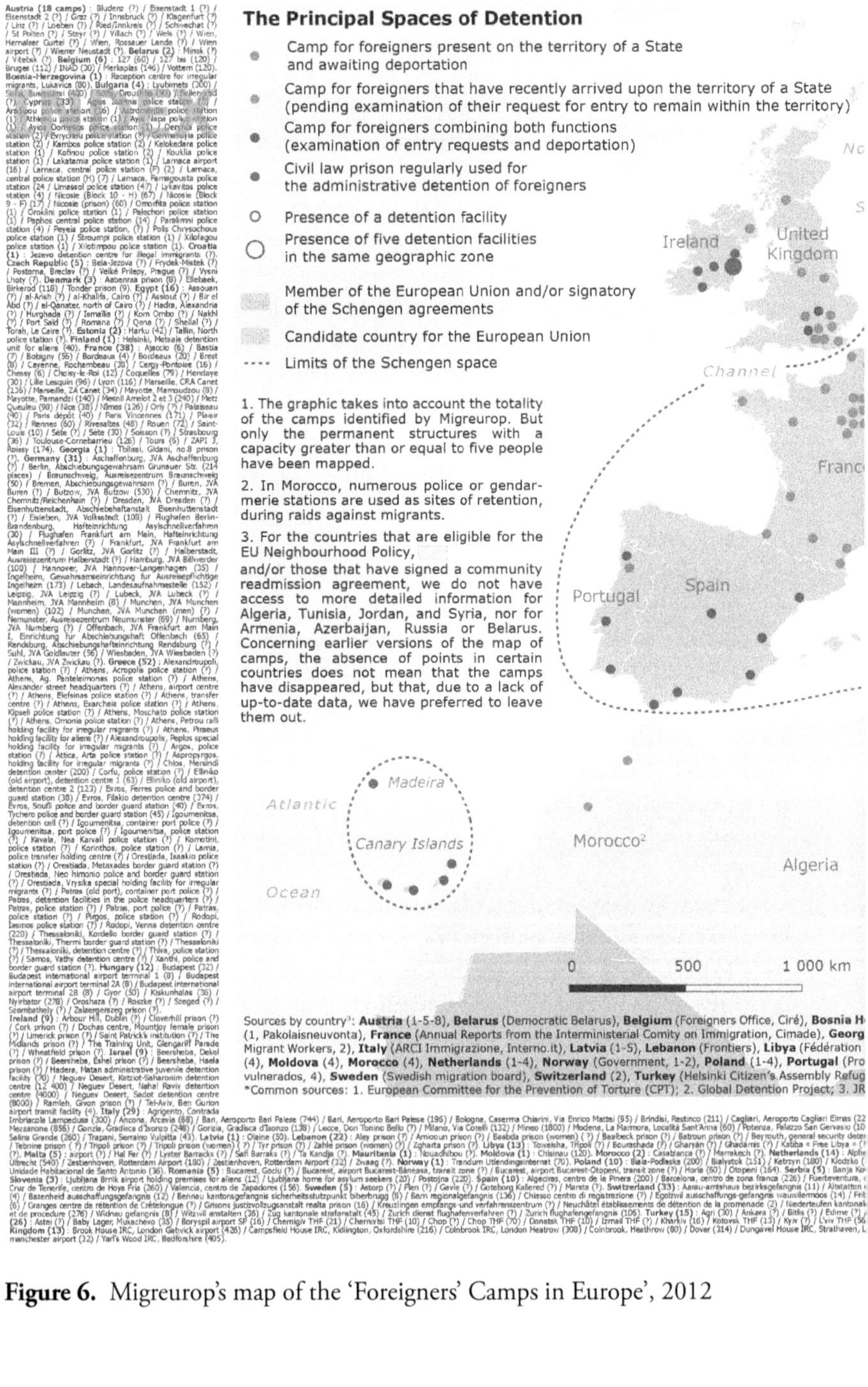


**Figure 6.** Migreurop's map of the 'Foreigners' Camps in Europe', 2012

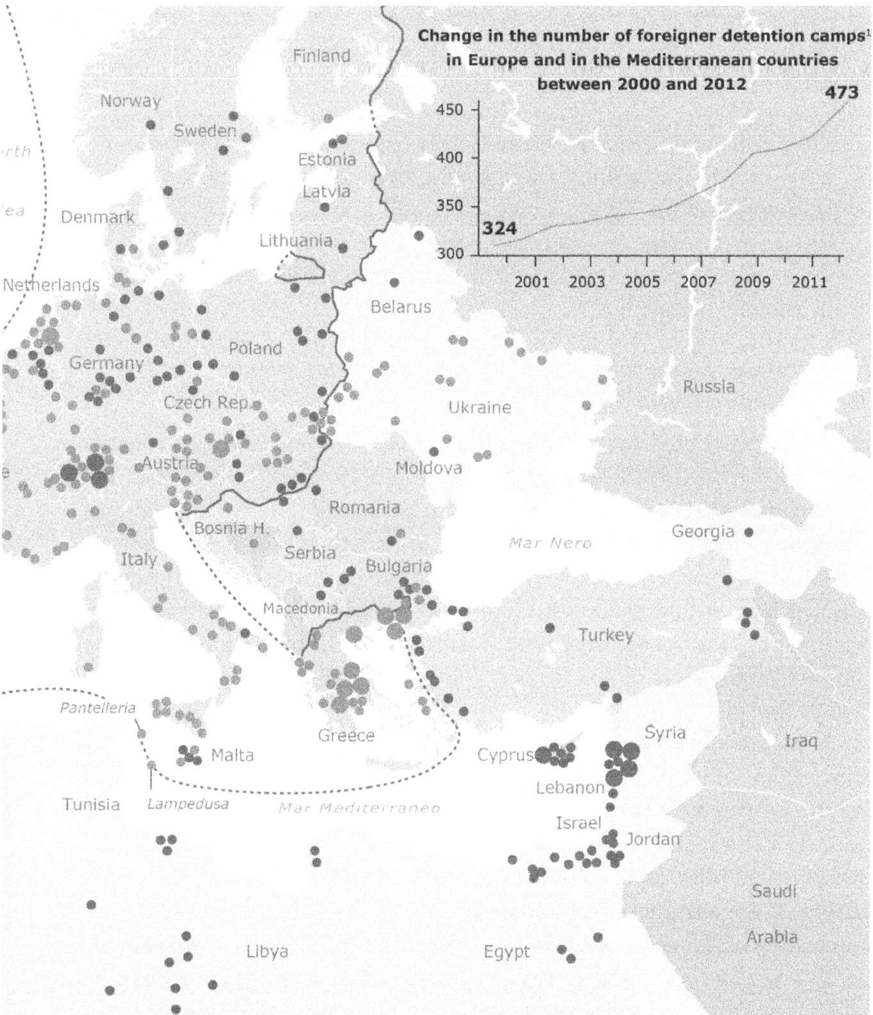


erzegovina (4), **Bulgaria** (1-4), **Cyprus** (Kisa, TerrFerme), **Croatia** (1-3-6), **Czech Republic** (1-5), **Denmark** (2-4), **Egypt** (2-4), **Estonia** (1-2-5), **Finland**
ia (4), **Germany** (Pro Asyl, 5), **Greece** (1-6-7-8, FRA), **Hungary** (Welcome to Europe network, 1-3), **Ireland** (Irish prison service, 1-2), **Israel** (Hotline for
internationale des droits de l'homme / FIDH, Justice sans frontières / JSF, 4), **Lithuania** (1-5), **Luxembourg** (4), **Macedonia** (IOM), **Malta** (JRS), **Mauritania**
vedor de justiça, Serviço de Estrangeiros e Fronteiras), **Romania** (TerrFerme), **Serbia** (4), **Slovakia** (1-5), **Slovenia** (1-5), **Spain** (APDHA, CIE, Derechos
ee Advocacy and Support Program), **Ukraine** (Border Monitoring Project Ukraine, GDISC, 1-3-6), **United Kingdom** (UK Border Agency, 4).
S Detention in Europe; 4. Migreurop; 5. European Parliament; 6. Human Rights Watch (HRW); 7. MSF; 8. Frontex

0) / Caltanissetta, Contrada Pian del Lago (96) / Caltanissetta, Contrada Pian del Lago (360) / Caserta, Santa Maria Capua Vetere (200) / Catanzaro, Lamezia Terme (80) / Crotone, Sant'Anna (875) / Crotone, Sant'Anna (124) / Foggia, Borgo
0) / Ragusa, Pozzallo (172) / Roma, Castelnuovo di Porto (650) / Roma, Ponte Galeria (360) / Taranto, Manduria (3300) / Torino, Corso Brunelleschi (180) / Trapani, Chinizia (206) / Trapani, Località Milo (204) / Trapani, Pantelleria (?) / Trapani,
ntion centre (700) / Beyrouth prison (women) (?) / Halba prison (?) / Jbeil prison (?) / Jeb Jannine prison (?) / Jezzine prison (?) / Maten prison (?) / Nabatieh prison (?) / Rachaya prison (?) / Ras Baalbeck prison ( ?) / Roumieh prison (2000)
) / Ganfuda (?) / Sabha (?) / Umm al Aranib (?) / Marzuq (?) / Al Qatrun (?) / Waw al Kabi (?) / Al Wigh (?) / Ghat (?) / Al Kufrah (?). **Lithuania (1)** : Pabrade (300). **Luxembourg (2)** : Findel (50) / Schrassig (25). **Macedonia (1)** : Skopje
n aan den Rijn (1300) / Alphen aan den Rijn (?) / Amsterdam, Schiphol-Oost (?) / Amsterdam, Schiphol-Oost (?) / Amsterdam, Schiphol-Oost (?) / Den Helder (?) / Dordrecht (496) / Ter Appel (?) / Veenhuizen (?) / Zaandam (576) / Zeist,
3) / Krosno Odrzanskie (66) / Lesznowola, Grojec (131) / Luban (9) / Okecie airport, Varsovie (41) / Przemysl (176) / Szczecin (33) / Unidade (?). **Portugal (6)** : Faro (24) / Funchal (?) / Lisboa (54) / Ponta Delgado (?) / Porto (24) / Porto,
ljaca (?) / Bogovadja (?) / Padinska Skela (120) / Subotica (?) / Vranje (?). **Slovakia (6)** : Bratislava, international airport (?) / Humenne (520) / Kosice, international airport (?) / Medvedov (152) / Opatovska Nova Ves (180) / Secovce (176).
entro de Matorral (?) / Lanzarote, airport terminal (?) / Las Palmas de Gran Cannas, centro de Branco Seco (168) / Madrid, centro de Carabanchel (240) / Malaga, centro de Capuchinos (44) / Murcia, centro de Sangonera la Verde (?) / Santa
mpfangs-und verfahrenszentrum (?) / Altstatten regionalgefangnis (18) / Appenzel kantonalen polizeigefangnis (6) / Basel empfangs-und verfahrenszentrum (?) / Basel-stadt ausschaffungsgefangnis (63) / Basel-stadt untersuchungsgefangnis
ourg central prison (9) / Geneva airport centre d'enregistrement et procédure (33) / Genève établissement concordataire de détention administrative de Frambois (20) / Genève maison d'arrêt de Riant-Parc (?) / Glarus kantonales gefangnis
e gefangnis (12) / Sarnen kantonspolizei (2) / Schaffhausen kantonales gefangnis (2) / Solothurn untersuchungsgefangnis (53) / Stans untersuchungs-und strafgefangnis (37 / Thurgau kantonalgefangnis (6) / Vallorbe centre d'enregistrement
' Erzurum (?) / Hakkari (?) / Hatay (?) / Istanbul, aéroport int. Ataturk (?) / Istanbul, Kunkapi (470) / Istanbul, Zeytinburnu (?) / Izmir (?) / Izmir, Jandarma Post (?) / Kirklareli (?) / Konya (150) / Van (?) / Van, Jandarma Post (65). **Ukraine**
) / Lugansk (12) / Luts'k THF (35) / Malniv THF (?) / Mostys'ka THF (16) / Odesa (16) / Odesa THF (10) / Rozsudic (239) / Seredina (16) / Shatsk THF (180) / Sumy THF (16) / Uzhgorod (?) / Velyka Pysarivka (6) / Zhuravychi (181). **United**
anarkshire (219) / Harmondsworth IRC, London Heatrow (623) / Haslar IRC, Gosport nr Portsmouth (160) / Larne House, Northern Ireland (22) / Morton Hall IRC, Lincolnshire (393) / Tinsley House IRC, Gatwick Airport (155) / Pennine House,

The figures in brackets indicate the holding capacity of the camps. The '?' indicate the absence of recent data.

The dynamic described by this activist has resulted in the centrality of the migration issue in the *EuroMayday* movement. This is clear in 'the EuroMayday 2008 call to action':

> From Milano to Helsinki, from Malaga to Berlin, MayDay Parades have spread throughout Europe and beyond. They express the common will to fight precarization and the criminalization of migrants, to make the daily struggles of the precarious visible, to work together to subvert and disrupt the flows of money and power in Fortress Europe.[57]

***The European delegations of the Ligue des droits de l'Homme and Amnesty International***

The cases constituted by the creation of *Amnesty International – European Office* (in the late 1990s) and of the *European Association for the Protection of Human Rights* (in 2000) correspond to a slightly different dynamic of Europeanization. It would be misleading to present this as the creation of alternative European networks because these two organizations cooperate on a regular basis with organizations like *ECRE*, *ENAR* or *PICUM*. They meet regularly and they coordinate their collective action. In addition, they are both active members of the *Brussels NGOs Platform on EU Migration and Asylum Policy*.

However, the creation of these two groups is still based on the logic of construction of alternative forms of mobilization. The French and German sections of *Amnesty International* and the French *Ligue des droits de l'Homme* worked (with a small group of sections from other European countries) for the creation of an office in Brussels because they were unsatisfied with the mobilization of the advocacy coalition already active at the EU level. Thus, after the creation of *Amnesty International – European Office*, *Amnesty International Section Française* has gradually stopped attending the meetings organized by *ECRE*. Therefore, in their own way (by entering the existing European advocacy coalition rather than by constructing an alternative one), these actors are also trying to change the rules of the game in the existing European field. They are also trying to impose new forms of discourses and collective actions. The innovative aspect of the repertoire of collective action brought about by *Amnesty* at the European level was underlined as follows in an interview:

> We (Amnesty International) are in a constant tension between different forms of mobilizations at the European level. We play on both fields: we try to influence the European institutions through face-to-face contacts and through a close monitoring of the European direc-

> tives. In this regard, we do the same job as the lobby groups that were already there before us. But we also try to launch campaigns of denunciation of the process of harmonization as a whole, in political terms. And when we do this, I think that we bring something new in comparison to what has been done before by the groups of NGO's established in Brussels.[58]

These 'campaigns of denunciation' take the form of mobilizations that are innovative in this particular European public policy field. Thus, in 2003, the *European Association for the Protection of Human Rights* launched a European petition to collect one million signatures of citizens across Europe.[59] In the same perspective, in 2004, *Amnesty International – European Office* managed to involve a majority of the actors of this advocacy coalition in the launching of a call for the withdrawal of the directive related to the procedures of examination of the statute of refugee.[60] In particular, these collective actions are innovative as they result from a strategy to 'make public' the debates relating to European asylum policies. These initiatives have been widely diffused in different networks and in the media across European countries.

Moreover, the discourse of these organizations contrasts with that of the European advocacy coalition which has been active since the beginning of the 1990s. The European delegations of *Amnesty International* and of the *LDH* tend indeed to politicize the discourse on EU asylum policies by presenting it in general terms and in a contentious way. This was underlined in an interview:

> We (Amnesty International) have a more principled discourse than that of most of our partners at the EU level. Their discourse is more pragmatic in the sense that they are more in a logic of negotiation, of advocacy, than in a logic of defence of fundamental principles.[61]

Thus, in an open letter to representatives of EU institutions, the *European Association for the Protection of Human Rights* argues against the readmission agreements concluded by the EU and urges the European power-holders to change radically the orientations of their immigration and asylum policies:

> On behalf of its leagues in the European countries, FIDH-AE deplores the multiplication of such readmission agreements and recalls that they contravene the commitments that the Member States have undertaken by ratifying International Conventions. We ask the leaders of the European Union to cease focusing their migration policy exclusively on the fight against clandestine immigration

> and to commit instead to an equitable asylum policy and an actual legal immigration policy. [. . .]
>
> FIDH-AE considers it unfortunate that the European Union, by these readmission agreements, commits to a policy of exclusion, closure and expulsion rather than to a project of positive migratory policy. FIDH-AE urges the Council not to yield to an isolationist temptation but to promote factual and equitable asylum and immigration policies that will represent our Community's responsibility on the international scene.[62]

In the same perspective, in an open letter to the UK presidency of the EU that was written after the tragic events in Ceuta and Melilla (September 2005), *Amnesty International – European Office* writes that these events are the direct consequences of the general orientations of EU policies on immigration:

> European Union countries are increasingly abandoning their responsibilities to protect refugees in an effort to combat 'illegal immigration', as the recent tragic events near the Spanish enclaves in North Africa show. [. . .]
>
> The human rights organization said not only was the direction of EU policy ill-guided, but individual countries such as Spain may be guilty of breaking their own EU and international commitments.
>
> In its Open Letter addressed to the UK Home Secretary Charles Clarke, Amnesty International calls for a radical rethink of EU refugee policy as EU Justice and Home Affairs ministers prepare to meet in Luxembourg tomorrow to discuss the new concept of 'regional protection programs' which are supposed to enhance refugee protection in host and transit countries. [. . .]
>
> Shamefully, EU Member States are shifting the burden of refugee protection to other countries which may be ill-equipped to deal with the ever increasing numbers of displaced people. In the process, international commitments to humane treatment and the principle of 'non-refoulement' are being violated. The overall effect is not only to strain the EUs own credibility, but to threaten the very integrity of the international refugee protection system.[63]

Finally, as is the case with the *Migreurop* network and for the informal networks of militants, the European delegations of *Amnesty International* and of the *Ligue des droits de l'Homme* have followed a strategy of globalization. Thus, for the same reasons as *Migreurop*, *Amnesty International* has carried out different missions in Morocco and has created a network of contacts with Moroccan associations. In the same vein, the *Ligue des droits de l'Homme* actively participates in the *Euro-Med Non-Governmental Platform* and has created an important network with associations from Northern Africa.

The strategies followed by *Amnesty International* and the *Ligue des droits de l'Homme* result in the progressive evolution of the groups active in Brussels since the beginning of the 1990s. Indeed, as they have transformed the 'rules of the game' within this field, these two groups have had an effect on the identity of the actors involved in it. Thus, as was evoked above, since the mid-2000s, they have involved actors such as *ECRE* or *ENAR* in new forms of actions at this level (more contentious actions that aim to involve public opinion). The best examples are probably the call for the withdrawal of the directive relating to the procedures of examination of the statute of refugee (2004), the joint letter (*Amnesty* and *ECRE*) to the European MPs against the 'Returns directive' (2008), and 'ECRE's call for suspension of Dublin transfers to Greece' (2008). This confirms the more general observation of a 'gradual "SMO-ization" of NGOs active at the EU level' (della Porta and Caiani 2009: 172). An empirical analysis of different types of actors active around EU institutions shows that in recent years, they tend to 'participate in less conventional forms of collective action and to express increasingly explicit criticism of EU policies' (della Porta and Caiani 2009: 172). Thus, as is shown by Hadden (2011) and Ruzza and Bozzini (2008), the protest of 'outsiders' environmental movements has progressively influenced the actions of the 'insiders' groups active around EU institutions, leading thus to a diversification of their repertoire. As is shown by Fella and Ruzza (2011) similar dynamics can be observed in the European anti-racist movements (see also Beyers 2004, and Parks 2009 more generally on the mobilizations of the groups active in Brussels).

## The mobilization of diversified resources as an alternative Europeanization strategy

In contrast to the group of organizations based in Brussels (which base their activities on expertise and social-organizational resources), politicized associations use a varied range of resources to construct Europeanized collective actions. They combine moral resources (a strong solidarity support) with social-organizational resources (the ability to construct wide networks of partner-associations and activists), expertise, experience, and 'savoir-faire' in terms of mobilization of public opinion. Due to the diversity of these resources, these SMOs develop different strategies of mobilization around

European immigration and asylum policies. This is best illustrated in this abstract of a document written by a member of the *Migreurop* network:

> **'Decoding' and 'Networking'**
> [. . .] *Migreurop* dedicates part of its activity to decoding the often disingenuous migration policies of the EU and its member states in order to convince informed groups, or others potentially receptive to its work, such as activist movements, of the validity of its analyses. To bring its message to the latter, *Migreurop* participates in several activist gatherings, while simultaneously reaching out to the academic and NGO worlds by participating in and organizing colloquia and educational seminars. Publishing articles in NGO journals or academic publications is another way that the group disseminates its policy analyses; most of these articles are simultaneously made available on the *Migreurop* website. The growing role that migration issues play in the concerns of activist and labour movements has made this milieu an important place to pass on information, and also for multiplying *Migreurop*'s contacts in and outside Europe. [. . .]
>
> **Turning Public Opinion Against the Creation of Camps on European Borders**
> In order to address the public at large, the strategy *Migreurop* chose was to raise the visibility of the camps and inform the public of their existence. The map 'Camps for Foreigners in Europe' (which includes camps at its borders), first distributed during the European Social Forum held in Paris in November 2003, has since been included in approximately forty publications and translated into three languages. The map has become the calling card of the network, and is regularly updated with information furnished by its correspondents. The successive versions of the map show an increasing number of dots, representing the multiplication of migrant camps, and demonstrating the dramatic expansion of the practice of holding migrants in detention centres. Between the lines, it also shows the growing number of links that the network is developing with new partners, and has been an important tool for the campaign launched by *Migreurop* in 2004 [. . .].[64]

This presentation of *Migreurop* shows how member-associations use diverse resources to elaborate different strategies of mobilization and highlights the way in which the activists have used their expertise in order to 'decode' European policies (see the reference to 'educational seminars') and in order to address different fields (the field of NGOs, the academic field, the EU political field, the journalistic field, etc.). It is also evoked how they have used their networks of activists from different horizons (the 'labour movement' is evoked, for example) in order to influence public opinion. And finally it is shown how they have used their experience and 'savoir faire' in terms of the mobilization of public opinion (the important role of the network's website is thus mentioned several times) to 'raise the visibility' of the phenomenon on which they are mobilizing.

These observations can be extended to all European networks of politicized associations mobilizing around EU immigration and asylum policies. Thus, the launching of a transnational petition for the European citizenship of residence on the part of the *European Association for the Protection of Human Rights* has required important 'savoir-faire' in terms of cross-national networking, an ability to establish contact with media, and knowledge of the EU agenda and policy-making process (the petition was strategically launched during the debates on the European constitutional treaty). It was also argued in an interview that *Amnesty* has more diversified resources than groups such as *ECRE* or *ENAR*:

> We have a wide range of tools that we can use in order to construct our European work. Being present in Brussels, we have now a very good knowledge of the mechanisms through which European policies are elaborated. And moreover, being here, we know the people inside the institutions. Said like that, it doesn't seem very important, but I think that it is crucial. It takes a long time to understand what is going on here and to know who is responsible for what. [. . .] We also use the experience that Amnesty has gained since its creation. That means that we know how to construct certain types of campaigns and how to use the media for example. And of course being Amnesty also means having an international dimension and an important public legitimacy. This gives us somehow more authority when we address institutions. In this sense (the experience, the international dimension and the public legitimacy), we are maybe different from groups with which we work here in Brussels, who base their work on their 'européanitude'. Of course I don't mean that they don't have experience or public legitimacy, but I think that they are from a different kind.[65]

Finally, the analysis shows that the European networks for the regularization of undocumented migrants and against border controls base their action on their ability to construct transnational networks and to influence public opinion (through websites, mailing lists and the large diffusion of documents), as well as on their ability to produce knowledge and analysis on realities that are not handled by the mainstream media (see for instance the information and analysis produced by *No Border* on the deportation procedures in the beginning of the 2000s). Finally they base their Europeanized collective action on the experience of the activists in their home country. In particular, the protests of the *sans-papiers* in France in 1996–1997 have served as a reference for the movements of undocumented migrants in other countries. Thus, at the end of the 1990s, the leaders of the movement in France travelled all over Europe to share their experience with activists from other countries. This experience was moreover largely diffused through the analysis presented on the movement's website.

The analysis of the resources used for the construction of transnational collective actions allows us to understand the different levels of Europeanization of politicized associations. It has been underlined during the interviews that the associations that have the most diversified resources at the national level play a leading role in the European movements. Thus, SMOs like *Gisti*, *Cimade*, the *LdH*, *Kein Mensch Ist Illegal* or *Pro Asyl*, who have disposed of a wide range of resources in their history, are the most active associations within these movements. Conversely, associations like *FASTI*, the *Flüchtlingsräte* or the *Aktionsbündnis Gegen Abschiebung Rhein-Main*, who traditionally base their collective action on a narrower range of resources, are less active. More generally, this analysis permits us to have a better understanding of the alternative contention fields that they are constructing. It shows that these actors organize collectively at the European or transnational level by pooling their resources. In order to dispose of a range of resources that is as diversified as possible, these networks bring together all the resources of the member-associations and activists (which can be more or less specific) in order to construct joint mobilizations. The dynamic through which they construct Europeanized collective actions is thus completely different from the European advocacy coalition that is present in Brussels (in which the actors have very similar resources and consequently act through a method of task-sharing). This argument was raised in an interview:

> The utility of the *Frassanito* network is to put in common what different groups and different activists have. We [the association Kanak Attak] do not construct transnational campaigns alone. We don't have the capacity to do it because we are a small association and it would be completely useless. Together however, we find the tools that allow us to do more interesting things. Organizing together means basic things like having more people, more time and more

> competences. It means also that we can learn from experiences and about situations that we didn't necessarily know about. Therefore it is interesting for us to organize with groups and people that come from different horizons.[66]

This interview illustrates that the pooling of diversified resources is fundamental for the construction of transnational collective actions. Moreover, this observation permits us to note a difference between the French and the German case. In the French case, the SMOs that are the most active within these networks are those that have a history of joint mobilizations at the national level. In particular, as was developed in chapter one, *Gisti*, *Cimade*, the *LdH* and *Act Up* share a common history of mobilizations since the beginning of the 1990s. Due to their experience of collective work, these SMOs have found it easy to pool their resources in order to mobilize (with associations from other European countries) at the European level. In the German case, associations do not have such a history of common mobilizations at the national level. In fact, it was underlined in several interviews that the emergence of transnational mobilizations has been perceived as an opportunity to overcome the constraints of the national context of mobilization. Indeed, German associations have seen the construction of European mobilizations as an opportunity to work together in a new context. This is particularly true for the associations and activists who created *No Border*. One of the key actors of this network commented that 'we [the German activists mobilizing on immigration and asylum] know each other much better since we are a European movement'.[67] In the French case, the Europeanization of protest was thus facilitated by the fact that associations tend traditionally to pool their resources at the national level. Conversely, in the German case, this process facilitated their coordination. This remark is important because it leads us to draw conclusions on the cross-national comparison of the Europeanization of social movements. Depending on their national context of mobilization, SMOs will have different incentives to Europeanize. However, the emerging European protest creates a new context of mobilization which permits them to overcome national specificities. This remark will be further developed in the conclusion to this chapter and in the general conclusion.

Concluding more generally on this question of resources, the alternative fields of contention that are emerging around European immigration asylum policies since the early 2000s have different characteristics and different 'rules of the game' from those established since the early 1990s. The European advocacy coalition that is part of the EU public policy field is led by a small group of 'elite associations' that have the same specific resources.

Consequently, this particular field is structured in a centralized way and the actions of the associations involved in it are oriented by a method of task-sharing. This leads to the construction of separated and multilevel collective actions (with each of the organizations specializing in a particular issue at a specific level of mobilization). In contrast, the alternative fields of contention emerging around politicized associations are constituted through diversified resources. Consequently, these fields are less centralized and the actions of the SMOs involved in them are oriented by a method of pooling of their resources, leading to the construction of common, more horizontal, mobilizations.

## Conclusions

Two main conclusions can be drawn from the analysis developed in this chapter.

The first conclusion is empirical. The results presented in this chapter permit us to discuss the general hypothesis of the 'NGOization' of associations that move from the national or local level to the European level. As I have reiterated, this hypothesis originates from one fundamental idea: the construction of Europeanized mobilizations would be easier for NGOs than for SMOs that traditionally tend to rely more often on protest because EU institutions actively promote lobbying and because NGOs have the resources that are necessary to act at this level. From this, two main hypotheses can be deduced: associations that have a profile that is close to that of NGOs (humanitarian associations) would Europeanize more than 'grass-roots' associations (politicized associations); associations (whatever identity they have initially) that follow a process of Europeanization would adapt their profile and become close to NGO-type associations.

The analysis of the Europeanization of French and German pro-asylum movements reveals that the idea of the 'NGOization' has to be revised. I have observed that humanitarian associations are not the only types of associations that move from the national to the European level. It is true that the Europeanization of humanitarian associations has been facilitated by the existence of a particular public policy field in which NGOs and lobby groups interact with European institutions through a relation of inter-dependence. However, in parallel to the Europeanization of these associations, I could observe that SMOs who privileged more contentious forms of actions at the national level could also progressively move to the EU level. Through the construction of alternative European coalitions and transnational networks, politicized associations have been able to construct significant mobilizations at the EU level since the beginning of the 2000s. The two main hypotheses that lie behind the idea of the 'NGOization' can thus be specified. First, humanitarian associations do not tend to Europeanize more than politicized associations. In the case of the French and German pro-asylum movements, both groups of organizations have followed a process of Europeanization. Moreover, SMOs do not tend to adapt their characteristics (in particular their repertoire of collective action) to the organizations that are in permanent interaction with European institutions. I have indeed observed that politicized organizations construct mobilizations at the European level through transnational public campaigns of protest.

Finally, the empirical analysis does not point to cross-national differences in terms of social movements' processes of Europeanization. I have shown that, even if they come from contrasted national contexts of mobilization, French and German SMOs follow dynamics of Europeanization that are determined by the same logics: the modes of Europeanization of French and German humanitarian associations are similar, as are those of French and German politicized associations. This leads me to say that the process of Europeanization of an SMO is determined more by its profile and history than by the context from which it comes. More generally, the Europeanization of immigration and asylum policies creates a new context of mobilization (with its own dynamics) that tends to transcend national specificities. As I will develop in the general conclusion, these empirical results confirm those of studies which have analysed the Europeanization of social movements 'from below' (della Porta and Caiani 2009).

The second conclusion is theoretical. As I have developed in this chapter, the use of the concept of field leads to an original understanding of the Europeanization of social movements and, more generally, of the interactions between institutional and non-institutional actors within the EU venue. I have shown how a group of actors with specific characteristics (the lobby groups and NGOs active in Brussels) organize strategically in order to constitute themselves as a group of 'elites' within a specific EU public policy field. This approach has moreover permitted me to observe on which resources these actors base their 'social power', and to identify the nature of the cultural practices and values that are attached to this particular field. Finally, it has allowed me to observe the 'rules of the game' that are established in this field. I have thus shown that the European advocacy coalition created in the beginning of the 1990s is formed of organizations with specific characteristics: they share a similar perception of the asylum issue (a technical, fragmented and de-politicized framing); a similar repertoire of collective action (based on lobbying techniques); and a similar associative culture (professionalized and centralized). I have then shown that these organizations have specific resources that allow them to maintain a monopoly of the interactions with European institutions. They have a high level of expertise and significant social-organizational resources composed of their personal contacts within European institutions. These specific characteristics and resources lead them to base their activities on highly Europeanized (or 'Brussels-based') cultural practices and values: they have similar cultural practices to those of the agents of the European Commission and they share the belief that the rights of asylum-seekers and refugees have to be guaranteed through a technical process of norm-making at the EU level. These elements evoke particular 'rules of the game'. In particular, I have underlined that this field is de-politicized and fragmented, that public opinion is kept distant from it, that it is euro-centric (in the sense that only actors from European member-states are involved), and that it is separated from other public policy fields. I have moreover shown through this approach that actors with different characteristics (SMOs that have a politicized profile) have developed diversified strategies of Europeanization (a strategy of proactive inclusion and of creation of alternative fields of mobilization) in order to act around EU immigration and asylum policies. These actors follow these strategies with the same perspective: they aim to change the 'rules of the game' established within this field. They aim in particular to politicize the immigration and asylum issue, to involve public opinion on these matters, to involve actors from outside Europe, and to construct cross-issue movements.

Summing up, an analysis in terms of fields leads one to focus on the identity of the actors and on their strategies in order to highlight which are the 'rules of the game' in a particular venue (and to observe the effects of these rules). The concept of field permits an understanding of how the characteristics and actions of agents are constitutive of structures (the 'rules of the games') which – in return – determine their actions. This approach has been conceived and applied at the national level, but is relatively new for studies on Europeanization and on the European Union (Bigo 1996; Cohen and Vauchez 2007; Favell 2000, 2008). As I will discuss in the conclusions below, this type of analysis can be understood as a contribution to the recent development of sociological approaches in European studies (Favell and Guiraudon 2009; Fligstein 2008).

## Notes

1 See, for example, the report by *Human Rights Watch*, 'Libya: Stranded Foreign Workers Need Urgent Evacuation', March 2011.

2 See, for example, *The Guardian*, 'How a migrant boat was left adrift on the Mediterranean', 28 March 2012.

3 'Joint Letter to the European Council. The need for a protection-oriented European response to migrant and refugee flows resulting from the recent developments in North Africa', June 2011.
4 Ibid.
5 *Migreurop*, 'A Flotilla to Stop Death in the Mediterranean', July 2011.
6 Ibid.
7 *Migreurop*, 'Boats4People presentation', 2012.
8 The objective here is to analyse the features of the advocacy coalition active at the European level prior to the process of Europeanization of national associations. In this sense, *Human Rights Watch*, *Amnesty International – European Office* and the *European Association for the Protection of Human Rights* have to be considered as particular cases. In the early 2000s, they entered into an advocacy coalition that had already been active for years. Therefore, these cases will not be analysed immediately. As will be developed in the following parts of this chapter, their inclusion into this specific field corresponds to a particular dynamic: they aim to diversify the range of actions used in this field.
9 *Migration Policy Group*, 'Five years of EU migration and asylum policy-making under the Amsterdam and Tampere mandates', May 2004.
10 According to the analyses of the *Migration Policy Group*, the main agendas are as follows: asylum; family reunification; visas and border controls; illegal immigration; expulsion; Schengen; immigration policy; re-admission agreements and cooperation with third countries; and the fight against racism and discrimination.
11 Interview number 16.
12 www.ecre.org.
13 www.migpolgroup.com.
14 This will be confirmed by an analysis of their repertoire of collective action.
15 See the presentation of its 'policy and advocacy work' on its website www.ecre.org.
16 *Brussels NGO Platform on EU Migration and Asylum Policy*, 'Fact sheet on the Brussels NGOs Platform on EU Migration and Asylum Policy', September 2005, p.1.
17 Even if *Amnesty International – European Office*, the *European Association for the Protection of Human Rights* and *Human Rights Watch* represent now important actors, they were not taken in account here because their involvement in the field came later (see below).
18 'Refugee and Human rights organizations across Europe call on EU to scrap key asylum proposal', March 2004.
19 *Brussels NGOs Platform on EU Migration and Asylum Policy*, 'Fact sheet on the Brussels NGOs Platform on EU Migration and Asylum Policy', September 2005, p.2.
20 www.ecre.org.
21 http://ec.europa.eu/dgs/home-affairs/financing/fundings/migration-asylum-borders/refugee-fund/index_en.htm.
22 This last point will be further developed in the next sections of the chapter.
23 *Brussels NGOs Platform on EU Migration and Asylum Policy*, 'Fact sheet on the Brussels NGOs Platform on EU Migration and Asylum Policy', September 2005, p.3.

24 Interview number 8.
25 www.ecre.org.
26 See, for example, the organizational structure of *ECRE* which is presented through a complex chart on the website www.ecre.org.
27 www.migpolgroup.com.
28 It is thus particularly important to note that the umbrella structures active in Brussels bring together only associations from European countries.
29 www.ecre.org.
30 *Forum Réfugiés*, 'L'action européenne de Forum Réfugiés' (author's translation).
31 Interview number 16.
32 Interview number 10.
33 Interview number 16.
34 www.erso-project.eu/.
35 Interview number 3.
36 Interview number 25.
37 Interview number 7.
38 Through the *European Association for the Protection of Human Rights*.
39 With the exception of *Cimade*, which is very active in the *Churches' Commission for Migrants in Europe* and *Pro Asyl*, which is very active in *ECRE*.
40 'Common principles on removal of irregular migrants and rejected asylum seekers', August 2005.
41 This network is constituted by associations that are part of *ECRE* and it benefits from the funds of the European Refugee Fund. Its work, however, differs from that of service-providing associations that access these funds. It aims at constructing a structure that is able to address European institutions critically on the basis of the experience of its member-associations.
42 'Introduction to the Migreurop network', www.migreurop.org.
43 'La démocratie en danger: des camps d'étrangers en Europe', June 2003.
44 'Maps of the camps for foreigners in Europe', September 2003.
45 As was developed above, these are the frames of anti-racism and anti-discrimination, the defence of fundamental rights, the promotion of new fundamental rights, international solidarity, the broader opening of borders, the fight against precariousness and social inequalities, the fight against repression and persecution, and the humanitarian frame.
46 *Migreurop*, 'European appeal against the creation of camps at European borders', October 2004.
47 Interview number 21.
48 With the exception of two activists who have been employed by the network since the end of the 2000s.
49 Interview number 21.
50 *Migreurop*, 'Euro-African Non-Governmental Manifesto on Migrations, Fundamental Rights and Freedom of Movement', 1 July 2006.
51 'PARIS 27 MARS 1999. SANS PATRIES NI FRONTIÈRES. Manifestation européenne, pour la régularisation des sans papiers, pour la libre circulation et contre les centres de retention' (author's translation).
52 www.noborder.org.

53 *Migreurop*, 'Derrière le mot camp', www.migreurop.org (author's translation).
54 www.deportation-alliance.com.
55 'Call for a 3rd Day of Migration-Related Actions on 7 October 2006, all over Europe and beyond . . .', October 2006.
56 Interview number 22.
57 'EuroMayday 2008 Call to Action', April 2008.
58 Interview number 5.
59 'Tous Égaux! Tous citoyens! Un million de signatures pour une citoyenneté européenne de residence', December 2003.
60 'Refugee and Human rights organizations across Europe call on EU to scrap key asylum proposal', March 2004.
61 Interview number 20.
62 *European Association for the Protection of Human Rights*, 'The European Association for the protection of Human Rights (FIDH-AE) calls on the European Union to renounce the conclusion of Readmission Agreements and to commit its Future Cooperation to the creation of equitable asylum and immigration policies', March 2004.
63 *Amnesty International – European Office*, 'EU countries compromising global refugee protection', October 2005.
64 Claire Rodier, 'The Migreurop Network and Europe's Foreigner' Camps', October 2006.
65 Interview number 20.
66 Interview number 24.
67 Interview number 14.

# Conclusion

## The Europeanization of Social Movements and the Emergence of a European Public Sphere

> We know much more about participation in consultative committees in the five square kilometers of Euroland in Brussels than we do about contention over the effects of their decisions among the 375 million people who have to live with their consequences. (Imig and Tarrow 2001: 7)

> Between February and October 2008 a series of events, protests and actions will take place in various cities and countries all over Europe and beyond: against the border regime, against detentions and deportations, against the exploitation of migrant labour and for legalization of all migrants. This transnational chain of struggles builds on the three action days for freedom of movement and the right to stay, which happened in previous years. But with this chain of events we are aiming for something more. We strongly believe that the transnational expression of migrants' struggles against the 'monster' of migration controls must be something more than a one day event once a year. We believe that the transnational space must be understood as a unified space of migrants' struggles, happening everyday and right now.[1]

> These are the starting points of our project, and to follow it we have to improve political communication, we have to find out feasible ways of cooperation and organization on a transnational level, we have to build up political bridges in order to cross the borders without denying differences, difficulties, obstacles. One thing is clear: transnationalization is already going on. We have to be up to the challenge.[2]

The two last quotations are taken from calls published before and after a 'transnational chain of migration related actions' organized by the European networks mobilizing for the regularization of undocumented migrants in 2008. As they clearly illustrate, Europeanization (or transnationalization) is not only a strategy for social movements. The construction of a 'unified space of struggles' is also an end in itself. As was stated by Imig and Tarrow (2001), we know little about the protest against decisions taken at the EU level. This phenomenon is however a crucial 'project' that has led to the transformation of many social movements in the last decades. In this research on the Europeanization of French and German pro-asylum movements, I have come to three main conclusions about the construction of this 'project'. After summarizing them briefly, I will present how they can be related more generally to the understanding of European integration and the emergence of a 'European public sphere'.

## Pro-asylum movements and the European Union: three conclusions

### A move to the European level

The first, and most evident, empirical result of this research is that pro-asylum movements traditionally mobilizing at the local or national level tend to Europeanize. Since the end of the 1990s the principal SMOs which form these movements in France and in Germany construct linkages and solidarities across countries, they produce frames that have European dimensions, and they organize mobilizations that address European power-holders (directly or indirectly). I have shown in chapter three that SMOs Europeanize their networks, frames and collective actions to different degrees: some associations play a crucial role in the construction of European mobilizations whereas other associations tend to remain principally at the national level. It emerges however from these empirical results that, even if not all of these SMOs have the same importance in the European movements against 'Fortress Europe', the large majority of them are concerned by the harmonization of asylum policies and thus increasingly consider the European Union as a new target of mobilization.

### Europeanization processes do not depend on the national contexts in which social movements are traditionally active

The second result that emerged from this analysis is that pro-asylum SMOs coming from different contexts Europeanize to the same extents and through the same modes. In other words, the traditional context of mobilization of an association neither impedes nor favours the Europeanization of its networks, frames, or collective actions. Neither does it lead this association to Europeanize its network, frames, and collective action in a particular way. I have shown in chapter one that French and German pro-asylum SMOs have faced different contexts of mobilization since the beginning of the 1990s. For this reason, they are characterized by different degrees of cohesion and of embeddedness in society: the French movement is made of denser and more durable inter-associative coalitions (and is therefore more cohesive), and is supported by a set of more diversified external actors (and is therefore more embedded in society) than the German movement. I have however shown in chapters three and four that these factors did not have an influence on the degrees and modes of Europeanization (in terms of networks, frames and collective actions) of the associations composing these movements.

These empirical results contradict the general idea that social movements coming from countries in which they have access to more resources (those who are better organized and more supported) Europeanize differently and to a greater extent than those coming from countries in which they have access to fewer resources. They also contradict those presented by various studies that have shown how the variations between different local or national contexts impeded (or at least made difficult) the construction of Europeanized mobilizations. In their comparison of the mobilizations of farmers in Galicia and the Netherlands, Klandermans et al. (2001) have shown that, depending on their local environment, farmers had different knowledge of the importance of EU agricultural policies, and that this prevented them from constructing European solidarities (even if EU competences are high in agricultural policies). Closer to my own object of study, Giugni and Passy (2002) and Koopmans et al. (2005) have shown that the differing national paradigms in terms of citizenship policies (the policies of integration of migrants and minorities) in Europe impeded the construction of European social movements on this issue: migrants continue to address national institutions.

However, my results have led me to conclude that the emergence of a European asylum policy has created a context of mobilization that overcomes traditional national specificities. When they move to the European level, the French and German pro-asylum movements create new spaces of mobilization in which they are able to construct new forms of solidarities and perceptions, and so to go beyond national differences. However, the reference to the literature brings to mind two factual elements. First, when one analyses asylum policies, one is referring to an issue that is global by nature (see the introduction) and that is thus less entrenched in the local level than, for example, agricultural policies. Also, when one analyses the asylum policy, one is referring to a policy for which EU competences are high (see the Introduction), and that is thus less dependent on national paradigms, such as citizenship policies. In conclusion, European social movements that overcome national specificities are more likely to emerge around the contestation of policies that relate to global issues and that constitute a priority in the agenda of European institutions.

## European pro-asylum movements emerge in distinct spaces of mobilization characterized by different dynamics

In the course of the empirical analysis, I have underlined the fact that the mobilizations related to the European asylum policies are constructed in different spaces of mobilization (see chapter four):

- the national space: when activists from different countries address power-holders of one member-state involved in the process of harmonization of asylum policies;
- the transnational space: when activists from different countries construct mobilizations in different member-states simultaneously, addressing power-holders of different member-states and of European institutions; these mobilizations have as their object EU asylum policies, but they do not necessarily address European institutions directly;
- the European space: when activists from different countries address directly and exclusively power-holders of European institutions.

Therefore different types of associations tend to Europeanize through their involvement in different spaces of mobilization. First, looking at the identity of the actors of the pro-asylum movements, I have shown in chapter two that two groups of associations are separated, in France and Germany, by a cleavage: humanitarian associations (characterized by a non-critical and pragmatic discourse, a non-protesting repertoire of collective action and a centralized and professionalized organizational structure) and politicized associations (characterized by a critical and principled discourse, a repertoire of collective action including protest and an activist-based organizational structure). I have then shown in chapter four that French and German humanitarian associations tend to Europeanize through a mode of externalization: they construct mobilizations in the national and European spaces, addressing national and European institutions separately. However, French and German politicized associations tend to Europeanize through the modes of construction of transnational and multilevel movements: they construct mobilizations in the transnational European spaces, addressing national and European institutions simultaneously.

Focusing on causal mechanisms, my research highlights the fact that these different Europeanization processes are largely determined by relational dynamics (the ability of SMOs to find partner-associations at the European level). I have thus shown that, due to the closeness of their profile, humanitarian associations have coordinated their activities with a coalition of NGOs and lobby groups mobilizing directly around EU institutions. On the other hand, politicized SMOs have Europeanized through the construction of transnational and multilevel movements in order to find partner-organizations with characteristics that are closer to their own profile. Using Bourdieu's theory of field, I have moreover underlined in chapter five that different spaces of mobilizations are characterized by different 'rules of the game', which, according to this theory, define different fields. The space of mobilization in which humanitarian associations are involved is characterized by a non-conflictual relationship towards power-holders (which means in particular that public opinion is rarely involved in the mobilizations), a technical and fragmented perception of the asylum issue and a centralized and professionalized inter-associative cooperation. In contrast, the space of mobilization in which politicized associations are involved is characterized by a conflictual relationship towards power-holders (involving public opinion in the mobilizations), a politicized and global perception of the asylum issue and a non-centralized and non-professionalized inter-associative cooperation. In brief, these results show that the emerging social movement mobilizing around EU asylum policies is fragmented: the mobilizations against 'fortress Europe' are defined in different spaces, through different dynamics and by different types of coalitions. As shown by Schmitter (2003), European governance is not only multilevel, it is also 'poly-centric': European policies are constructed in different venues, which have different (and sometimes competing) logics. The mobilization of the European pro-asylum movements in different spaces can substantiate this idea: through their different strategies, social movements address different actors and for different objectives, thereby showing the poly-centric nature of the European Union.

One of the objectives of this study was to examine the hypothesis of the NGOization of mobilizations around EU policy issues: the associations that are able to mobilize at the EU level are those that can adapt to the discourse of expertise and lobbying techniques promoted by EU institutions and that can rely on important material and human resources necessary for the construction of European wide collective actions. From this perspective, the construction of Europeanized mobilizations on the part of politicized associations is improbable. More generally, the occurrence of actions of protest at the European level is unlikely. My results show that politicized SMOs privileging protest are clearly under-represented (in fact almost absent) among the groups active directly around EU institutions. However, they are still able to construct contentious European mobilizations, through their involvement in more transnational arenas. In doing so, they address European institutions indirectly, through the involvement of public opinion. Moreover, EU protest can have an influence on the groups who are active exclusively in Brussels, leading to a diversification of their frames and repertoires of collective action. My results show thus more generally that EU-level protest is expanding.

## The 'statization' of power relations, the emergence of a European public sphere and the construction of a European identity?

The general idea of democratic deficit is both central and recurrent in European Union studies (Hix 2008; Rohrschneider and Dalton 2002; Streeck and Schmitter 1991). It is also a common argument found in mass media and public opinion at large (Weiler et al. 1995). As shown by these studies, the lack of responsiveness of EU institutions with regard to voters' preferences leads to a general apathy (or mistrust) about European politics in public opinion. In a similar perspective, the analysis of the Europeanization of social movements (and in particular those on immigration and asylum policies) leads to a more general reflection on the relation of individuals to European institutions. As I will discuss below, three points which have been presented in the introduction can be developed: the question of the 'statization' of power relations at the EU level; that of the emergence of a European public sphere; and that of the construction of a European identity.

### A 'statization' of power relations at the European level

As has been developed in Charles Tilly's (1978, 1984, 2004) work, social movements follow in their scope of mobilization and in their form the emergence of political systems: the construction of modern nation-states in Europe from the eighteenth to the end of the nineteenth century has led to the organization of protest (through the construction of social movements) at the national level. The progressive transfer of power from the local to the national level has led protesters to move the scope of their mobilization from the local to the national level and to organize social movements that are able to formulate long-term demands (in contrast to spontaneous episodes of contention such as charivaris). Following this analysis, can one observe analogies between this process and the emergence of Europeanized social movements in the last decades?

First, the evolution in the scope of mobilization of pro-asylum movements clearly shows that European institutions constitute an increasingly important political system. These movements have Europeanized in order to address, directly or indirectly, these institutions. This shows thus the increasing role of European institutions in the elaboration and in the implementation of immigration and asylum policies since the 1990s. However, can one deduce from this fact that nation-states have been transferring their power to the European level in this matter? In other words, is the fact that social movements are Europeanizing a sign that European power is replacing nation-state power (in the same way that the power of nation-state replaced local power from the eighteenth to the end of the nineteenth century)?

The observation of the mobilizations constructed by pro-asylum movements shows that this is not the case. These movements have not transferred their activities to the European level. Rather, they have enlarged their scope of mobilization in order to include – in addition to their mobilization at the national level – the European level. Moreover, when they mobilize around EU asylum policies, French and German associations address both European and national power-holders (whether separately in the case of the humanitarian associations or simultaneously in the case of politicized associations). The process of harmonization of asylum policies creates a new context of mobilization: it takes place in an emerging political system. But this new context of mobilization does not replace the traditional national contexts: the growing importance of this political system does not mean that the traditional ones (the nation-states) lose competences. This corroborates theories on European integration which analyse the EU as a system of multilevel governance (Hooghe and Marks 2001; Kohler-Koch and Eising 1999). It is the sense of Imig and Tarrow's definition of the European Union as a 'composite polity'; that is:

> A system of political relations in which actors at various levels and in different geographical units within a loosely linked system face both horizontal and vertical interlocutors and find corresponding opportunities for alliance building across both axes. (Imig and Tarrow 2001: 15)

In this composite polity, social movements do not act differently to how they act in traditional political spaces. This compels a refining of the analysis proposed by Marks and McAdam (1996) who have considered (on the basis of Tilly's analysis) that, because lobbying prevails over protest at the European level, the European Union is a new type of polity in comparison to nation-states. For them, this new type of polity implies the emergence of new types of relationships between institutional and non-institutional agents. My results allow me to state that these conclusions can be revised. The configuration of the European mobilizations increasingly resembles that of mobilizations at the national level: since the end of the 1990s EU immigration and asylum policies have also been subject to protest. More generally, the emergence of protest in European mobilizations has been observed by recent studies on other EU public policies (della Porta and Caiani 2009). The European Union is less and less a new type of power in comparison to the power of nation-states: the relationships between institutional and non-institutional agents are increasingly similar to those traditionally existing in nation-states.

The fact that the diversification of the repertoires of action at the European level concerns EU immigration and asylum policies has to be underlined. As I developed in the introduction, immigration and asylum policies are historically fundamental public policies through which nation-states have defined and implemented their power (Joppke 1999; Noiriel 1998): it is through these policies that they have been able to exclude categories of people from individual, political and social rights and thus to define their territory as a homogeneous political space (Sassen 1999; Sayad 2004). From this perspective, one can argue that the protest against European immigration and asylum policies indicates that a process of 'statization' of power relations at the European Union level is occurring.

## The emergence of a diffuse and fragmented European public sphere

The analysis of the Europeanization of social movements leads then to ask if a European public sphere is emerging. The concept of the public sphere is subject to much theoretical controversy and its use in European studies can be problematic (Sintomer 2003). However, analysing the role of social movements in the European Union, one cannot avoid this question (Chabanet 2003; della Porta and Caiani 2009; Koopmans and Statham 2010). Following Habermas' (1993) classical analysis, a public sphere is a space of inter-mediation between institutions and the private sphere (Risse 2003). In this 'symbolic space', 'discourses (most often contradictory) between the different social, religious, cultural and political actors composing a society are exchanged' (Mercier 2003: 10). In this regard, social movements are fundamental components of the public sphere: they are important actors taking part in these exchanges of discourses. Can one thus consider that the construction of Europeanized social movements is the sign of the emergence of a European public sphere? Going further, can it be considered a 'pre-condition' for the emergence of a European public sphere?

First, the fact that the large majority of French and German pro-asylum movements follow a process of Europeanization clearly shows that they recognize the increasingly important role of European institutions. This can be interpreted as a sign that European institutions create an 'imagined community' (Anderson 1983), and thus a European public sphere. In this emerging European public sphere, social movements are collective actors which contest the form of this community such as it is constructed by European institutions:[3] they contest the fact that it constructs itself by excluding migrants.

It is a remarkable fact that, even if coming from traditional contexts of mobilization characterized by different dynamics, French and German SMOs could not be clearly differentiated in terms of their levels and modes of Europeanization. This has led me to conclude that the dynamics of the emerging European context of mobilization overcome the specificities of the contexts of mobilization in which social movements are traditionally mobilizing (the nation-states). Consequently, the emerging European public sphere in which Europeanized social movements evolve does not simply superimpose itself on existing national public spaces. In other words, it is not plural: it creates a new context of mobilization that is common to social movements coming from different countries. However, neither does it replace the national public spaces: in parallel to the mobilizations that they construct at the EU level, the social movements which Europeanize continue to mobilize at the national level. One can thus say that the emerging European public sphere is diffuse within the traditional national public spheres: it creates a new space of inter-mediation between European Union institutions and the private sphere which does not decrease the importance of the traditional spaces of inter-mediation (between the national institutions and the private sphere).

The idea of a diffusion of the European public space within national public spaces is similar to that presented by Gerhards' (1993, 2000) analysis on media in Europe: he emphasized that the emergence of a European public sphere would not occur through the creation of a genuinely supranational European public sphere in the singular but rather through the Europeanization of the various national public spheres. In other words, the actors intervening in the national public spheres would increasingly refer to European perspectives (without these perspectives replacing the national references). This idea echoes the analysis presented by Eder, Kantner and Trenz

(2000), and by Koopmans and Erbe (2003), who evoke a 'parallelization' of national public spheres 'in the sense that increasingly the same themes are discussed at the same time under similar criteria of relevance' (Koopmans and Erbe 2003: 4).

My analysis leads me, however, to specify that the emerging European public sphere is fragmented: it is a sphere in which different (and often disconnected) spaces of mobilization emerge. Thus, as I have mentioned above, the (humanitarian) associations who lobby in the European political space are generally disconnected from those (the politicized associations) organizing protests at the transnational level. Even if they address the same actors, they act through different strategies, they construct different forms of discourses and collective actions, and they mobilize different types of resources.

To conclude, my analysis suggests the emergence of a European public sphere which is diffuse within national public spheres and which is fragmented. The analytical categories which have been used for the analysis of the national public spheres have thus to be qualified when one moves to the European level.

## A contested European identity

In an emerging European public sphere, do social movements base themselves upon and generate European identities? This question is particularly relevant if one focuses on the social movements organizing protest at the transnational level. Indeed, the literature on social movements shows that protest, in contrast to lobbying, is based upon and creates identities because it is geared towards the mobilization of public opinion (Touraine 1978). As a matter of fact, participants get involved in protest when there is an important sense of belonging to a political community (Fantasia, 1988). In return, protests are 'eventful' (della Porta 2008; Sewell 1996; Monforte and Dufour 2013): they create the conditions for the construction or reinforcement of identities. Thus, can the emergence of protest at the European level be interpreted as a sign (and as a factor) of the emergence of a European identity?

As the construction of a Europeanized 'identity frame' in associative discourses has shown, it is true that French and German movements mobilizing around the asylum issue increasingly consider themselves as being European social movements. Moreover, they are often involved in cross-issue networks at that level, participating in the construction of new forms of identities (della Porta and Caiani 2009). However, the question of the emergence of a European identity goes beyond this statement. Indeed, considering that Europeanized social movements are, in an emerging European public sphere, agents of inter-mediation between the private sphere and European institutions, the question is whether they act through – and promote – the construction of a European identity at the individual level. In other words, do French and German movements act increasingly at the European level because they consider that French and German citizens have increasingly manifested a European identity? Do they 'presuppose, generate and mobilize, directly or not, identities which can then produce a feeling of belonging to a political community' (Chabanet 2003: 64)?

This is less than evident if one considers the meaning of the mobilizations relating to immigration and asylum policies. The objective of these mobilizations is to denounce the exclusion of migrants by European institutions. These are the limits of this European public sphere that are contested. In fact, these social movements are not based upon (and do not generate) a European identity. Rather, they are based on (and generate) a questioning of the European identity such as it is defined by European institutions. This questioning concerns their very 'raison d'être'. This is clearly expressed in a text published by an activist of the network *Migreurop*:

> Europe is enlarging to twenty-five and allows almost hundred millions of chosen people to enter the club of those it recognizes as part of the family. In the meantime, the cartographers who carry out studies on the place of immigration in the continent will have to draw, beside the traditional arrows representing migration flows, increasingly numerous marks representing the camps in which Europe locks up those it does not want to see. The right to circulate freely into a 'space of security, freedom and justice', which has been solemnly re-asserted by the future European constitution for the EU citizens, has always had as corollary the restrictions to exercise this right for foreigners.[4]

## Notes

1 'Fighting the border regime! Transnationalization now! Common Call for a Transnational Chain of Migration related Actions In the 'heart of the monster'', February 2008.
2 'Transnationalization Now!', November 2008.
3 Throughout my research, it was clear that the associations I analyse do not contest the process of European construction as such and thus cannot be described as 'anti-European' or 'Euro-sceptic'. What they contest is the direction of this process in the immigration and asylum issue. For more on this perspective, see Dufour (2010).
4 Claire Rodier (2003), 'Les camps d'étrangers, nouvel outil de la politique migratoire de l'Europe', *Mouvements* 30 (author's translation).

# Interviews

Interview 1: Activist in the networks *Kein Mensch Ist Illegal* and *No Lager*, 20 June 2006
Interview 2: Project coordinator for 'Eastern-Europe', *European Council on Refugees and Exiles*, 12 October 2007
Interview 3: Spokesperson for European development, *Forum Réfugiés*, 19 January 2007
Interview 4: Spokesperson for European development in *Gisti*, and director of *Migreurop*, 20 December 2005
Interview 5: Coordinator of the 'Refugees' section, *Amnesty International Section Française*, 23 December 2005
Interview 6: Spokesperson for European development, *France Terre d'Asile*, 19 December 2005
Interview 7: Spokesperson for the 'Refugees' section, *Amnesty International Deutschland*, 22 June 2006
Interview 8: Director of the *Platform for an International Cooperation on Undocumented Migrants*, 11 October 2007
Interview 9: Spokesperson for European development, *Flüchtlingsrat Hamburg*, 8 June 2006
Interview 10: Spokesperson for European development, *Secours Catholique*, 21 December 2006
Interview 11: Spokesperson for the section on immigration, *European Network Against Racism*, 23 October 2007
Interview 12: Spokesperson for European development, *Cimade*, 6 January 2006
Interview 13: Coordinator of the section on refugees, *Evangelische Akademie zu Berlin*, 19 May 2006
Interview 14: Activist in the networks *Kein Mensch Ist Illegal* and *Frassanito*, 24 June 2006
Interview 15: Spokesperson for European development, *Pro Asyl*, 6 June 2006
Interview 16: Spokesperson for European development, *Caritas Deutschland*, 7 July 2006
Interview 17: Activist in *The Voice Refugee Forum* and the *Karawane für die Rechte der MigrantInnen und Flüchtlinge*, 23 May 2006
Interview 18: General Secretary of the *Churches Committee for Migrants in Europe*, 24 October 2007
Interview 19: Activist in the networks *Kein Mensch Ist Illegal, No Lager* and *Frassanito*, 19 June 2006
Interview 20: Executive Officer Justice and Home Affairs, *Amnesty International European Office*, 24 October 2007
Interview 21: Spokesperson for the network *Migreurop*, 24 July 2007
Interview 22: Spokesperson for European development in *Act Up Paris*, and member of *Migreurop*, 5 January 2006
Interview 23: Spokesperson for the *Jesuit Refugee Service Europe*, 23 October 2007
Interview 24: Activist in *Kanak Attak*, 15 June 2006

Interview 25: General Secretary of the *Ligue des droits de l'Homme*, and Vice-President of the *European Association for the Defence of Human Rights*, 5 January 2006

Interview 26: Spokesperson for the *Flüchtlingsrat Berlin*, 1 June 2006

Interview 27: Activist in *Initiative Gegen Abschiebhaft*, 17 June 2006

Interview 28: Coordinator of the section on refugees, *Human Rights Watch Europe*, 27 September 2007

Interview 29: Coordinator of the 'Foreigners' section, *Arbeiterwohlfahrt*, 4 July 2006

# References


Abdallah, M. 2000. *J'y suis, j'y reste ! Les luttes de l'immigration en France depuis les années soixante*. Paris: Reflex.

Adler-Nissen, R. 2011. 'On a Field-Trip with Bourdieu', *International Political Sociology* 5(3): 327–345.

Adler-Nissen, R. and I. Sommier (eds). 2005. *Radiographie du mouvement altermondialiste: le second forum social européen*. Paris: La Dispute.

Anderson, B. 1983. *Imagined Communities. Reflections on the Origin and Spread of Nationalism*. London: Verso.

Arendt, H. 1951 (2001). *The Origins of Totalitarianism*. New York: Harcourt.

Aspinwall, M. and J. Greenwood (eds). 1997. *Collective Action in the European Union: Interests and the New Politics of Associability*. London: Routledge.

Bade, K. 2000. *Europa in Bewegung, Migration vom späten 18. Jahrhundert bis zur Gegenwart*. Munich: Beck.

Balibar, E., C. Chemillier-Gendreau, J. Costa-Lacoux and E. Terray. 1999. *Sans-Papiers, L'Archaïsme Fatal*. Paris: La Découverte.

Balme, R. and D. Chabanet. 2002. 'Introduction: Action collective et gouvernance de l'Union Européenne', in R. Balme, D. Chabanet and V. Wright (eds), *L'Action Collective en Europe*. Paris: Presses de Sciences Politiques, pp. 21–120.

_______. 2008. *European Governance and Democracy. Power and Protest in the European Union*. Lanham: Rowman & Littlefield.

Balme, R., D. Chabanet and V. Wright (eds). 2002. *L'Action Collective en Europe*. Paris: Presses de Sciences Politiques.

Bandy, J. and J. Smith. 2005. *Coalitions across Borders: Transnational Protest and the Neoliberal Order*. Lanham: Rowman & Littlefield.

Bigo, D. 1996. *Polices en Réseaux: L'Expérience Européenne*. Paris: Presses de la Fondation nationale des sciences politiques.

Bigo, D. and E. Guild (eds). 2005. *Controlling Frontiers: Free Movement Into and Within Europe*. Aldershot: Ashgate.

Bojadzijev, M. 2002. 'Antirassistischer Widerstand von Migrantinnen und Migranten in der Bundesrepublik. Fragen der Geschichtsschreibung', *Zeitschrift für Sozialgeschichte des 20. Un 21. Jahrhunderts*, 17 (1): 125–152.

Borkert, M. and W. Bosswick. 2007. 'Migration Policymaking in Germany. Between National Reluctance and Local Pragmatism', IMISCOE Working Paper No. 20.

Bourdieu, P. 1992. *Les Règles de l'Art. Genèse et Structure du Champ Littéraire*. Paris: Seuil.

_______. 2000. *Propos sur le champ politique*. Lyon: Presses Universitaires de Lyon.

Bouteillet-Paquet, D. 2001. *L'Europe et le droit d'asile*. Paris: L'Harmattan.

_______. 2002. 'Quelle protection subsidiaire dans l'Union européenne?', *Hommes et Migrations* 1238: 75–86.

Branch, A. 2002. 'The Impact of the European Union on the Trade Union Movement', in R. Balme, D. Chabanet and V. Wright (eds), *L'Action Collective en Europe*. Paris: Presses de Sciences Politiques, pp. 279–312.

Bright, C. and S. Harding (eds). 1984. *Statemaking and Social Movements: Essays in History and Theory*. Ann Arbor: University of Michigan Press.

Brubaker, R. 1992. *Citizenship and Nationhood in France and in Germany*. Cambridge: Cambridge University Press.

_______. 2001. 'The Return of Assimilation? Changing Perspectives on Immigration and its Sequels in France, Germany, and the United States', *Ethnic and Racial Studies* 24(4): 531–548.

Caporaso, J., M.G. Cowles and T. Risse-Kappen (eds). 2000. *Transforming Europe: Europeanization and Domestic Change*. New York: Cornell University Press.

Carrère, V. 2002. 'Sangatte. Un Toit Pour les Fantômes', *Hommes et Migrations* 1238(1): 13–22.

Cefaï, D. and D. Trom (eds). 2001. *Les Formes de l'action collective. Mobilisations dans les arènes publiques*. Paris: Editions de l'Ecole des Hautes Etudes en Sciences Sociales.

Chabanet, D. 2001. 'L'Européanisation de l'Action collective? Quelques Hypothèses, Tendances et Perspectives', in D. Chabanet (ed.), *Action collective, représentation des intérêts et intégration européenne*. Lettre de la Maison française d'Oxford: Oxford University Press, pp. 5–15.

_______. 2002. 'Les marches européennes contre le chômage, la précarité et les exclusions', in R. Balme, D. Chabanet and V. Wright (eds), *L'Action Collective en Europe*. Paris: Presses de Sciences Politiques, pp. 461–494.

_______. 2003. 'Vers une européanisation de l'action collective?', in A. Mercier (ed.), *Vers un espace public européen? Recherches sur l'Europe en construction*. Paris: L'Harmattan.

_______. 2008. 'When the Unemployed Challenge the EU: The European Marches as a Mode of Externalisation of Protest', *Mobilization* 13(3): 311–322

Cinalli, M. 2004. *Horizontal Networks vs. Vertical Networks within Multi Organisational Alliances: A Comparative Study of the Unemployment and Asylum Issue-Fields in Britain*. European Political Communication Working Paper Series Issue 8/04.

Cissé, M. 1999. *Paroles de Sans-Papiers*. Paris: La Dispute.

Clayes, P., C. Gobin, I. Smets and P. Winand (eds). 1998. *Lobbyisme, pluralisme et intégration européenne*. Brussels: Presses Interuniversitaires Européennes.

Cohen, A. and A. Vauchez. 2007. *Anatomie d'un 'Moment Constituant' Européen. Élites, Mobilisations, Votes*. Brussels: Presses de l'Université libre de Bruxelles.

Costa-Lascoux, J. 1997. 'Les sans-papiers de Saint Bernard', *Revue Française des Affaires Sociales* 51(2).

Crépeau, F. 1995. *Droit d'asile: De l'hospitalité aux contrôles migratoires*. Brussels: Bruylant.

Crettiez, X. and I. Sommier (eds). 2006. *La France rebelle: tous les mouvements et acteurs de la contestation*. Paris: Michalon.

Crossley, N. 2002. *Making Sense of Social Movements*. London: Open University Press.

Curtis, R. and L. Zurcher. 1973. 'Stable Resources of Protest Movements. The Multi-Organisational Field', *Social Forces* 52(1): 53–61.

Dauvin, P. and J. Siméant (eds). 2004. *ONG et humanitaire*. Paris: L'Harmattan.

Della Porta, D. 2003. *The Europeanization of Protest: A Typology and Some Empirical Evidence*. EUI Working Paper SPS N° 2003/18, Florence.

_______. 2008. 'The Emergence of European Movements? Civil Society and the EU', *European Journal of Legal Studies* 1(3): 1–37.

Della Porta, D., M. Andretta, L. Mosca and H. Reiter. 2006, *Globalization From Below: Transnational Activists and Protest Networks*. Minneapolis: University of Minnesota Press.

Della Porta, D. and M. Caiani. 2007. 'Europeanization from Below? Social Movements and Europe', *Mobilization* 12(1): 1–20.

_______. 2009. *Social Movements and Europeanization*. Oxford: Oxford University Press.

Della Porta, D. and M. Diani. 2006. *Social Movements. An Introduction*. Oxford: Blackwell.

Della Porta, D. and M. Piazza. 2008. *Voices of the Valley, Voices of the Straits: How Protest Creates Communities*. Oxford: Berghahn Books.

Diez Medrano, J. 2003. *Framing Europe: Empire, WWII and Attitudes toward European Integration in Germany, Spain, and the United Kingdom*. Princeton: Princeton University Press.

_______. 2008. 'The Public Sphere and the European Union's Political Identity', in P. Katzenstein and J. Checkel (eds), *European Identity*. Cambridge: Cambridge University Press, pp. 81–108.

Dufour, P. 2010. 'Mobilization Against the 2005 Treaty Establishing a Constitution for Europe: A French Mobilization for Another Europe', *Social Movement Studies* 9(4): 425–441.

Earl, J., A. Martin, J. McCarthy and S. Soule. 2004. 'The Use of Newspaper Data in the Study of Collective Action', *Annual Review of Sociology* 30(1): 65–80.

Eder, K., C. Kantner and H.-J. Trenz. 2000. *Transnationale Öffentlichkeit und die Strukturierung politischer Kommunikation in Europa*, online: http://www2.rz.hu-berlin.de/struktur/forschung/transoeff/Euro-DFG-Antrag.pdf

Edwards, B. and J. McCarthy. 2004. 'Resources and Social Movement Mobilization', in D. Snow, S. Soule and H. Kriesi (eds), *The Blackwell Companion to Social Movements*. Oxford: Blackwell Publishing, pp. 116–152.

Einwohner, R. 2006. 'Identity Work and Collective Action in a Repressive Context: Jewish Resistance on the "Aryan Side" of the Warsaw Ghetto', *Social Problems* 53(1): 38–56.

Fantasia, R. 1988. *Cultures of Solidarity. Consciousness, Action, and Contemporary American Workers*. Berkeley: University of California Press.

Favell, A. 2000. 'L'européanisation ou l'émergence d'un nouveau "champ politique": le cas de la politique d'immigration', *Cultures et Conflits* 38–39: 153–186.

Favell, A. and V. Guiraudon. 2009. 'The Sociology of the European Union. An Agenda', *European Union Politics* 10(4): 550–576.

Fillieule, O. 2006. 'Requiem pour un concept. Vie et mort de la notion de "structure des opportunités politiques", in G. Dorronsoro (ed.), *La Turquie conteste*. Paris: Presses du CNRS, pp. 201–219.

Fritz, F. and F. Groner. 2004. 'Erlaubt? Geduldet? Illegal? Ausländer und Asylrechtliche in Deutschland un Ihre Auswirkungen auf die Soziale Arbeit mit Flüchtlinge', in *Wartesaal Deutschland. Ein Handbuch für die Soziale Arbeit mit Flüchtlinge*. Stuttgart: Lucius.

Gamson, W. 1992. 'The Social Psychology of Collective Action', in A. Morris and C. Mueller (eds.), *Frontiers in Social Movement Theory*. New Haven: Yale University Press, pp. 53–76.

Geddes, A. 1998. 'The Representation of Migrants' Interests in the European Union', *Journal of Ethics and Migration Studies* 24(4): 695–713.

_______. 2000. 'Lobbying for Migrant Inclusion in the European Union: New Opportunities for Transnational Advocacy?', *Journal of European Public Policy* 7(4): 632–649.

_______. 2000. *Immigration and European Integration. Towards Fortress Europe?* Manchester: Manchester University Press.

Geddes, A. and V. Guiraudon. 2004. 'The Emergence of a European Union Policy Paradigm Amidst Contrasting National Models: Britain, France and EU Anti-Discrimination Policy', *West European Politics* 27(2): 334–353.

Georgakakis, D. 2008. 'La Sociologie Historique et Politique de l'Union Européenne. Un Point de Vue d'Ensemble et Quelques Contre Points', *Politique Européenne* 25(2): 53–85.

Gerhards, J. 1993. 'Westeuropäische Integration und die Schwierigkeiten der Entstehung einer europäischen Öffentlichkeit', *Zeitschrift für Soziologie* 22: 96–110.

_______. 2000. 'Europäisierung von Ökonomie und Politik und die Trägheit der Entstehung einer europäischen Öffentlichkeit', in M. Bach (ed.), *Die Europäisierung nationaler Gesellschaften*, Sonderheft 40 der Kölner Zeitschrift für Soziologie und Sozialpsychologie. Wiesbaden: Westdeutscher Verlag, pp. 277–305.

Giugni, M. 2004. *Social Protest and Policy Change: Ecology, Antinuclear, and Peace Movements in Comparative Perspective*. Lanham: Rowman & Littlefield.

Giugni, M. and F. Passy. 2001. *Political Altruism? Solidarity Movements in International Perspective*. Lanham: Rowman & Littlefield.

_______. 2002. 'Le champ politique de l'immigration en Europe: opportunités, mobilisations et héritages de l'Etat national', in R. Balme, D. Chabanet and V. Wright (eds), *L'Action Collective en Europe*. Paris: Presses de Sciences Politiques, pp. 433–460.

Graziano, P. and M. Vink (eds). 2006. *Europeanization. New Research Agendas*. Basingstoke: Palgrave.

Greenwood, J. 1997. *Representing Interests in the European Union*. Basingstoke: Macmillan.

Grossman, E. and S. Saurugger. 2006. *Les Groupes d'Intérêt. Action Collective et Stratégies de Représentation*. Paris: Armand Colin.

Guild, E. 2000. 'Between Persecution and Protection. Refugees and the New European Asylum Policy', *Cambridge Yearbook of European Legal Studies* 3: 169–199.

Guiraudon, V. 2000. 'European Integration and Migration Policy: Vertical Policy-Making as Venue Shopping', *Journal of Common Market Studies* 38(2): 334–353.

_______. 2001. 'Weak Weapons of the Weak? Transnational Mobilization around Migration in the European Union', in D. Imig and S. Tarrow (eds), *Contentious Europeans. Protest and Politics in an Emerging Polity*. Lanham: Rowman & Littlefield, pp. 163–183.

_______. 2002. 'L'espace sociopolitique européen, un champ encore en friche?', *Cultures et Conflits* 38–39: 7–38.

_______. 2003. 'The Constitution of a European Immigration Policy Domain: A Political Sociology Approach', *Journal of European Public Policy* 10(2): 263–282.

_______. 2010. 'Les effets de l'européanisation des politiques d'immigration et d'asile', *Politique Européenne* 31(2): 7–32.

Haas, E. 1964, *Beyond the Nation-State, Functionalism and International Organization*. Stanford: Stanford University Press.

Habermas, J. 1993. *L'espace public*. Paris: Payot.

Heckmann, F. 2003. 'From Ethnic Nation to Universalistic Immigrant Integration: Germany', in F. Heckmann and D. Schnapper (eds), *The Integration of Immigrants in European Societies. National Differences and Trends of Convergence*. Stuttgart: Lucius, pp. 45–78.

Herbert, U. 2001. *Geschichte der Ausländerpolitik in Deutschland. Saisonarbeiter, Zwangsarbeiter, Gastarbeiter, Flüchtlinge*. Munich: Beck.

Hix, S. 2008. *What's Wrong with the European Union and How to Fix It*. London: Polity

Hooghe, L. and G. Marks. 2001. *Multi-Level Governance and European Integration*. Lanham: Rowman & Littlefield.

Imig, D. and S. Tarrow (eds). 2001. *Contentious Europeans. Protest and Politics in an Emerging Polity*. Lanham: Rowman & Littlefield.

Israel, L. 2003. 'Faire émerger le droit des étrangers en le contestant, ou l'histoire paradoxale des premières années du GISTI', *Politix* 62: 115–144.

Johnston, H. 2002. 'Verification and Proof in Frame and Discourse Analysis', in B. Klandermans and S. Staggenbord (eds), *Methods in Social Movement Research*. Minneapolis: University of Minnesota Press, pp. 62–91.

Joppke, C. 1999. *Immigration and the Nation-State: The United States, Germany, and Great Britain*. Oxford: Oxford University Press.

Jørgensen, K. and A. Wiener (eds). 2001. *The Social Construction of Europe*. London: Sage.

Kastoryano, R. 1996. *La France, l'Allemagne et leurs immigrés: négocier l'identité*. Paris: Armand Colin.

Keck, M. and K. Sikkink. 1998. *Activists Beyond Borders. Advocacy Networks in International Politics*. Ithaca: Cornell University Press.

Klandermans, B., M. De Weerd, J.M. Sabudeco and M. Rodriguez. 2001. 'Framing Contention: Dutch and Spanish Farmers Confront the EU', in D. Imig and S. Tarrow (eds), *Contentious Europeans. Protest and Politics in an Emerging Polity*. Lanham: Rowman & Littlefield, pp. 77–96.

Kohler-Koch, B. and R. Eising (eds). 1999. *The Transformation of Governance in the European Union*. London: Routledge.

Koopmans, R. and W. Duyvendak. 1994. *The Political Construction of the Nuclear Energy Issue and its Impact on the Mobilization of Anti-Nuclear Movements in Western Europe*. Berlin: Wissenschaftszentrum Berlin.

Koopmans, R. and J. Erbe. 2003. *Towards a European Public Sphere? Vertical and Horizontal Dimensions of Europeanized Political Communication*, Paper presented at the International Conference 'Europeanization of public spheres? Political mobilisation, public communication, and the European Union', Wissenschaftszentrum Berlin für Sozialforschung (WZB), 20–22 June.

Koopmans, R. and P. Statham. 2010. *The Making of a European Public Sphere: Media Discourse and Political Contention*. Cambridge: Cambridge University Press.

Koopmans, R., P. Statham, M. Giugni and F. Passy. 2005. *Contested Citizenship: Immigration and Cultural Diversity in Europe*. Minneapolis: University of Minnesota Press.

Kriesi, H., R. Koopmans, W. Duyvendak and M. Giugni. 1995. *New Social Movements in Western Europe. A Comparative Analysis.* Minneapolis: University of Minnesota Press.

Ladrech, R. 1994. 'The Europeanization of Domestic Politics and Institutions: The Case of France', *Journal of Common Market Studies* 32(1): 69–88.

Lahusen, C. 2004. 'Joining the Cocktail Circuit: Social Movement Organizations at the European Union', *Mobilization* 9(1): 55–71.

Laubenthal, B. 2007. *Der Kampf um Legalisierung. Soziale Bewegungen Illegaler Migranten in Frankreich,* Spanien und der Schweiz. Frankfurt am Mein: Campus.

Lavenex, S. 1999. *The Europeanization of Refugee Policies: between Human Rights and Internal Security.* Florence, European University Institute PhD Thesis.

_______. 2001. 'The Europeanization of Refugee Policy: Normative Challenges and Institutional Legacies', *Journal of Common Market Studies* 39: 851–874.

_______. 2006. 'Shifting Up and Out: The Foreign Policy of European Immigration Control', *West European Politics* 29(2): 329–350.

Lefébure, P. and E. Lagneau. 2002. 'Le moment Vilvorde: action protestataire et espace public européen', in R. Balme, D. Chabanet and V. Wright (eds), *L'Action Collective en Europe.* Paris: Presses de Sciences Politiques, pp. 495–529.

Lichterman, P. 2002. 'Seeing Structure Happen: Theory-Driven Participant Observation', in B. Klandermans and S. Staggenbord (eds.), *Methods of Social Movement Research.* Minneapolis, University of Minnesota Press, pp. 118–145.

McAdam, D., J. McCarthy and M. Zald (eds). 1996. *Comparative Perspectives on Social Movements.* Cambridge: Cambridge University Press.

Magnette, P. 2000. *L'Europe, l'Etat et la démocratie.* Brussels: Complexe.

Marcos, C. 2003. *La professionnalisation du militantisme associatif. L'exemple de la Cimade,* mémoire de DEA, département de Sciences Politiques, Université de Paris I-Panthéon Sorbonne.

Marks, G. and D. McAdam. 1996. 'Social Movements and the Changing Structure of Political Opportunity in the European Union', *West European Politics* 19(2): 249–278.

Marques-Pereira, B. 1998. 'Mort du néo-corporatisme?', in P. Clayes, C. Gobin, I. Smeth and P. Winand (eds), *Lobbyisme, pluralisme et intégration européenne.* Brussels: Presses Interuniversitaires Européennes, pp. 51–57.

Mathieu, L. 2007. 'L'Espace des Mouvements Sociaux', *Politix. Revue des Sciences Sociales du Politique* 77(1): 131–151.

_______. 2010. 'Soutenir les Familles Sans-Papiers', in D. Fassin (ed.), *Les Nouvelles Frontières de la Société Française.* Paris: La Découverte, pp. 317–338.

Maurer, S. and E. Pierru. 2001. 'Le Mouvement des Chômeurs de l'Hiver 1997–1998. Retour sur un "Miracle Social"', *Revue Francaise de Science Politique* 512(3): 317–407.

Mazzey, S. and J. Richardson. 1993. *Lobbying in the European Community.* Oxford: Oxford University Press.

_______. 2002. 'Pluralisme ouvert ou restreint? Les groupes d'intérêt dans l'Union Européenne', in R. Balme, D. Chabanet and V. Wright (eds), *L'Action Collective en Europe.* Paris: Presses de Sciences Politiques, pp. 123–161.

Melucci, A. 1989. *Nomads of the Present: Social Movements and Individual Needs in Contemporary Society*. London: Hutchinson Radius.

_______. 1995. 'The Process of Collective Identity', in B. Klandermans and H. Johnston (eds), *Social Movements and Culture*. Minneapolis: University of Minnesota Press, pp. 43–44.

Mercier, A. (ed.). 2003. *Vers un espace public européen? Recherches sur l'Europe en construction*. Paris: L'Harmattan.

Milward, A. 1992. *The European Rescue of the Nation-State*. Berkeley: University of California Press.

Monforte, P. and P. Dufour. 2013. 'Comparing the Protests of Undocumented Migrants Beyond Contexts: Collective Actions as Acts of Emancipation', *European Political Science Review* 5: 83–104.

Moravcsik, A. 1998. *The Choice for Europe. Social Purpose and State Power from Messina to Maastricht*. Ithaca: Cornell University Press.

Morgenstern, M. 1993. *Kirchenasyl in der Bundesrepublik Deutschland. Historische Entwicklung, Aktuelle Situation, Internationaler Vergleich*. Wiesbaden: Verlag für Sozialwissenschaften.

Niehr, T. 2000. 'Die Asyldebatte im Deutschen Bundestag – Eine "Sternstunde" des Parlaments? Untersuchungen zur Debattenkultur im Deutschen Bundestag', in A. Burkhardt and K. Pape (eds), *Die Sprache des Deutschen Parlamentarismus. Studien zu 150 Jahren Parlamentarischer Kommunikation*. Wiesbaden: Westdeutscher Verlag.

Noiriel, G. 1998. *Réfugiés et sans-papiers: la République face au droit d'asile, XIX-XXème Siècle*. Paris: Hachette.

Nugent, N. 1999. 'Decision-making', in E. Geoffrey and D. Spence (eds), *The European Commission*. Harlow: Longman Current Affairs, pp. 130–150.

Offerlé, M. 1998. *Sociologie des groups d'intérêt*. Paris: Montchrestien.

Passy, F. 1998. *L'Action altruiste: contraintes et opportunités de l'engagement dans les mouvements sociaux*. Geneva: Droz.

Péchu, C. 1996. 'Quand les Exclus Passent à l'Action', *Politix* 34: 114–133.

Piven, F. and R. Cloward. 1977. *Poor People's Movements: Why They Succeed, How They Fail*. New York: Pantheon Books.

Polletta, F. and J. Jasper. 2001. 'Collective Identity and Social Movements', *Annual Review of Sociology* 27(1): 283–305.

Prantl, H. 1993. 'Hysterie und Hilflosigkeit. Chronik der Asyldebatte seit der deutschen Einheit', in B. Blanke, *Zuwanderung und Asyl in der Konkurrenzgesellschaft*. Opladen: Leske und Budrich.

Radaelli, C. 2001. 'The Domestic Impact of European Union Public Policy: Notes on Concepts, Methods and the Challenge of Empirical Research', *Politique européenne* 5(1): 105–136.

Risse, T. 2003. *An Emerging European Public Sphere? Theoretical Clarifications and Empirical Indicators*, Paper presented to the Annual Meeting of the European Union Studies Association (EUSA), Nashville.

Rodier, C. 2003, 'Les Camps d'Etrangers, Nouvel Outil de la Politique Migratoire de l'Europe', *Mouvements* 30: 102–107.

Rohrschneider, R. and R. Dalton. 2002. 'A Global Network? Transnational Cooperation by Environmental Groups', *Journal of Politics* 64: 510–533.

Rootes, C. 2002. 'The Europeanization of Environmentalism', in R. Balme, D. Chabanet and V. Wright (eds), *L'Action Collective en Europe*. Paris: Presses de Sciences Politiques, pp. 377–404.

_______. 2004. 'A Limited Transnationalization? The British Environmental Movement', in D. Della Porta and S. Tarrow (eds), *Transnational Protest and Global Activism*. Lanham: Rowman & Littlefield, pp. 21–44.

Rucht, D. 2002. 'The EU as a Target of Political Mobilization. Is There a Europeanization of Conflict?', in R. Balme, D. Chabanet and V. Wright (eds), *L'Action Collective en Europe*. Paris: Presses de Sciences Politiques, pp. 163–194.

Ruzza, C. 2004. *Europe and Civil Society. Movement Coalitions and European Governance*. Manchester: Manchester University Press.

Sassen, S. 1999. *Guests and Aliens*. New York: New Press.

Sayad, A. 2004. *The Suffering of the Immigrants*. Cambridge: Cambridge University Press.

Schmitter, P. 2003. 'Neofunctionalism', in T. Diez and A. Wiener (eds), *European Integration Theory*. Oxford: Oxford University Press.

Schönbach, K. 1993. 'Ist "Bild" Schuld an Mölln? Offentliche Meinung, Gewaltbereitschaft in den Massenmedien', *Zeitschrift für Medien, Bildung, Kultur* 8(1): 52–56.

Sewell, W. 1996. 'Three Temporalities. Towards an Eventful Sociology', in T. McDonald (ed.), *The Historic Turn in the Human Sciences*. Ann Arbor, University of Michigan Press, pp. 245–280.

Siméant, J. 1998. *La Cause des Sans-Papiers*. Paris: Presses de Sciences-Politiques.

Sintomer, Y. 2003. 'L'espace public européen: les ambivalences d'une notion', in A. Mercier (ed.), *Vers un espace public européen? Recherches sur l'Europe en construction*. Paris: L'Harmattan.

Smith, A. 1999. '"L'espace public européen": une vue (trop) aérienne', *Critique Internationale* 2(2): 169–180.

Smith, J., C. Chatfield and R. Pagnucco. 1997. *Transnational Social Movements and Global Politics: Solidarity Beyond the State*. Syracuse: Syracuse University Press.

Snow, D. and R. Benford. 1988. 'Ideology, Frame Resonance, and Participant Mobilization', in B. Klandermans, H. Kriesi and S. Tarrow (eds), *From Structure to Action: Comparing Social Movements Research Across Cultures*. Greenwich: JAI, pp. 197–218.

_______. 1992. 'Master Frames and Cycles of Protest', in A Morris and C. McClurg Mueller (eds.), *Frontiers in Social Movement Theory*. New Haven: Yale University Press, pp. 133–155.

_______. 2000. 'Framing Processes and Social Movements: An Overview and Assessment', *Annual Review of Sociology* 26: 611–639.

Snow, D., B. Rochford, S. Worden and R. Benford. 1986. 'Frame Alignment Processes, Micromobilization, and Movement Participation', *American Sociological Review* 51: 464–481.

Streeck, W. and P. Schmitter. 1991. 'From National Corporatism to Transnational Pluralism: Organized Interests in the Single European Market', *Politics and Society* 19: 133–164.

Tarrow, S. 1994. *Power in Movement*. Cambridge: Cambridge University Press.

_______. 2001. 'Contentious Politics in a Composite Polity', in D. Imig and S. Tarrow (eds), *Contentious Europeans, Protest and Politics in an Emerging Polity*. Lanham: Rowman & Littlefield, pp. 233–252.

_______. 2002. 'La contestation transnationale', *Cultures et Conflits* 38–39: 187–223.

_______. 2005. *The New Transnational Activism*. Cambridge: Cambridge University Press.

Taylor, V. 1996. *Rock-a-by Baby: Feminism, Self-Help and Postpartum Depression*. London: Routledge.

Tilly, C. 1978. *From Mobilization to Revolution*. Englewood Cliffs: Prentice Hall.

_______. 1984. 'Social Movements and National Politics', in C. Bright and S. Harding (eds), *Statemaking and Social Movements: Essays in History and Theory*. Ann Arbor: University of Michigan Press, pp. 297–317.

_______. 2004. *Contention and Democracy in Europe, 1650–2000*. Cambridge: Cambridge University Press.

Touraine, A. 1978. *La Voix et le Regard*. Paris: Seuil.

_______. 1984. *Le Retour de l'Acteur*. Paris: Seuil.

Uba, K. and F. Uggla. 2011. 'Protest-Actions Against the European Union, 1992–2007', *West European Politics* 34(2): 384–393.

Valluy, J. 2007. *L'accueil étatisé des demandeurs d'asile: de l'enrôlement dans les politiques publiques à l'affaiblissement des mobilisations de soutien aux exilés*. TERRA-Editions, online: http://terra.rezo.net

Weil, P. 1995. *La France et ses étrangers*. Paris: Gallimard.

Weiler, J., U. Haltern and F. Mayer. 1995. 'European Democracy and its Critique', *West European Politics* 18: 4–39.

Weisbein, J. 2001. 'Le militant et l'expert. Les associations civiques face au système politique européen', *Politique Européenne* 4: 105–118.

_______. 2002. 'Le lobbying associatif à Bruxelles. Entre mobilisations unitaires et sectorielles', *Revue Internationale de Politique Comparée* 9(1): 79–98.

Zolberg, A. 1981. 'International Migrations in Political Perspective', in C. Keely and S. Tomasi (eds), *Global Trends in Migration: Theory and Research on International Population Movements*. New York: Centre for Migration Studies, pp. 225–252.

# Index

www.ingramcontent.com/pod-product-compliance
Ingram Content Group UK Ltd.
Pitfield, Milton Keynes, MK11 3LW, UK
UKHW021837100926
8556IPUK00004B/391

9 780857 459961